HUMAN RIGHTS ABUSES IN THE CONTEMPORARY WORLD

Cultures juridiques et politiques Vol. 3

Les conceptions du pouvoir, du droit et de l'ordre se réfèrent inévitablement à l'ensemble du système de représentations qu'est la culture de chaque société. Toute forme de culture ayant donc nécessairement une dimension politique et juridique, la collection «Cultures juridiques et politiques» publie des travaux, tels que des thèses, synthèses de recherches, ouvrages collectifs et actes de colloques, se proposant de faire connaître les systèmes politiques et juridiques des pays européens, d'évaluer les grandes tendances des processus d'intégration politique et d'harmonisation juridique en cours dans l'Union européenne et d'éclairer les interférences entre le politique, le juridique et les autres aspects «culturels» dans le contexte de ces processus.

RALF ALLEWELDT, RAPHAËL CALLSEN,
JEANNE DUPENDANT (EDS.)

HUMAN RIGHTS ABUSES IN THE CONTEMPORARY WORLD

TRI-NATIONAL WORKSHOP, TBILISI, SEPTEMBER 2011

PETER LANG
Bern · Berlin · Bruxelles · Frankfurt am Main · New York · Oxford · Wien

Information bibliographique publiée par
«Die Deutsche Nationalbibliothek»
«Die Deutsche Nationalbibliothek» répertorie cette publication dans la «Deutsche Nationalbibliografie»; les données bibliographiques détaillées sont disponibles sur Internet sous ‹http://dnb.d-nb.de›.

Réalisation de couverture: Didier Studer, Peter Lang AG

ISSN 2235-1078
ISBN 978-3-0343-1147-2 br.   ISBN 978-3-0352-0149-9 eBook

Hochfeldstrasse 32, CH-3012 Berne, Suisse
info@peterlang.com, www.peterlang.com

Imprimé en Suisse

Notice

This book is a trinational and trilingual publication. There are Georgian scholars writing in French, French scholars writing in German and German scholars writing in English. In order to respect the cultural background of each author, the editors chose not to standardize the citation and punctuation system.

Please note that the quotations, that are set back from the text, are presented without quotation marks.

Foreword

This volume contains the proceedings of the first tri-national research workshop, held on 6-9 September 2011 in Tbilisi (Georgia), organized jointly by the Caucasus University (Georgia), Potsdam University (Germany) and the University Paris Ouest Nanterre La Défense (France). The idea was born in July 2010 in Vilnius (Lithuania) in the course of conversations with students of the Caucasus University, who participated in the seventh edition of our traditional European Summer University. A preparatory meeting took place in September 2010 in Tbilisi, to which we had sent Raphaël Callsen. At this meeting our honored colleagues of the Caucasus University determined, according to our expressed wishes, the theme of the workshop corresponding to their research interests. The contributions presented at the workshop reflected well the variety of legal cultures and the discussions between the young researchers were a source of scientific enrichment. This event confirmed once again the importance of international cooperation. Our strategy of expanding the activities of our German-French course of study, established more than 20 years ago, already led to cooperation with countries such as Turkey, the Maghreb states, South Africa, States of the Near and Middle East, China, Canada or the USA. We are striving for cooperation with Eastern European countries outside of the European Union and we hope to establish it through our first workshop and future events in Georgia.

It is a particularly pleasant duty to thank all those who have helped my Potsdam co-organizer Professor Tilman Bezzenberger and me in the conceptualization, preparation and execution of this workshop. First of all the participants – doctoral candidates and other young researchers – who, through their lectures, made the workshop possible. Second, graduates of the German-French course of studies, namely Raphaël Callsen and Jeanne Dupendant, have played a great role in the organization of this event and have taken the responsibility to co-edit this volume. Mrs. Lechner (Potsdam) handled a good part of the administrative burden. The National Parliamentary Library of Georgia kindly put its magnificent conference hall at our disposal. The German and French Embassies gave valuable support and we will remember with pleasure the reception at the residence of Mrs. Gabriel. Last but not least we would like to address special thanks to those institutions whose financial support made this event and the publication of the present proceedings possible: the German-French University (DFH-UFA) and the German-French Youth Organization (DFJW-OFAJ).

Nanterre, May 2012

Otmar SEUL

Summary of Contents

Human rights and criminal law and enforcement

Human rights and private actors

Introduction

Raphaël CALLSEN, Jeanne DUPENDANT and Ralf ALLEWELDT

One might be surprised to read "human rights abuses" in the title of this volume. Of course, the aim of the tri-national workshop held in Tbilisi (Georgia) in September 2011 was not to list human rights violations. The presentations and discussions of the young researchers rather focused on the question how to effectively prevent such violations. Nonetheless, abuses offer an interesting starting point, which allows for a better understanding of to what extent human rights have a role to play. For instance, the finding that the enjoyment of human rights could be impaired by acts committed by private persons or entities, led international and domestic courts dealing with human rights cases to recognize their so-called "horizontal effect". Similarly, the observation that human rights violations often have irreversible consequences pushed the States to establish prevention mechanisms to ensure an efficient human rights protection.

Moreover, the subject of the workshop, which was chosen by our Georgian colleagues, also highlights that human rights abuses are a painful part of recent Georgian history which is still very present in the collective memory. After the collapse of the Soviet Union and the accession to independence in 1991, Georgia experienced ethnic conflicts and wars, especially in Abkhazia (1992-1993) and South Ossetia (2008).

The organization of the tri-national workshop opened new perspectives, not only because of the different legal backgrounds of the participants but also because of their different academic traditions. In order to benefit from this legal and cultural diversity and not to restrict the debates, we chose to start from a wide understanding of "human rights", *i.e.* the rights of individuals and groups that are recognized by international law, but also, if pertinent, by domestic law. The diversity of academic traditions is also reflected by the fact that this volume is a trilingual one and that the collected papers written in English, French or German by French, German and Georgian authors reflect different mindsets.

Unfortunately, it was not possible to publish all the twenty-seven presentations given in Tbilisi. The present selection of twelve papers, however, reflects well the different issues that have been presented and discussed by the participants. Sincere thanks are given to all of them.

The first section of this volume is dedicated to the human rights protection in Georgia and the Black Sea region. The evolution of the political system in Georgia since 1991 is described by Ioseb KELENJERIDZE, who explains how the human rights protection as framed by the Georgian Constitution has been consolidated after the accession to the European Convention on Human Rights (ECHR) in 1999. Giorgi ASATIANI then traces back the use and prohibition of the death penalty in Georgia from feudal times to nowadays and underlines the role of international instruments in precluding this form of punishment during both peace and wartime. In a detailed study, Ralf ALLEWELDT analyzes the reports of the European Committee for the Prevention of Torture (CPT) on Armenia, Bulgaria, Georgia, Turkey and Ukraine from 1990 to 2011. Although there are still difficulties, he identifies positive evolutions and concludes that CPT recommendations effectively contribute to prevent torture.

In the second section, Jean-Marc THOUVENIN explores whether there is a contradiction between the principle of self-determination of peoples and the principle of territorial integrity. This question of particular sensitivity in Georgia, due to the conflicts in Abkhazia and South Ossetia and reflected in Article 1 of the Georgian Constitution, is answered in the negative as, in the view of the author, these principles do not collide with each other.

The third section deals with current issues regarding the application of human rights in armed conflicts. Nina KAPAUN takes the stand that targeted killings of individuals by states, *e.g.* Osama Bin Laden, which do not always take place within armed conflicts, have to primarily be evaluated according to human rights law. After detailed considerations of the extraterritorial applicability of human rights and of the content of the right to life, she clarifies the conditions under which a targeted killing might be allowed. Olaf SEIRING, on the other hand, advocates an extension of international human rights law and international humanitarian law obligations to non-state parties involved in an armed conflict.

The relationship and interactions between human rights and criminal law are illustrated in the fourth section. Eliette MIRAU-GONDOIN, on the one hand, underlines the need and traces the long way to establish effective criminal sanctions at the international level to prevent and sanction sexual violence. Rieke ARENDT, on the other hand, undertakes a comparative study showing how Articles 5 and 7 ECHR limit preventive detention of persons deemed likely to commit a crime.

In the fifth and last section the analysis focuses on the role that human rights may play in relations between private actors. Two studies examine the impact of human rights in private international law. Raphaël CALLSEN demonstrates the relevance of German and French discussions about an immediate application of human rights for Georgian choice-of-law cases. He explains why it is preferable to opt for the public policy exception in order to discard foreign law, when it conflicts with fundamental values and especially human rights of the forum state. Romuald DI NOTO, in contrast, explores a positive dimension of human rights in choice-of-law cases. In his opinion, a "method of recognition" based on Article 8 ECHR could compel the recognition of *e.g.* a registered partnership or same-sex marriage regularly registered in a foreign country even if this is not permitted by the legislation of the forum. The two final contributions investigate the possibility of direct human rights obligations for transnational corporations. Jeanne DUPENDANT analyzes the United Nations Global Compact. She underlines the lack of efficiency of this voluntary corporate responsibility initiative, notably due to its lack of notoriety, but agrees that it could contribute to the emergence of positive human rights obligations, possibly under international law. Finally, Caroline BRETON examines the possibility for victims of human right violations committed by a subsidiary or subcontractor of a transnational firm to engage the civil liability of the latter. She observes, however, that a lack of jurisdiction of the domestic courts and the structure of the corporations often impedes such actions for extraterritorial civil liability in the corporation's home state.

Regional human rights protection

Protection régionale des droits de l'Homme
Regionaler Menschenrechtsschutz

Les rapports entre démocratie et droits de l'Homme – L'exemple du Conseil de l'Europe et de la Géorgie

Ioseb KELENJERIDZE*

Bien que la notion soit ancienne, la protection des droits de l'Homme a réellement émergé sur le plan international après 1945 et la création de l'Organisation des Nations Unis. Parallèlement des mécanismes régionaux de promotion et de protection des droits de l'Homme et de la démocratie ont été développés. Le Conseil de l'Europe a notamment joué un important rôle de promoteur en la matière. Depuis sa création, il n'a cessé de se développer d'un point de vue matériel, par le développement de nouveaux instruments juridiques, et d'un point de vue géographique, il compte aujourd'hui 47 Etats membres.

La Géorgie est le premier Etat du Caucase à avoir adhéré au Conseil de l'Europe en 1999. Depuis l'effondrement de l'Union Soviétique, la Géorgie a été secouée par des conflits, notamment ethniques, ce qui a fortement endommagée son économie en transition, déjà fragile. Malgré des difficultés, elle a réalisé d'importantes réformes économiques et démocratiques marquant la volonté politique du peuple géorgien de s'intégrer au Conseil de l'Europe et de mettre tout en œuvre pour y parvenir.

Cet article vise à présenter les grandes lignes du système constitutionnel géorgien et à expliquer comment son adhésion au Conseil de l'Europe a soutenu sa transition démocratique.

---

* Doctorant à l'Université du Caucase (Caucasus University), Tbilisi (Géorgie).
Merci à Jeanne DUPENDANT pour ses nombreuses relectures et corrections.

I. Les acquis démocratiques du système politique géorgien depuis 1991

La Géorgie est un Etat indépendant, uni et indivisible, comme l'ont confirmé le référendum national du 31 mars 1991[1] et la proclamation du 9 avril 1991 sur le rétablissement de l'indépendance nationale de la Géorgie. La Constitution instaure un régime semi-présidentiel avec d'une part un Président élu au suffrage universel direct (mandat de 5 ans, renouvelable une seule fois), d'autre part un parlement (mandat de 4 ans), qui définit les grandes orientations politiques, vote les lois et contrôle l'activité du Gouvernement.

Le parlement est actuellement monocaméral, l'article 4 de la constitution envisage toutefois la création, à terme, d'une seconde chambre :

> lorsque les conditions appropriées seront réunies et que, sur l'ensemble du territoire géorgien, auront été formées des collectivités territoriales s'administrant librement, le Parlement de Géorgie comportera deux chambres: le Conseil de la République et le Sénat.[2]

La composition, les compétences et les procédures d'élections des chambres seront précisées par une loi organique. Les membres du Conseil de la République seront en principe élus au suffrage universel direct par circonscriptions. Les membres du Sénat devraient être des représentants élus de l'Abkhazie, de la République autonome d'Adjarie[3] ainsi que des autres unités territoriales de la Géorgie. Cinq membres additionnels seront désignés par le Président.

---

1 Référendum réalisé sur tout le territoire y compris dans la République socialiste soviétique autonome d'Abkhazie et dans l'ex-région autonome d'Ossétie.

2 Art. 4 de la Constitution de Géorgie adoptée le 24 août 1995.

3 Juridiquement l'autonomie de l'Ossétie du Sud n'existe pas suite à l'arrêté du Président de la Géorgie du 11 décembre 1990. Aujourd'hui, conformément à la Constitution géorgienne, il n'y a que deux Républiques autonomes sur le territoire de la Géorgie – l'Adjarie et l'Abkhazie.

En cas de violation de la Constitution, constatée par la Cour constitutionnelle, de haute trahison ou de crime grave, constaté par la Cour suprême [4], le parlement peut démettre le Président de ses fonctions. La mise en accusation doit être votée par un tiers au moins des membres du Parlement. Si le Parlement ne se prononce pas par un vote dans un délai de trente jours, la motion est considérée comme retirée et aucune mise en accusation pour ces mêmes faits ne peut à nouveau être déposée pendant un an. Ce délai ne fait bien sûr pas obstacle à une nouvelle mise en accusation en cas de nouveau crime du Président. Le Parlement n'est pas autorisé à débattre ou à prendre une décision au sujet de l'accusation portée contre le Président en cas de guerre, d'état d'exception ou de loi martiale. Dans ce cas, aucune accusation ne peut être déposée contre le président.

Les séances du Parlement et de ses chambres sont publiques. Les débats du Parlement, sauf pour ce qui concerne les questions considérées comme secrètes, sont publiés dans les comptes rendus des séances du Parlement. Un projet de loi est considéré comme adopté s'il recueille la majorité des voix des membres présents et au moins un tiers des voix des députés. Une révision de la Constitution est considérée comme adopté si elle recueille au moins trois cinquièmes des voix des membres du Parlement. Un projet de loi organique est considéré comme adopté s'il recueille la majorité des voix de tous les membres du Parlement au scrutin par appel nominal. La décision du parlement est adoptée sous forme de décret sauf si d'autres conditions sont prévues par la Constitution. Le droit d'adopter d'autres types de décisions est défini dans le règlement du Parlement.

Le Gouvernement assure l'exercice du pouvoir exécutif, c'est-à-dire la politique extérieure et intérieure de l'Etat conformément à la législation. Le Gouvernement est responsable devant le Président et devant le Parlement. Le Premier ministre est le chef du

---

4 La Cour suprême de Géorgie est la plus haute Cour de cassation. Elle révise les décisions rendues par les tribunaux. Les décisions de la Cour suprême sont sans appel. La Cour Constitutionnelle est un organe du contrôle de la Constitution. Elle se prononce sur la conformité à la Constitution des lois et des actes normatifs du Président et du Gouvernement.

Gouvernement. Il nomme les ministres avec l'accord du Président. La démission du Premier ministre ou la cessation de ses fonctions entraîne la fin des pouvoirs des autres membres du Gouvernement. En cas de démission ou de révocation d'un autre membre du Gouvernement, le Premier ministre pourvoit au poste dans les deux semaines. Le Parlement peut déposer une motion de censure à l'égard du Gouvernement. Si le Parlement approuve la censure du Gouvernement à la majorité des trois cinquièmes du nombre total de ses membres dans un délai de 15 à 20 jours après le dépôt de la motion, le Président doit révoquer le Gouvernement. Si le Parlement ne vote pas la censure, il est interdit de déposer une motion de censure contre le Gouvernement pendant six mois suivants.

En ce qui concerne le pouvoir judiciaire, les juges ne sont en théorie soumis qu'à la Constitution et à la loi. Seul le Conseil suprême de Justice, dont les compétences sont établies par une loi organique, peut révoquer les juges. La procédure est conduite conformément aux principes de l'égalité des parties et du contradictoire. La justice est rendue par des tribunaux de droit commun. L'établissement de tribunaux militaires n'est autorisé qu'en cas de guerre et uniquement au sein du système judicaire du pays. La procédure des tribunaux ordinaires y est applicable. L'établissement de tribunaux d'exception et de tribunaux spéciaux n'est pas autorisé. Pour les affaires civiles, les citoyens ont toutefois la possibilité de recourir à l'arbitrage.

II. La construction d'un système de protection des droits de l'Homme

La constitution géorgienne est le principal fondement de la démocratie et du système de protection des droits de l'Homme. Les grands principes du Conseil de l'Europe y ont été intégrés et comme dans tous pays démocratiques, la défense des droits de l'Homme y a été rendue prioritaire.

La Constitution fait un lien direct avec le droit international des droits de l'Homme en posant d'une part le principe de la supériorité des traités internationaux sur les lois, d'autre part en stipulant dans son article 7 que :

> la Géorgie reconnaît et respecte en tant que valeurs immuables et supérieures de l'humanité les droits de l'Homme et les libertés fondamentales universellement reconnus. Dans l'exercice du pouvoir, le peuple et l'Etat sont tenus de respecter ces droits et libertés au même titre que le droit en vigueur.

La constitution garantit notamment l'égalité devant la loi (art. 14), le droit à la liberté (art. 18), la liberté d'expression (art. 19), d'association (art. 25), de manifestation (art. 33) et de confession (art. 9).

Pour les non ressortissants, l'article 47 de la Constitution dispose que les étrangers et les apatrides vivant en Géorgie ont des droits et obligations égaux aux citoyens de Géorgie, sauf exception explicitement prévue par la Constitution et la loi. De plus, l'article 142 du Code pénal punit les actes discriminatoires basés sur la race, la couleur, la langue, le sexe, l'appartenance nationale, ethnique ou sociale.

La Constitution comporte des dispositions limitant l'exercice de certains droits et libertés, afin de sauvegarder la sécurité publique ou l'intégrité territoriale, de lutter contre la criminalité, ou encore de protéger les droits et la dignité d'autrui. Ainsi, en cas d'état d'urgence ou d'état de guerre, le Président de la Géorgie peut imposer, dans l'ensemble ou partie du territoire, des restrictions à certains droits et libertés (liberté de la personne, liberté de la vie privée et du domicile, liberté de circulation, liberté de recevoir et de diffuser des informations, liberté de réunion et de manifestation, droit de propriété, droit de travailler librement, droit de grève, droit d'accès à certains documents officiels). Dans ces cas, le Président est tenu de soumettre sa décision à l'approbation du Parlement dans les 48 heures. S'il ne le fait pas, ou que le parlement rejette les restrictions, ces dernières sont nulles (art. 46).

La Constitution prévoit la création d'un poste de Médiateur de la République (art. 43), qui peut dénoncer publiquement tous faits constituant une violation des droits et libertés de la personne et en informer les autorités et personnes compétentes. Le Médiateur peut agir sur la base des plaintes et informations qui lui sont adressées ou de sa propre initiative. Toute mesure faisant obstacle à son activité est punie par la loi.

Suite à l'entrée en vigueur de la Constitution, le cadre législatif relatif aux droits de l'Homme a été rapidement mis en place, grâce aux intenses efforts du Parlement. Les lois nécessaires pour le bon fonctionnement des tribunaux et de la Cour constitutionnelle (1996) ont notamment été adoptées. La création de la Cour constitutionnelle marque un pas important vers le respect de la Constitution. Les individus ont à présent le droit de s'adresser directement à la Cour constitutionnelle s'ils estiment qu'un acte normatif porte atteinte aux droits et aux libertés garantis par la Constitution.

Conformément à la Constitution et à la loi sur le Ministère Public[5], les fonctions du Procureur sont conformes aux principes démocratiques. Le contrôle général du système judiciaire, qui faisait partie des pouvoirs de la « prokuratura »[6] sous le régime soviétique, a été aboli.

Au sein du Parlement, un Comité chargé des droits de l'Homme composé de onze députés a été mis en place. Outre son travail législatif, ce comité examine des plaintes et requêtes des citoyens relatives à la violation des droits de l'Homme dans le système pénitentiaire. Chaque citoyen peut déposer les requêtes auprès de ce comité. Le comité établit également la liste des prisonniers susceptible d'être gracier par le Président.

---

5 Loi sur le Ministère Public. 21 octobre 2008.N 382 – IIS.

6 « La prokuratura » désigne le ministère public en URSS. Les magistrats du parquet étaient centralisés en un système unique pour tous les pays de l'URSS et étaient indépendants des juridictions.

Enfin, l'Etat accorde une grande importance au développement de ce qu'il est convenu d'appeler le « secteur tiers » constitué d'organisations non gouvernementales (ONG), (internationales et locales), spécialisées dans la protection des droits de l'Homme. A ce jour, plus de 1000 organisations de ce type ont été enregistrées au Ministère de la justice. Certes, il convient de noter que le développement quantitatif des organisations non gouvernementales n'a pas encore trouvé son expression sur le plan qualitatif. A cet égard, il faut tenir compte de l'absence de traditions dans ce domaine, des lacunes méthodologiques et du manque de moyens matériels des ONG, tributaires de l'aide des donateurs. En particulier, le problème du perfectionnement de la formation de leurs employés et bénévoles se pose avec acuité.

III. L'adhésion au Conseil de l'Europe : Consolidation du système de protection des droits de l'Homme

Dès juillet 1992, la Géorgie nouvellement indépendante est admise aux Nations Unies et à la Banque mondiale. Puis, à la fin de l'année, elle devient membre de l'Organisation pour la Sécurité et la Coopération en Europe (OSCE). Elle intègre le Programme de Partenariat pour la Paix, accord de coopération militaire limitée avec l'Organisation du Traité de l'Atlantique Nord (OTAN) en 1994.

La Géorgie a été la première République de l'ancienne URSS à prendre des mesures, en 1991, en vue d'abolir la peine de mort[7]. Tout d'abord, le 20 mars 1991, le Parlement géorgien a aboli la peine de mort pour quatre sortes de délits économiques ne comportant pas de violence (art. 88, 89, 96* et 186 de l'ancien Code pénal de 1975). Puis, le 2 août 1991, la peine de mort a été abolie pour deux délits supplémentaires : le refus d'accomplir son service militaire actif

7 V. la contribution de Giorgi ASATIANI dans le présent ouvrage.

(art. 82 du Code pénal) et les détournements d'avion (art. 242-2). Enfin, après un moratoire de fait sur la peine de mort déclaré en février 1995 et un moratoire officiel déclaré en décembre 1996, la peine de mort a été totalement abolie à l'automne 1997 par voie d'amendement au code pénal. Les peines de mort déjà prononcées ont été commuées en peine d'emprisonnement de longue durée.

Dès 1996, la Géorgie a participé à diverses activités du Conseil de l'Europe dans le cadre des programmes intergouvernementaux de coopération et d'assistance ainsi qu'aux travaux de l'Assemblée parlementaire de l'organisation (APCE) et de ses commissions par le biais de sa délégation d'invités spéciaux. Considérée comme l'élément stabilisateur du Caucase, la Géorgie a déposé une demande d'adhésion au Conseil de l'Europe, le 14 juillet 1996 et s'est déclarée prête à respecter les principes relatifs aux droits de l'Homme et des libertés fondamentales énoncés à l'article 3 du Statut du Conseil de l'Europe. A la demande du Bureau de l'APCE, une délégation d'éminents juristes[8] s'est alors rendue en Géorgie pour examiner la conformité de l'ordre juridique géorgien avec les principes fondamentaux du Conseil de l'Europe, notamment les principes relatifs au respect de la démocratie pluraliste, de l'Etat de droit et du respect des droits de l'Homme. Selon leur rapport, de nombreux progrès avaient été achevés en matière de respect des droits de l'Homme :

> Aujourd'hui, le pays possède une constitution qui peut se comparer avec celle des démocraties traditionnelles. Dans une large mesure, les droits fondamentaux sont également respectés en pratique, avec certaines exceptions ça et là et, parfois, un reste d'appréhension et d'insécurité, par exemple en ce qui concerne la liberté de réunion. Il serait probablement excessif de dire que la norme évoquée dans l'article 3 du statut du Conseil de l'Europe a déjà été pleinement atteinte, mais nous avons eu l'impression qu'il y a un mouvement résolu dans la

8 M. Stefan Trechsel, Président de la Commission Européenne des Droits de l'Homme et M. Isi Foighel, Juge à la Cour Européenne des Droits de l'Homme.

bonne direction qui justifie l'espoir qu'un niveau pleinement compatible sera bientôt réalisé.[9]

Estimant, sur la base de ce rapport, que la Géorgie est une société démocratique pluraliste respectueuse des droits de l'Homme et de l'Etat de droit, qu'elle est en mesure et a la volonté de poursuivre les réformes démocratiques engagées afin de se conformer aux standards européens en la matière, et que l'adhésion au Conseil de l'Europe devrait servir un tel objectif, l'APCE se déclare favorable à l'adhésion de la Géorgie. La Géorgie devient ainsi membre du Conseil de l'Europe le 27 avril 1999.

Les premières années de l'adhésion sont complexes et douloureuses : corruption rongeant le système démocratique, difficultés économiques et sociales, exacerbées par les tensions et conflits ethniques avec les régions séparatistes d'Abkhazie et d'Ossétie du Sud. La Géorgie a eu du mal à remplir son engagement auprès du Conseil de l'Europe et à réaliser toutes les réformes démocratiques promises. La démission, le 23 novembre 2003, du Président Chevardnadze, au pouvoir depuis 1992, suite à la « révolution des roses » menée par l'opposition en raison de suspicions de fraudes lors des élections législatives, puis rapidement raliée par la rue, a fait jaillir de nouveaux espoirs en matière de droits de l'Homme et de démocratie en Géorgie.

IV. Les reformes considérables réalisées depuis la « Révolution de Roses »

Depuis 2004 les autorités géorgiennes procèdent à des réformes institutionnelles, juridiques et socio-économiques, avec une étroite

9 Rapport des « éminents juristes » du 7 novembre1997, AS/Bur/Géorgie (1997)1, annexe 1.

coopération des experts du Conseil de l'Europe. Ce processus s'inscrit dans la dynamique d'adaptation de la législation géorgienne aux standards européens.

Les autorités géorgiennes ont accompli des efforts importants, passant par des arrestations et des licenciements, mais aussi une revalorisation des salaires, pour réformer l'administration, notamment la police, réputée très corrompue. Ces réformes sont allées de paire avec la construction de nouveaux bâtiments équipés des dernières technologies à l'architecture symbolique : de nombreux bâtiments en verre symbolisent la transparence, l'ouverture et la lumière de la nouvelle politique.

Parallèlement, la Géorgie a conduit des réformes visant à une meilleure indépendance de la justice, notamment en établissant des procédures plus objectives et transparentes en matière de nomination, sanction et révocation des juges. Le Conseil Suprême de Justice travaille actuellement à la révision des standards de nomination et de démission des juges, ainsi que des mesures disciplinaires prononcées à leur encontre.

Ces dernières années, le Bureau de Médiateur de la République a également connu des changements considérables. Le Médiateur peut notamment à présent exercer des contrôles sur place des organismes étatiques afin d'exiger des explications de la part des agents. Ces derniers ont l'obligation de lui fournir tous les documents demandés en moins de dix jours[10].

En octobre 2010, le nouveau code de procédure pénal a introduit le procès avec jury, en cas de meurtre aggravé. Le jury ne se prononce que sur la culpabilité ou non de l'accusé, il revient ensuite à un juge de définir la peine. Les jurés délibèrent en toute indépendance, mais sont toutefois techniquement assistés par un juge professionnel dans leurs fonctions. Selon les autorités, cette innovation vise à promouvoir le droit à un procès équitable, mais il semble que le concept et les implications du procès avec jury, y compris le rôle des jurés, ne soient

---

10 Article 18 de la loi organique sur le Médiateur de la République. Le 16 mai, 1996. N 220 – 2S.

pas encore clairs pour le public. D'autre part, il existe un risque que l'absence d'une décision motivée du jury ne satisfasse pas aux exigences de la Convention européenne de sauvegarde des Droits de l'Homme et des Libertés fondamentales[11].

La réforme constitutionnelle de 2010 a introduit la nomination à vie pour l'ensemble des juges, exception faite des juges de la Cour suprême, qui conformément à l'article 90 de la Constitution continuent à être désignés pour une durée de dix ans au minimum. Les candidatures sont présentées par le Président au Parlement, qui nomme les juges de la Cour suprême.

Depuis 2010, les responsables des organes exécutifs et représentatifs des autorités locales sont élus. Les autorités locales ont compétences pour toutes les questions locales, sous réserve de ne pas porter atteinte à la souveraineté de l'Etat, conformément à la législation géorgienne.

Des améliorations ont également été apportées en matière de protection des droits et libertés fondamentales. Depuis 2010, le droit de propriété et d'hériter sont reconnus et garantis par la Constitution (art. 21). Le Gouvernement respecte la liberté religieuse. Il en va de l'égalité de traitement de tous les citoyens, quelles que soient leurs convictions religieuses ou philosophiques. Depuis le 5 Juillet 2011, les organisations religieuses minoritaires peuvent, à coté de la puissante Eglise orthodoxe, être enregistrées comme personnes morales de droit public (art. 1509 du Code Civil géorgien). La loi permet aux groupes religieux ayant « des liens étroits historiques » avec la Géorgie, ainsi qu'aux groupes reconnus en tant que religion par des Etats membres du Conseil de l'Europe, de choisir de devenir soit une entité de droit privé , soit une entité de droit public.

En ce qui concerne la lutte contre le racisme et la situation des minorités nationales, l'Etat géorgien tend à offrir des conditions égales pour le développement culturel de tous les groupes ethniques. La législation en vigueur en Géorgie est relativement protectrice envers les droits des minorités. Chaque individu peut facilement employer sa

---

11 V. CEDH, *Taxquet c. Belgique*, arrêt du 17 novembre 2010.

langue maternelle dans la vie privée et publique[12]. Le Code pénal géorgien fait de certaines infractions ordinaires des infractions spécifiques dès lors qu'elles revêtent un caractère raciste.

Les progrès réalisés vers une société démocratique pluraliste respectueuse des droits de l'Homme et de l'Etat de droit sont plutôt encourageants, mais la Géorgie doit encore fournir un effort considérable pour consolider le fonctionnement de ses institutions démocratiques et améliorer la protection des droits de l'Homme. Le Conseil de l'Europe soutient largement la transition de la Géorgie pour renforcer l'Etat de droit et le processus démocratique.

---

12 Cela est notamment révélé par l'existence de nombreuses écoles ou classes en langues étrangères ou régionales : Il existe des établissements préscolaires en géorgien, mais aussi en russe, arménien, en azerbaïdjanais et en ossète. On compte 183 écoles arméniennes, environ 200 écoles russes (des écoles maternelles, ainsi que des départements de russe dans les principales universités). 159 écoles azéries (et des écoles maternelles, ainsi que des départements d'azerbaïdjanais dans deux universités). De plus, les Grecs peuvent apprendre le grec dans des classes grecques. Les Kurdes bénéficient des mêmes avantages en kurde, ainsi que les Juifs en yiddish. Il existe aussi des écoles bilingues pour les minorités linguistiques : russo-arménien, russo-azeri, russe-ossète, russo-abkhaze, russo-géorgien, russo-yiddish, armenien-géorgien, azeri-géorgien, etc. On compte des écoles trilingues en géorgien-russe-ossète. De même, si la plupart des journaux indépendants sont en géorgien, les minorités nationales disposent de plusieurs journaux. Les médias géorgiens diffusent massivement en géorgien, mais les russes disposent d'émissions radiophoniques et télévisées quotidiennes dans leur langue. Les Arméniens bénéficient d'une émission radiophonique d'une heure par jour, les Azerbaïdjanais de 30 minutes et d'un programme de musique, les Kurdes d'un programme hebdomadaire de 15 minutes.

Questions of the death penalty in Georgia and former Eastern Bloc countries

Giorgi ASATIANI*

It is a great honor for me to address this respected audience. I appreciate the opportunity to inform you about the current situation with application of the death penalty as the extreme penalty in Georgia. I will try to describe the way passed by Georgian Law in connection with this subject from the distant historical past up to the present. I would also like to tell you about the experience of Georgia regarding abolition of the death penalty.

The death penalty is the most extreme and the oldest form of punishment in different times used almost in all countries. In this respect Georgia is not an exception. In Georgian Law the death penalty for a serious crime was used as one of the penalty measures as far back as in the feudal time. Feudal monuments of Georgian Law preserved the indication of methods of punishment and of those crimes commission of which entailed the use of these sanctions against a criminal. Though it should be mentioned that in the 12th century, in the golden age of Georgia, when the country was under Queen Tamar, at the time when the state system reached its high point, the society of that time opposed to the death penalty and in Georgia, for a certain period of time, the death penalty was abolished. However, later, with weakening of king's centralized authority and in the age-old period of occupation government the Georgian State again faced the necessity of introducing this kind of punishment.

The death penalty as a punishment was also used in the eighteenth century when the Russian Empire abolished the king's power in Georgia and the country became a part of the Russian Empire. Justice

---

* Lawyer, lecturer and PhD candidate at Caucasus School of Law, Tbilisi, Georgia; the oral style of the presentation has been maintained.

in this period was exercised according to the Russian legislation and these sanctions were generally used against state criminals or recidivists.

The use of the death penalty as an extreme penalty in Georgia reached an unprecedented scale during the first 30 years of Communist government. In this period shooting as a form of the death penalty strongly dominated quantitatively over other forms of punishment. In Soviet Georgia a death sentence was imposed not only for the most serious crimes, but also for such crimes as, for example, pilferage. However, if the individual was suspected of disloyalty to the Soviet government, this meant inevitable death. It should be emphasized that in this period a sentence was often imposed not by court authorities, but by the famous Soviet "Trinity" who "out of court and investigation" passed and executed death sentences. These methods used on the pretext of a struggle against "people's enemies" served, on the one hand, for terror and frightening of the population, and on the other hand, gave the governing elite of that time an opportunity to get rid of elements dangerous for them, to suppress even a possibility of dissidence in the society. In the history of the Soviet republics this period is known as "Red Terror" that eventually destructed millions of human victims throughout the whole Soviet Union.

In the 1970s and 1980s, when the Soviet Union reached its peak in corruption in the public sector, the power of that time took a decision to increase significantly the struggle against so-called bribe-takers and persons who were in criminal relations with them. In this period a death sentence was given to bribe-takers blamed in most serious crimes, and less frequently – for state crimes.

Executions in the Soviet Republics after 1945 are fully applicable to the countries of the Central Europe of the former Eastern bloc. After World War II their laws were copies of soviet laws. In the late 1940s/early 1950s in Hungary, Czechoslovakia, Bulgaria etc. were conducted trials of the "Enemies of People" on the soviet model, which usually ended by hanging or shooting. From 1990, after "Velvet

Revolutions" in these republics, including Romania, the death penalty was canceled.

Today, Belarus is the last country, where the death penalty is applied. The death penalty in Belarus is carried out by shooting. The death penalty is imposed for 12 categories of crimes in peace time and 2 in war time. In November 1996 a republican referendum showed, that against the abolition of death penalty, voted 80.50% of citizens.

In conditions of independent Georgia the death penalty as one of the forms of punishment existed only 5 years. In 1997 the Parliament of Georgia adopted a law according to which courts were prohibited to pass death sentences to the accused. But let us put it chronologically: in the early 1990s Article 13 of the Criminal Code of Georgia envisaged the death penalty for crimes of different kinds of heaviness. At that time the society supported application of the death penalty. Non-governmental organizations, free press and some groups in the Government oriented to reforms played an important role in turning the public opinion against the death penalty. The result of the efforts of these groups was the consensus reached in the society regarding abolition of the death penalty. In 1995-1996 a moratorium was declared, however courts continued to impose death sentences when necessary, though they were not executed. The last death sentence in Georgia was executed on 14 February 1995. On 12 October 1996 a group of non-governmental organizations founded a Coordination Center for struggle against the death penalty that later was joined by many other non-governmental organizations. For a short period of time, the Center conducted a large-scale elucidative campaign against the death penalty in Georgia. It took various measures, organized press-conferences, published articles, etc. This campaign was also actively supported by mass-media. This activity of the society allowed the reformers in legislative bodies to increase their struggle in the Parliament for adoption of new legislation that would not envisage the death penalty as a form of punishment. As a result, at the end of 1996, the number of articles stipulating for the death penalty was reduced. Their number decreased from 13 to 4 articles. Then, during the whole year, the same organizations and private persons conducted PRcampaigns for full and final abolition of the law that envisaged the death penalty in Georgia. According to the statistical data, at the end of 1995 and at the beginning of 1996, after the campaign conducted throughout the whole country, only 10-20% of the population supported abolition of this special measure of punishment. At the end of 1997, the study of public opinion showed that this figure reached 50-55%. Finally, on 11 November 1997 the Parliament of Georgia abolished officially the death penalty.[1] And for the persons who at that time were waiting for execution of the death sentence, the death penalty was replaced by life-imprisonment and in some cases – by 20-year imprisonment. Georgia, after Moldova, became the second post-Soviet country that did away with this extreme form of punishment. Later, the death penalty was abolished in a number of post-Soviet countries, such as Azerbaijan, Armenia, Lithuania, Latvia, Estonia, Turkmenistan, Ukraine and the Kyrgyz Republic. The most important thing is, that abolition of the death penalty did not challenge increase of the criminal level and new legislation gave chance to Georgia to become a member of several international organizations.

Of special mention should be the attitude of the international community to the above problem: the international community regards the death penalty as the extreme penalty. In the international legislation the problems of the death penalty and protection of rights of individuals sentenced to death are governed by several international agreements. One of the most important agreements is the "International Covenant on Civil and Political Rights" adopted in 1966. In Article 6 of the aforesaid Covenant it is specified that a death sentence may be imposed only for most serious crimes in accordance with the law in forth and not contrary to the provisions of this Covenant.[2] Here the rights of the people sentenced to death to seek pardon or commutation of the sentence are explained. The second

---

1 Gela Nikolaishvili. Human Rights in Georgia. Critical Analysis/UNDP, Tbilisi, Georgia 1998.

2 International Covenant on Civil and Political Rights of 16 December 1966, UNTS no. 999, p. 171 <http://www2.ohchr.org/english/law/ccpr.htm#part3> (26.06.2012).

optional protocol to the "Covenant on Civil and Political Rights" regarding abolition of the death penalty was adopted in 1990 and is also valid to the present day. The states that signed the Protocol believe that abolition of the death penalty "contributes to enhancement of human dignity and progressive development of human rights" (preamble). The above Protocol demands from the state parties to suspend capital punishment and to take all possible measures to abolish it. No reservation is admissible to this Protocol, though states may reserve the right to use the death penalty during wartime against persons who committed most serious crimes of a military nature. However, all states that joined this agreement are to notify the Secretary-General of the United Nations on the time of the beginning and the end of this war.[3]

As we see, today the international law condemns unambiguously the death penalty. At the end of the 20th century such political environment was created when the majority of international organizations adopted conventions and protocols related to abolition of the death penalty, though some states have not yet resorted to these actions. Today, the death penalty still exists, for example, in Saudi Arabia, China, Iran, as well as in some of the US states, etc. The International Covenant shows vividly the attitude of the international community to the death penalty. Article 6 contains the appeal to the states where this extreme penalty still exists to be careful in using this form of punishment.

For years there has been a dispute between supporters and opponents of abolition of the death penalty. Both parties have serious arguments. But allow me to express my own position and join the ranks of opponents of application of the death penalty as a punishment since the death penalty as a punishment contradicts in its essence the purpose of punishment. The purpose of punishment is to prevent a crime, to reform a criminal and to return him as a full-bodied member of the society. Indeed, we can argue how far the forms of punishment spread in the modern society facilitate correction of criminals and

---

3 Rona K. Smith, International Human rights, Blackbone Press 2003.

changing them into full-bodied members of the society, but one thing is indisputable – the death penalty exceeds the limits of humanism and principles of modern values. When the death penalty as an extreme penalty is used, a state and a society become like a machine possessed by the lust of vengeance and wish, using barbarian methods, to pay back to the individual who committed a crime. We, on the one hand, censure and condemn a criminal for a most serious crime committed by him, but on the other hand, we give the right to another individual, the judge, to decide a person's death and life fate. Sentences are passed by normal people and nobody is safeguarded against mistakes. A question arises whether a state has the right to authorize one or another person to deprive a man or, let us say, a criminal of life by taking a decision even in full conformity with law. If we proceed from the point that deprivation of human life is evil, by passing a death sentence we, on the one hand, free the society from crime, but at the same time we obtain another murderer, a person who executes the death sentence imposed by the court. One crime entails another crime.

The modern democratic society recognizes the principle of human equality, yes, everybody is equal to law, nobody has the right to take away another man's life. Based on this principle, the application of the death penalty as a punishment is, to put it mildly, anti-constitutional and strongly violates the norms recognized by the international community.

And finally, our common debt is to think, at least for one minute, which is the worse punishment for a criminal – to spend his whole life in a cell, in four walls, isolated from the society, or to finish his life by one shot?

Summary of Discussion

During the discussion one of the participants of the conference asked the presenter a question on abolition of death penalty as the highest measure of punishment in Georgian legislation. Namely, it touched the fact when in 1997 Georgian Parliament abolished, but not withdrew from the legislation, the use of death penalty as the highest measure of punishment. Concerning the question the presenter answered that the death penalty as the highest measure of punishment was abolished in Georgia on 11 November 1997 when the Georgian Parliament adopted the legal act "On total abolition of death penalty as a special punishment measure". The adoption of this legal act was significantly derived from Georgia's motivation to become a member of Council of Europe and to harmonize its own legislation with the European standards of human rights protection. On 17 June 1999, Georgia signed the 16th Protocol on abolition of death penalty during peaceful period of time of Protection of Human Rights and Freedoms of European Convention. On 3 May 2002, Georgia signed the 13th Protocol on abolition of death penalty during wartime. On 22 March 1999, Georgia joined the 2nd optional protocol on abolition of death penalty of the International Pact on Civil and Political Rights that came into force on 22 June 1999. Thus, Georgia together with the internal legal norms gained international liabilities that totally excluded death penalty as the special measure of punishment both during the peace and wartime.

Moreover, one of the participants of the conference got interested about the public opinion on abolition of death penalty as the highest measure of punishment while decisions were being made on this issue and about their opinion today. The presenter answered that 10-20% of the population throughout the country supported the abolition of such special measure of punishment at the beginning of 1996. At the end of 1997 according to polls it reached 50-55%. This kind of a change is connected to the active campaign throughout the country both by the representatives of non-governmental organizations and some groups in governmental sector oriented on reforms. This decision became for Georgia one of the promoting factors on the way of integration with the European structures. Today, large portion of Georgia's population considers unacceptable the issue of death penalty because this phase has already passed and modern society fully agrees with the principles of international humanism. Besides, it is considered as remains of communist legislation which on its part was a weapon in the hands of the then authorities in order to strengthen their ideology and to use it against those masses that had opposite opinion.

Also, there was a question on how the abolition of death penalty as the highest measure of punishment affected the criminal situation of the country. The questioner was interested whether this kind of abolition caused the worsening of the criminal situation and the increase of grave crimes. The presenter answered that heavy punishments don't always solve the problem and the fear towards the punishment doesn't force the criminal from refraining committing unlawful act. Concerning the criminal situation in Georgia after the abolition of death penalty it has not changed much. Moreover, if we compare the official statistics of the late 90s and present situation we'll see that the number of grave crimes, that according to the modern legislation presume live imprisonment, is considerably declined.

Prevention of torture in the Black Sea region – progress or stagnation?

An assessment of developments in Armenia, Bulgaria, Georgia, Turkey and Ukraine, 1990-2011

Ralf ALLEWELDT*

Is it possible to fight torture effectively? And if so, how? In this paper, I want to deal with this question, by examining approaches to the prevention of torture in the Black Sea region. This region is of particular interest for the participants of the workshop held in Tbilisi in September 2011 during which this paper was presented. At the same time, although many countries in the Black Sea region face similar problems concerning torture and its prevention, the approaches taken by governments show a remarkable degree of diversity.

I. The prohibition of torture

Torture is prohibited by international law. Article 7 of the International Covenant on Civil and Political Rights[1] states:

> No one shall be subjected to torture or to cruel, inhuman or degrading treatment or punishment. [...]

---

* Dr. iur., Interim Professor of Law, University of Munich, Germany.

1 International Covenant on Civil and Political Rights of 16 December 1966, UNTS no. 999, p. 171.

A similar provision is contained in Article 3 of the European Convention on Human Rights[2]. Since the phenomenon of torture was considered to be a particularly serious human rights problem, governments agreed to conclude a specific Convention against Torture in 1984[3].

The prohibition of torture is a very unique human right, in that it allows for no exceptions or restrictions in the interests of the community. Even in times of war or other emergency situations threatening the life of a nation, no derogation is possible[4]. Specific rules against torture are dealing with certain situations in the context of armed conflicts, namely with regard to the treatment of prisoners of war[5].

In spite of this very clear legal situation, torture and other forms of ill-treatment of detainees still persist in more than 100 countries[6]. Torture is a very serious violation of human dignity. It inflicts immediately very cruel suffering to the victims, and it causes serious long-term problems for their physical and psychological health. Some victims die under torture or a short time afterwards. Many survivors suffer from a trauma which makes it very difficult for them to enjoy life again, and which even may lead them to committing suicide[7].

---

2 Convention for the Protection of Human Rights and Fundamental Freedoms of 4 November 1950, ETS no. 5.

3 Convention against Torture and Other Cruel, Inhuman or Degrading Treatment of Punishment of 10 December 1984, UNTS no. 1465, p. 85.

4 Cf. Article 4 of the International Covenant on Civil and Political Rights, Article 15 of the European Convention on Human Rights, Article 2 of the Convention against Torture.

5 See the Regulations concerning the law and customs of war on land, 18 October 1907, Article 4.

6 A picture of the situation has been given recently by Manfred Nowak, Study on the phenomena of torture, cruel, inhuman or degrading treatment or punishment in the world, including an assessment of conditions of detention. Addendum to the Report of the Special Rapporteur on torture and other cruel, inhuman or degrading treatment or punishment, 5 February 2010, UN Doc. A/HRC/13/39/Add.5, para. 9, including a number of proposals for action, paras. 140-166.

7 Typical consequences of torture and possibilities of rehabilitation are described by Manfred Nowak, Interim Report of the Special Rapporteur on torture and

Accordingly, many will understand the necessity that international law not only contains a prohibition of torture, but that it also provides for mechanisms and procedures for the implementation of this prohibition.

II. Individual complaint procedures: achievements and limitations

In Europe, including in all countries of the Black Sea region, all persons who feel that their human rights are violated are entitled to apply to the European Court of Human Rights. This court has the power to determine, in a binding judgment, whether human rights have in fact been violated and, if this is the case, to order the respondent State to provide the victim with "just satisfaction", usually in the form of a financial compensation for pecuniary and non-pecuniary damage[8]. The European system is considered to be one of the most effective international human rights protection mechanisms in the world. Individual complaint mechanisms in general reflect a revolutionary development in international law: individuals have human rights and may enforce them in the international sphere, even against their own government.

Victims of torture may use these individual complaint procedures, and in fact many cases alleging torture have been brought to the European Court in the last few years and decades[9]. Still, although these procedures are extremely important for human rights protection, they are not sufficient for eliminating torture effectively, because

---

other cruel, inhuman or degrading treatment or punishment, 10 August 2010, UN Doc. A/65/273, paras. 63 et seq.

8 Cf. Articles 41, 46 of the European Convention on Human Rights.

9 Starting from Ireland v. United Kingdom, judgment of 18 January 1978, Series A no. 25. For a list of recent cases see European Court of Human Rights, Annual Report 2011, pp. 91-93, 112-116, <www.echr.coe.int>.

cases of alleged torture differ considerably from other human rights cases.

We may understand that if we consider the typical emotional situation of someone who has recently been subjected to torture. The main emotion of such a person is likely to be fear: fear from taking any steps against their government, fear from being tortured again, fear from other reprisals. Indeed, cases have occurred where individual applicants in proceedings before the European Court of Human Rights have been killed or have died under unclear circumstances, or being subjected to pressure from government authorities to withdraw their application [10] . Understandably, governments object to allegations of torture. They will dispute the facts and may even prosecute the applicant for libel or similar offences. Since torture usually takes place in secrecy, victims typically have problems to prove their case. The European Court of Human Rights will find a violation of Article 3 if the underlying facts are proven "beyond reasonable doubt"[11]. For individual applicants there is no certainty that those time-consuming procedures will be successful in the end. And, very practically, not all victims of torture are in a position and willing to pay the considerable cost of a competent lawyer to bring their case to Strasbourg.

For all these reasons, many victims of torture are reluctant to introduce any kind of application concerning their treatment, and, as stated by Antonio Cassese, the first President of the European Committee for the Prevention of Torture, it is likely that most cases of

---

10 See the judgments of the European Court of Human Rights in Aksoy v. Turkey, 18 December 1996, paras. 101 et seq., and Bitiyeva and X. v. Russia, 21 June 2007, paras. 3, 7, 127-136, as well as International Helsinki Federation for Human Rights (ed.), The assault on human rights defenders in the Russian Federation, Belarus and Uzbekistan, 2006, p. 16 et seq.

11 European Court of Human Rights, Ireland v. United Kingdom, judgment of 18 January 1978, Series A no. 25, para. 161; Nachova and others v. Bulgaria, judgment of 6 July 2005, Reports 2005-VII, para. 147.

torture or ill-treatment are never examined in any kind of legal or other procedure[12].

The most important reason why complaint procedures should be complemented by other mechanisms is, however, that any official finding that a person has been tortured will come, in a way, too late. The consequences of torture, as described above, cannot be removed by any kind of declaration or compensation. Even in those cases where a victim of torture receives compensation in a simple procedure, this will not remove the physical and psychological scars. Normally where the law is violated, restitution or compensation is possible, in particular where merely economic interests are at stake. Such compensation does hardly work for victims of torture. In these cases, typically either the law is respected or it is irreparably violated. Accordingly, in the fight against torture additional protection mechanisms are necessary which aim to prevent acts of torture from happening. In this context, "prevention is the key"[13].

III. Mechanisms for the prevention of torture. The CPT

As a consequence, specific mechanisms for the prevention of torture have been created which have the right to visit places of detention, to examine the situation of the detained persons, and to give recommendations to governments how such persons can be protected effectively against torture and other forms of ill-treatment. The first and most important prevention mechanism is the European Committee for the Prevention of Torture (CPT). It was established through the

12 Antonio Cassese, Inhuman States, 1996, p. 17.

13 Antonio Cassese, "A new approach to human rights. The European Convention for the Prevention of Torture", American Journal of International Law 83 (1989), p. 128 (129).

European Convention for the Prevention of Torture (ECPT[14]) in 1987, and took up its activities in 1990. Following many years of negotiations, a similar institution was created at the universal level in 2006, namely the Sub-Committee for Prevention of the Committee against Torture of the United Nations (SPT). Its legal basis is the Optional Protocol to the UN Convention against Torture (OPCAT)[15]. This Protocol requires State Parties, in addition, to create National Mechanisms for the Prevention of Torture (NPMs).

The focus of this paper is on the activities of the European Committee for the Prevention of Torture, and I will concentrate on the problem of physical ill-treatment by the police and other security forces. This area is only part of the field of activities and recommendations of the CPT, the other important part being the conditions of detention and their improvement. I will examine the development of torture prevention in selected countries of the Black Sea Region, namely Georgia, Armenia, Turkey, Ukraine and Bulgaria.

The practical task of the CPT is to establish the relevant facts during visits to places of detention and, on this basis, to give recommendations as to the prevention of ill-treatment of the detained persons[16].

CPT visits are carried out without a specific invitation of the government concerned. During the preparation of such a visit, non-governmental organisations may communicate their complaints or reports to the CPT. By these means, the committee may develop a concrete idea even before the visit as to where are the practical problems in a given country. During the visits, members of the visiting delegation conduct private conversations with detainees and carry out, if necessary, medical examinations. The CPT will consult

---

14 European Convention for the Prevention of Torture and Inhuman or Degrading Treatment or Punishment of 26 November 1987, ETS no. 152. Website of the CPT: <www.cpt.coe.int>.

15 Optional Protocol to the Convention against Torture and other Cruel, Inhuman or Degrading Treatment or Punishment of 18 December 2002, UNTS no. 2375, p. 237.

16 See Articles 7-9 ECPT.

the custody register and any relevant medical records. The CPT is entitled to request and acquire any information concerning the conditions of detention and treatment of detainees which is necessary for assessing the situation. Sometimes the delegation of the CPT finds torture cells or tools for ill-treatment; such discoveries are of course a very credible basis for expressing convincing recommendations related to the prevention of torture towards the government[17].

On the basis of the information obtained during a visit, the CPT gives recommendations to the government as to how to ensure human treatment of detained persons. Such recommendations are written down, together with a description of the facts found, in a report to the government. This report is confidential but may be published with the consent of the government. In the case of the CPT, such publication usually takes place one or two years after the visit. Publication is the rule now for all contracting states of the European Convention, with the important exceptions of Russia and, partly, Azerbaijan[18].

Unlike court proceedings, the activities of the CPT are based on the principle of cooperation[19], not confrontation. The success of the Committee is dependent on the attitude of the government. The Committee may issue recommendations, if necessary repeat them several times, but there are no means to enforce them and to ensure their implementation. The only thing the Committee may do if the government fails to cooperate or to improve the situation in the light of the recommendations of the CPT, is to issue a "public statement"[20]. Such an event occurs very rarely; in the 25 years of the CPT's existence only six public statements were made.

In the following sections of this paper, I will describe the situation in the Black Sea Region countries under review at the beginning of the

---

17 See Antonio Cassese, Inhuman States, op. cit., p. 16; and, to give some examples, CPT, Public Statement on Turkey, 15 December 1992, CPT/Inf (93) 1, para. 20; Report on the visit to Ukraine in 2009, CPT/Inf (2011) 29, paras. 13; Report on the visit to Croatia in 1998, CPT/Inf (2001) 5, para. 22.

18 See Article 10 ECPT.

19 Article 3 ECPT.

20 Article 10, para. 2 ECPT.

CPT's activities, and subsequently I will compare this situation with the situation found during the latest visits made by the CPT. The first visits to these countries took place, dependent on the date of ratification of the Convention by the country in question, between 1990 (Turkey) and 2002 (Armenia). The latest reports refer to visits within the period between 2009 (Turkey) and 2011 (Ukraine).

IV. The beginning of the CPT's activities in the Black Sea region

When the CPT visited Turkey for the first time in 1990, it found that torture and other forms of severe ill-treatment where "important characteristics" of police custody in that country[21]. During its first visits to Bulgaria (1995), Ukraine (1998), Georgia (2001) and Armenia (2002), the CPT concluded in very similar wordings that persons deprived of their liberty by the police or militia in these countries run a "significant risk of being ill-treated" at the time of their apprehension or while in police custody, in particular when being interrogated, and on occasion resort may be had to severe ill-treatment or torture[22].

The forms of ill-treatment, as alleged by the detainees, included slaps, punches, kicks, beating on the soles of the feet ("falaka"), blows with a truncheon or other hard objects, the infliction of electric shocks (all countries), asphyxiation by using a gas mask or plastic bag (Georgia, Ukraine), suspension by the body in an inverted position (Georgia, Ukraine), suspension by the arms or wrists, including behind the body (Turkey), squeezing of fingers with pliers (Armenia),

---

21 CPT, Public Statement on Turkey, 15 December 1992, CPT/Inf (93) 1, para. 4.

22 See the CPT Reports on the visits to Bulgaria in 1995, CPT/Inf (97) 1, para. 27; to Georgia in 2001, CPT/Inf (2002) 14, para. 23; to Ukraine in 1998, CPT/Inf (2002) 19, para. 28; to Armenia in 2002, CPT/Inf (2004) 25, para. 17, 19.

squeezing of the genitals (Turkey, Ukraine), sexual humiliation of women (Ukraine), severe psychological humiliation, hosing with pressurised cold water, threats of torture to the detained person or to others, incarceration for lengthy periods in very small, dark and unventilated cells (Turkey). This list is likely to be incomplete.

In sum, although the situation was not identical in all of the countries under review, it was to a large extent similar, and it may be fairly described as rather serious.

V. The present situation

If we compare the most recent CPT reports with those reports which were drawn up after the first visits, we may see that in some of these countries the treatment of persons by the police has improved considerably. In others, the CPT did not find any significant changes.

With regard to Ukraine and Armenia, the CPT in its latest reports uses more or less the same words as it did in 1995 and 2002. During the 2009 visit to Ukraine, the Committee again received "a substantial number of allegations of recent physical ill-treatment". Like 1995, some of the methods used could be described as torture (infliction of electric shocks; asphyxiation using a plastic bag or gas mask, with tear gas or cigarette smoke being poured into the mask; sexual humiliation, "falaka"; extensive beating while the person was handcuffed and suspended). The CPT found supporting medical evidence as well as some unusual objects which could be used for beatings (a baseball bat, a crowbar)[23]. Apparently the situation had not changed by the time of a follow-up visit in late 2011[24]. In Armenia, during the 2010 visit "a significant number" of credible and consistent allegations were made

23 CPT, Report on the visit to Ukraine in 2009, CPT/Inf (2011) 29, paras. 12, 13.

24 CPT, Preliminary observations by the delegation which visited Ukraine in 2011, CPT/Inf (2012) 8, p. 6.

of recent physical ill-treatment, consisting mainly of punches, kicks and blows inflicted with truncheons, bottles filled with water or wooden bats. Like in 2002, some of the methods used could be said to amount to torture (extensive beating; infliction of electric shocks with stun batons; blows to the soles of the feet)[25].

Apparently some change has been achieved in Bulgaria. During the CPT visit to this country carried out in 2006, the majority of the persons in police custodyfelt that they had been "correctly treated". Numerous persons with considerable experience of the police stated that there had been "a change for the better" in recent years as regards the manner in which they were treated by police officers. Still, a "significant number" of persons, including juveniles, complained about physical ill-treatment at the time of their apprehension or subsequent questioning by police officers. The ill-treatment alleged mainly consisted of kicks, punches, slaps and blows with truncheons or other hard objects. Some detained persons claimed to have been subjected to psychological pressure in order to make them confess to a crime[26]. The findings following the CPT's visit to Bulgaria four years later, in 2010, were very similar, however, in addition, a small number of detainees complained about the use of electric shocks. In spite of positive developments, the CPT concluded that "the problem of police ill-treatment persists"[27].

The CPT found that significant developments had taken place in Georgia and Turkey.

During the visit to Georgia in 2010, the "great majority" of persons interviewed by the CPT indicated that they had been treated in a correct manner. The delegation received a few allegations of physical ill-treatment by the police, relating for the most part to excessive force (punches, kicks) at the time of apprehension, but including some allegations related to ill-treatment during questioning.

---

25 CPT, Report on the visit to Armenia in 2010, CPT/Inf (2011) 24, para. 12.

26 CPT, Report on the visit to Bulgaria in 2006, CPT/Inf (2008) 11, para. 12.

27 CPT, Report on the visit to Bulgaria in 2010, CPT/Inf (2012) 9, paras. 13, 14.

The findings of this visit confirm, according to the CPT, the "generally positive impression" already obtained during the previous visit in 2007[28], that the situation as regards the treatment of detained persons in Georgia has "considerably improved", and this impression was confirmed by various interlocutors like NGOs and representatives of the Public Defender's Office. The CPT thinks that the "series of measures" taken over the last few years by the Georgian authorities are "bearing fruit"[29].

In the report on its 2005 visit to Turkey, the CPT stressed from the outset that the facts found in the provinces visited (Adana, Istanbul and Van) are "encouraging". The great majority of detainees stated that they had not been physically ill-treated, several of them emphasised the contrast with the situation some years ago. Various interlocutors like prosecutors, bar associations or non-governmental organisations indicated that torture was now "exceptional" and there had been a "very significant decrease" of other forms of ill-treatment. In the report on the 2009 visit, the Committee was "pleased to note" the continuing "downward trend" in the incidence of ill-treatment, and apparently the great majority of detainees stated that they had been treated correctly while in police custody. In one part of the country (area of Diyarbakır), however, detainees allegedly had been subjected to beatings during transportation, blows with batons und threats of a sexual nature, as well as cigarette burns.

If we come back now to our initial question whether the prevention of torture in the Black Sea region is in a state of progress or stagnation, we see that we cannot give a clear, uniform answer to this question. None of the countries can be described as ideal as regards the treatment of detained persons, and we may say that each country finds itself within a process from the rule of ill-treatment to the rule of fair treatment of detainees. Having said this, it appears clearly from the

---

28 CPT, Report on the visit to Georgia in 2007, CPT/Inf (2007) 42, paras. 6, 10-11.
29 CPT, Report on the visit to Georgia in 2010, CPT/Inf (2010) 27, paras. 13-14.

CPT reports that in some countries there is more progress and in others more stagnation as regards the prevention of torture.

In the following section, I want to look into the reasons for such differences, and to find out about typical steps that a government may take which may prove effective in the fight against torture. In particular, in order to find out how such progress might be connected to the activities of the CPT, I want to look into the typical recommendations given by the CPT and the degree to which they have been implemented in the countries in question.

VI. Analysis of typical CPT recommendations and their implementation

A. The CPT standards

The CPT has developed a "corpus of standards" regarding the treatment of persons in police custody. This is a set of recommendations which was originally contained in the annual general reports of the CPT, and they are part of almost each and every country report in countries where there is a problem concerning torture and ill-treatment by the police, including the countries which are under review in this article.

The first condition – which is not in itself sufficient, but absolutely necessary – is that the political leadership of the country gives a clear, audible message to all subordinates that torture and ill-treatment of detained person is a totally unacceptable behaviour, and that it will have negative consequences for any perpetrator, including such of a criminal nature. In short, the government should proclaim a "zero tolerance" policy as regards torture[30].

30 CPT, 14th General Report, CPT/Inf (2004) 28, para. 42.

The key recommendations on prevention are based on the experience that the period immediately following arrest is when the risk of physical ill-treatment is greatest[31]. At this point in time, the police has full control and power over the detained person and torture happens when this power is abused.

Effective prevention of torture accordingly requires that the opportunities for such abuse are reduced as far as possible. For this purpose the CPT recommends that the law should limit police custody to a relatively short duration (72 hours or less), and that authorities ensure that such rules are respected in reality[32].

During detention, any contact with the outside world or other persons not belonging to the police forces contributes to prevention. The CPT recommends that any detained person should be brought promptly before a judge who should have the right, and duty, to order appropriate investigation and other measures if a person complains about ill-treatment, or if other evidence of ill-treatment, like visible injuries, come to light[33].

In addition, the CPT recommends to governments to adopt three fundamental safeguards against ill-treatment: the right of detainees, from the very beginning of custody, to inform a family member or friend about their detention, the right to access to a lawyer, and the right to request a medical examination by a doctor. All detainees should be expressly informed about these rights. Any possibility for authorities to delay the exercise of one of these rights should be clearly defined and limited in time. In order to exclude any possibility

---

31 CPT, 6th General Report, CPT/Inf (1996) 21, para. 15; 12th General Report, CPT/Inf (2002) 15, para. 41.

32 Cf. CPT, Report on the visit to Bulgaria in 2010, CPT/Inf (2012) 9, paras. 10-11; Report on the visit to Ukraine in 2009, CPT/Inf (2011) 29, paras. 9-11; Report on the visit to Georgia in 2010, CPT/Inf (2010) 27, para. 10; Report on the visit to Armenia in 2010, CPT/Inf (2011) 24, paras. 9-10; Report on the visit to Turkey in 2009, CPT/Inf (2011) 13, para. 13.

33 CPT, 12th General Report, CPT/Inf (2002) 15, para. 45; 14th General Report, CPT/Inf (2004) 28, para. 28.

of retaliation in the context of medical examinations, they should take part out of the hearing and normally out of the sight of policemen[34].

I will now look into the question as to what extent the CPT's recommendations have been implemented in the countries under review in this article.

B. Developments in Turkey (1990 - 2009)

The most important activities taken by the Turkish government on the recommendation of the CPT may be summarized as follows[35]:

The Turkish government repeatedly issued public statements about a "zero tolerance" policy towards torture[36]. Many legislative reforms have taken place. In particular, the maximum period of police custody has been considerably reduced. In the beginning in 1990, it was in some cases admissible to detain a person up to 30 days before he or she was brought before a judge[37]. This period has been reduced to 1 to 4 days[38]. The right to notify a relative or friend is now established in Turkish law and, as a rule, respected in reality[39]. The right to immediate access to a lawyer has been introduced in law, and increasingly, though not always, the police is complying with this

34 CPT, 2nd General Report, CPT/Inf (92) 3, paras. 36-38; 6th General Report, CPT/Inf (96) 21, paras. 14-16; 12th General Report, CPT/Inf (2002) 15, paras. 41-44.

35 See, in particular, CPT, Report on the visit to Turkey in 2005, CPT/Inf (2006) 30, para. 12.

36 CPT, Report on the visit to Turkey in 2005, CPT/Inf (2006) 30, para. 16.

37 CPT, Public Statement on Turkey, 15 December 1992, CPT/Inf (93) 1, paras. 29-30.

38 CPT, Report on the visit to Turkey in 2005, CPT/Inf (2006) 30, para. 13; Report on the visit to Turkey in 2009, CPT/Inf (2011) 13, para. 13.

39 CPT, Report on the visit to Turkey in 2005, CPT/Inf (2006) 30, paras. 13, 22; Report on the visit to Turkey in 2009, CPT/Inf (2011) 13, para. 19.

requirement[40]. There is also a system of medical examinations at the beginning and at the end of police custody, however, its implementation apparently leaves something to be desired[41].

In contrast to the previous situation, there are now detailed custody registers[42]. Public prosecutors conduct monitoring visits to police stations in order to examine the treatment of detainees[43]. Higher sentences have been introduced for officials who have committed the crime of torture[44]. Finally, intense efforts have been made with regard to the professional training of policemen[45].

C. *Developments in Bulgaria (1995 - 2010)*

In Bulgaria, reforms in police training have taken place, as well as other legislative reforms[46]. Independent monitoring of police stations is carried out by the Bulgarian Helsinki Committee and other actors[47]. Regional commissions on human rights and police effects have been established and are working[48]. Fundamental safeguards (information on family, access to a lawyer and a doctor) are in place legally, though

---

40 CPT, Report on the visit to Turkey in 2005, CPT/Inf (2006) 30, paras. 13, 23; Report on the visit to Turkey in 2009, CPT/Inf (2011) 13, paras. 20-22 with critical remarks about the introduction, in 2006, of exceptions to this right.

41 CPT, Report on the visit to Turkey in 2005, CPT/Inf (2006) 30, paras. 13, 26; Report on the visit to Turkey in 2009, CPT/Inf (2011) 13, para. 23.

42 CPT, Report on the visit to Turkey in 2005, CPT/Inf (2006) 30, paras. 13, 21; Report on the visit to Turkey in 2009, CPT/Inf (2011) 13, paras. 29-30 with some critical remarks.

43 CPT, Report on the visit to Turkey in 2005, CPT/Inf (2006) 30, paras. 13, 27; Report on the visit to Turkey in 2009, CPT/Inf (2011) 13, para. 35, including critical remarks as to the thoroughness of some of these visits.

44 CPT, Report on the visit to Turkey in 2005, CPT/Inf (2006) 30, paras. 13, 14.

45 CPT, Report on the visit to Turkey in 2005, CPT/Inf (2006) 30, para. 29.

46 CPT, Report on the visit to Bulgaria in 2006, CPT/Inf (2008) 11, para. 15; Report on the visit to Bulgaria in 2010, CPT/Inf (2012) 09, para. 14.

47 CPT, Report on the visit to Bulgaria in 2006, CPT/Inf (2008) 11, paras. 15, 36; Report on the visit to Bulgaria in 2010, CPT/Inf (2012) 09, para. 14.

48 CPT, Report on the visit to Bulgaria in 2006, CPT/Inf (2008) 11, para. 15.

they are not always implemented[49]. In particular the CPT noted that it "is still rare for detained persons to benefit from a lawyer during police custody"[50]. In addition, the CPT was concerned that the exact time of apprehension was not always recorded properly by the police[51].

D. Developments in Georgia (2001 - 2010)

In Georgia, the CPT found that the 72 hours time limit for police custody is now generally respected[52]. A number of new staff in the field of internal affairs has been recruited and trained, including in areas relevant for the prevention of torture[53]. A code of police ethics has been adopted[54]. Modern equipment for interrogation had has been acquired, including video and audio equipment [55]. Standardised custody records have been introduced, as well as a special system to monitor injuries of newly admitted persons to a detention establishment[56].

Furthermore the reliance on confessions in the criminal procedure has been reduced. Important procedural reforms have been introduced, in particular a rule that information obtained during police interviews cannot be the basis of a conviction unless the relevant statement is repeated by the person in court[57]. Independent monitoring of the

---

49 CPT, Report on the visit to Bulgaria in 2006, CPT/Inf (2008) 11, paras. 26-33; Report on the visit to Bulgaria in 2010, CPT/Inf (2012) 09, paras. 20-25.

50 CPT, Report on the visit to Bulgaria in 2010, CPT/Inf (2012) 09, para. 22.

51 CPT, Report on the visit to Bulgaria in 2010, CPT/Inf (2012) 09, paras. 11, 25.

52 CPT, Report on the visit to Georgia in 2007, CPT/Inf (2007) 42, para. 9; Report on the visit to Georgia in 2010, CPT/Inf (2010) 27, para. 10.

53 CPT, Report on the visit to Georgia in 2007, CPT/Inf (2007) 42, para. 12; Report on the visit to Georgia in 2010, CPT/Inf (2010) 27, para. 15.

54 CPT, Report on the visit to Georgia in 2007, CPT/Inf (2007) 42, para. 12.

55 CPT, Report on the visit to Georgia in 2007, CPT/Inf (2007) 42, para. 12.

56 CPT, Report on the visit to Georgia in 2007, CPT/Inf (2007) 42, para. 12; Report on the visit to Georgia in 2010, CPT/Inf (2010) 27, para. 32.

57 CPT, Report on the visit to Georgia in 2007, CPT/Inf (2007) 42, para. 12.

police is carried out by the public defender's office and non-governmental organisations[58].

E. Developments in Ukraine and Armenia (1998 - 2010)

In its latest reports concerning Ukraine and Armenia, the CPT considered it necessary to remind the respective governments that the principle of cooperation (Article 3 ECPT) requires decisive action to be taken on the Committee's recommendations. The CPT expressed its concern that "a number of positive developments is overshadowed by little or no progress in several key areas", including the treatment of persons detained by the police[59]. While some developments were appreciated by the CPT, like the independent investigation of one particular case of alleged ill-treatment and death in custody (Armenia[60]) and efforts in the field of training and supervision (Ukraine[61]), the Committee expressed its concern about other issues, such as the fact that in a number of cases the time of deprivation of liberty was not properly recorded in the custody register, and that such registers contained inaccurate or misleading information[62]. The CPT saw "hardly any improvement" concerning the fundamental safeguards against ill-treatment, including the right to notify a relative or third person of custody, the right to have access to a lawyer and a doctor, as well as the right to be informed about these rights[63].

---

58 CPT, Report on the visit to Georgia in 2007, CPT/Inf (2007) 42, para. 12; Report on the visit to Georgia in 2010, CPT/Inf (2010) 27, para. 9.

59 CPT, Report on the visit to Armenia in 2010, CPT/Inf (2011) 24, para. 6; similar words in the Report on the visit to Ukraine in 2009, CPT/Inf (2011) 29, para. 6.

60 CPT, Report on the visit to Armenia in 2010, CPT/Inf (2011) 24, paras. 21-22. See however the critical remarks about other investigations, paras. 23-26.

61 CPT, Report on the visit to Ukraine in 2009, CPT/Inf (2011) 29, para. 14.

62 CPT, Report on the visit to Armenia in 2010, CPT/Inf (2011) 24, para. 37: Report on the visit to Ukraine in 2009, CPT/Inf (2011) 29, paras. 10, 33.

63 CPT, Report on the visit to Armenia in 2010, CPT/Inf (2011) 24, paras. 28-36; similar criticism in the Report on the visit to Ukraine in 2009, CPT/Inf (2011) 29, paras. 26-32.

VII. Summing up: what works?

It was only possible, in the context of this paper, to give a sketchy overview of the developments in the region. For a comprehensive picture, a much more detailed analysis would be required. Some caveats are necessary: It is assumed that CPT reports are reflecting reality, at least to a large extent, but of course there can be no guarantee that this is always the case, that the CPT sees everything, that all available information in one particular country finds its way into one of the CPT reports. Even if in one country some progress is achieved as regards the treatment of detainees by the police, other problems, like prison overcrowding, may persist.

Still, even within these limitations, it emerges from our brief overview that there is, in all likelihood, a correlation between the extent to which CPT recommendations are implemented, and the subsequent improvements in the human rights situation in a given country. A variety of effective measures may be taken by governments in order to prevent torture. Public statements on "zero tolerance" are easy to implement, and they are relevant. They show that the government has recognised the treatment of detainees as a real problem, and they make clear that there is no acquiescence by the government as regards the use of torture. Another rather relatively simple way of preventing ill-treatment is to reduce the admissible period of police custody in the law and to make sure that such maximum period is effectively respected.

It appears that fundamental safeguards (information of the outside world, access to a lawyer and a doctor) can be very useful in preventing torture. These safeguards are not directly related to the ill-treatment of detainees, but their implementation creates a framework where it is much more difficult to carry out such treatment. Of course, the prohibition of torture and its prevention must be an important part of police training.

It is clear from this paper that the problem of torture and other ill-treatment has not yet been solved in the Black Sea Region. It shows, however, that progress can be achieved: torture is a part of reality, but not a necessary one. Preventing torture effectively is not an ideal, but an imperative, even if it is sometimes difficult and time-consuming. The activities of the CPT and other institutions involved in the fight against torture show that torture and its prevention can be influenced by government policy. Governments may take a choice. They may choose not to subject themselves to international prevention mechanisms, or to ignore their recommendations, and their country is likely to remain a torture state. They may choose to implement such recommendations, to improve the situation of persons deprived of their liberty, and to prevent those willing to use torture from doing so. They may take a choice in favour of civilisation and humanity.

Self-determination of peoples

Droit des peuples à disposer d'eux-mêmes
Selbstbestimmungsrecht der Völker

Is there a contradiction between self-determination and territorial integrity ?

Jean-Marc THOUVENIN*

The question raised in the title of this contribution is the one I will deal with in the following pages and, for sure, this could hardly be seen as an easy task, as this question is one of the most highly controversial in international law, especially since the recent independence of South Sudan, and the declaration of independence of Kosovo. Indeed, this question is also at the heart of the disputes, or "situations", in the terms of the UN Charter, related to South Ossetia, Abkhazia, and some others. In this context, my goal is certainly not to go into the details of all these disputes. It is simply to expose what are the international law rules we are talking about, in order to better understand to what extent they are relevant to explain and resolve such or such dispute or "situation". Then, I will aim to answer three questions: What is the meaning of these "principles" of self-determination and territorial integrity? (I) Do they contradict each other? (II) And, finally: Which of these two principles should prevail? (III).

* Professor of International Law, Director of the *Centre de droit international* (CEDIN), University Paris Ouest Nanterre La Défense.

I. The meaning of the principles

A. Self-determination

As to the first question, it's necessary to remind where the principle of self-determination comes from. Obviously, it is a concept very close to the so-called "principle of nationality". It appears quite clearly in the *political* speeches at the end of World War I, especially in President Wilson's words. Concerning the *legal* status of self-determination in international law, it has been discussed in the *Aaland Islands* Case in 1920, and the conclusion, as reflected in the reports of the case, is that self-determination was not a positive legal principle in 1920. The Commission of jurists established to deal with this case thus said:

> Positive international law does not recognize the right of national groups as such to separate themselves from the State of which they form part by the simple expression of a wish[1].

The Commission of Rapporteurs established on the same subject added, in 1921:

> to concede to [...] any fraction of a population the right of withdrawing from the community to which they belong, because it is their wish or their good pleasure, would be to destroy order and stability within States and to inaugurate anarchy in international life.
> The separation of a minority from the State of which it forms a part and its incorporation in another State can only be considered as an altogether

1 Report of the International Committee of Jurists Entrusted by the Council of the League of Nations with the Task of Giving an Advisory Opinion upon the Legal Aspects of the Aaland Islands Questions', Official Journal of the League of Nations, Special Supplement No. 3, Oct. 1920.

> exceptional solution, a last resort when the State lacks either the will or the power to enact and apply just and effective guarantees[2].

At the end of World War II, the authors of the UN Charter decided to introduce references to the principle of self-determination in several articles. It has been applied primarily in favour of colonial peoples, since the adoption of Resolution 1514(XV) containing the *Declaration on the Granting of Independence to Colonial Countries and Peoples.* In this particular context, the principle means that the peoples covered by the resolution have a right, not an obligation, to complete independence: they can create a new State, or prefer to opt for an association with an independent State, or for integration in an already existing and independent State. It has been discussed what is a "people" having this right, or more specifically, what is a "colonial people". Beyond the words of Resolution 1514(XV), which focuses on peoples under alien subjugation, domination or exploitation, the simple, and probably the only answer as far as UN Law is concerned, is that a "colonial people" is any people considered as such by the UN General Assembly. This pragmatic "definition" calls for two more remarks. First, the notion of "people" is not equivalent to the notion of "minority"; specific rules are made for minorities[3] . Second, the notion of "people" referred to in the self-determination principle is not equivalent to the notion of "indigenous people". There again, specific rules are made for this notion[4] .

Currently, the process of decolonization has been largely completed, through the implementation of the principle of self-determination, qualified here as "external" as it is taking place at the international level. But the principle of self-determination stays in force, and new questions as to its meaning and scope of application

---

2 Report of the Commission of Rapporteurs, League of Nations Council Doc., B7/21/68/106, 16 April 1921.

3 See art. 27 of the 1966 UN Covenant on Civil and Political Rights, the UN Declaration of 1992, res. 47/135, and the Framework Convention on the Protection of National Minorities of the Council of Europe, 1995.

4 See the UN Declaration on the Rights of Indigenous peoples, 2007.

have emerged. The current debate can be summarized as follows: is the right to self-determination relevant for every people, even for those not under a colonial subjugation? Does the right to self-determination confer to every people a right to separate from the existing State under the sovereignty of which they are placed?

As to the first of these two questions, the answer is "for sure". Every people, colonized or not, has the right to self-determination. The first article of the two Covenants on human rights adopted in 1966 clearly states: "All peoples have the right to self-determination. By virtue of that right, they freely determine their political status and freely pursue their economic, social and cultural development". And there is no doubt that in modern international law, the legal principle of self-determination "serves to safeguard human rights"[5] , and means that every people has the right to choose its own destiny freely and through its participation in the definition of its political, economic, social and cultural future.

This "side" of self-determination, distinct from the concept as implemented in the context of decolonization, is often called the "internal" self-determination, as it reverts to the fact that a people is entirely free to decide its internal matters, on the basis of participation. At the very least, it means that no State has the right to decide in the name of the people of another State. Currently, it also means that a State must be organized in a democratic manner. In this regard, one could observe that the UN Human Rights Committee emphasized that the realization of the right to self-determination is an "essential condition for the effective guarantee of individual rights", among which one will find freedom of expression, of assembly, of association, to take part in the conduct of public affairs, and to vote[6].

As to the second question, two positions have emerged from the doctrine: the first position is radical and says that in no way self-determination gives a right to secession; the second position admits

---

5 Opinion 2 of the Arbitration Commission for the former Yugoslavia, presided by R. Badinter.

6 CCPR *General Comment No. 12.*

that in principle self-determination does not give a right to secession, save in exceptional circumstances, where the State behaves like an oppressor against the people. This is the "remedial secession" theory. My own view is that there is no right to secession in international law, whatever the situation is. I will explain this position later. At this stage, we can sum up what has already been seen by saying that if every people has a right to *internal* self-determination, "colonial peoples" also have another right, the right to *external* self-determination, according to which they have a right to independence.

B. Territorial integrity

Now, let us turn to the principle of territorial integrity. There is absolutely no doubt that this principle is one of the very founding principles of international law. It was already stipulated in the League of Nations Covenant (art. 10), and it has been restated many, many times, in a huge number of international instruments. This principle means that no State has the right to challenge the territorial integrity of another State. It also means that an international organization like the UN has no right to challenge the territorial integrity of sovereign States. This is what explains why the UN organs frequently remind this principle when confronted to civil wars and internal secessionist movements. But it does not mean anything else. Particularly, it does not mean, contrary to what Serbia has repeatedly asserted during its pleadings in the *Kosovo* Case, that internal claims for independence are in breach of it. In other words, as far as international law is concerned, a secessionist movement is not in breach of this principle when it is claiming for secession.

II. Contradiction?

Is there a contradiction between the legal principle of self-determination and the one of territorial integrity? As can be concluded from the remarks already done, my view is that, normally, the two principles are never directly confronted one to the other. Situations where a people would, at the same time, be granted an international right to secession, and be precluded from secession by international law, simply cannot happen.

In effect, no people has a right to secession. When colonized peoples acceded to independence, it was not a phenomenon of "secession", but a process of "decolonization", which is not the same because the territory object of a "decolonization" is not supposed to have ever been under the territorial sovereignty of its colonial power. The UN has always considered that "the territory of a colony or other Non-Self-Governing Territory has, under the Charter, a status separate and distinct from the territory of the State administering it"[7]. But let me be clear: saying that self-determination does not entail a right to secession is not saying that it forbids secession. By law, self-determination has simply nothing to do with secession: it does not give a right to it, but it does not preclude it as well. This being said, it is clear that the right to self-determination is not in contradiction with the principle of territorial integrity.

If we now turn more specifically to the principle of territorial integrity, we see that this principle does not apply to "peoples", but to States - and international organizations. And even when self-determination grants a right to independence – which is the case for colonial peoples, it does not undermine territorial integrity because, as already said, the territory under colonial domination cannot be viewed as being part of the territory of the colonial State. Therefore, the independence of a State under colonial occupation is clearly not an

7 *Declaration on Principles of International Law, Friendly Relations and Cooperation among States in Accordance with the UN Charter*, 1970.

infringement to the principle of territorial integrity. Moreover, far from being opposite, the two principles complete each other, as the principle of *uti possidetis,* which regulates the accession to independence of colonial peoples, ensures precisely that the process of self-determination is implemented in respect of territorial boundaries as they existed at the very moment of the independence.

III. Prevalence of one principle over the other?

As there is supposedly no contradiction between the two principles, I should not have to deal with the question whether one principle prevails over the other one. Nevertheless, allow me to deal here with the doctrine according to which even if territorial integrity normally prevails over the right of self-determination, internal self-determination gives, in exceptional circumstances, a right to secession.

Legally it cannot be said that, territorial integrity usually prevails. As we said, territorial integrity is not opposable to peoples, but to States. But, for the sake of argument, let us agree on that, in order to analyze this so-called "remedial" secession theory. According to this theory, when a State denies the people living on its territory any role in its own government, either through its own institutions or the general institutions of the State, this people would have a right to secession. This doctrine finds its basis, in international law, notably in the *Aaland Islands* Arbitration, already quoted above[8]. It is also sustained by the following sentence included in the UN General Assembly Declaration of 1970 also referred to above, stating that:

> [n]othing in the present declaration shall be construed as authorizing or encouraging any action which would dismember or impair, totally or in part, the territorial integrity or political unity of sovereign and independent State conducting themselves in compliance with the principle of equal rights and self

8 See *supra*, par. 2.

> determination of peoples [...] and thus possessed of a government representing the whole people belonging to the territory without distinction as to race, creed or color.

Now, could these statements be understood, *a contrario*, as validating in positive international law that in case of oppression, a people is recognized an international right to secession?

The question was not answered by the Canadian Supreme Court, in the *Quebec Secession Case* decided in 1998, nor by the International Court of Justice in the *Kosovo* Case. But virtually all the States pleading in this latter case provided their views on it. A number of them, including the USA, the U.K. and Russia, accepted it. Others, led by Serbia, took an opposite view, including Spain and China. In this context, it is quite clear that there is no *opinio juris* in favor, or against, the doctrine of "remedial secession".

In my view, this means that international law does not positively admits the idea of a right to secession as a remedy to a gross human rights violation, notably the violation of the right to internal self-determination. But it does not mean that a people will never achieve secession in such a context. If this people succeeds in its enterprise, and gains its independence, then the secession will occur, as it has been the case for Kosovo or South Sudan. This solution will be at best negotiated with the "parent State", at worst achieved only with arms and soldiers. But in this latter case, it is obviously the duty of the International Community to do whatever it can to help find a peaceful settlement.

Human rights and armed conflicts

Droits de l'Homme et conflits armés
Menschenrechte und bewaffnete Auseinandersetzungen

Human rights aspects of targeted killings

Nina KAPAUN*

This paper deals with several human rights aspects of targeted killings, a policy that has become more and more popular during recent years, as a tool in the so-called war on terror, with its latest example, the killing of Osama bin Laden by the US Army in May 2011.[1]

The killing of Osama bin Laden was conducted by a special force unit of the United States Army, called the Navy Seals. They shot him in his house in Abbottabad, Pakistan, where he had been living and hiding for supposedly years.[2] Afterwards, when the specific circumstances of the forceful action were revealed, it turned out that Osama bin Laden was not killed during combat, that he was not armed when the Navy Seals approached him, though he was said to have a gun within reach.[3]

---

* PhD candidate at the University of Cologne.

1 Due to the time restriction of the oral presentations on the occasion of the tri-national workshop this paper does not aim to thoroughly discuss the various human rights aspects of targeted killings in length.

2 For detailed information on the raid see New York Times, 9 May 2011, The Death of Osama bin Laden, <http://topics.nytimes.com/top/reference/timestopics/people/b/osama_bin_laden/i ndex.html> (04.10.2012).

3 Shortly after the killing was conducted and communicated, it was still assumed that Bin Laden "resisted the assault force" and was killed in the middle of an intense gun battle, see New York Times, 1 May 2011, <http://www.nytimes.com/2011/05/02/world/asia/osama-bin-laden-is-killed.html?pagewanted=all> (04.10.2012). Later it was revised to say that he was unarmed, see New York Times, 09 May 2011, The Death of Osama bin Laden, <http://topics.nytimes.com/top/reference/timestopics/people/b/osama_bin_laden/index.html> (04.10.2012).

In my judgement, despite the statement of US President Obama that "justice has been done"[4], this killing, like any other targeted killing, is not easily justified and raised complex legal questions.

This paper will give a short overview about the characteristics of a targeted killing, followed by an illustration of the two different legal settings in which targeted killings take place, *i.e.* in an armed conflict, weather international or non-international, or in times of peace respectively outside armed conflict scenarios.

"Targeted killing" is not a term specifically defined under international law, but was introduced in 2000 after Israel made public a policy of targeting alleged terrorists in the Palestinian territories.[5] There is still no universally accepted definition of targeted killing, but one can say that as a common denominator, according to the UN Special Report on Extrajudicial, Summary, or Arbitrary Executions, targeted killings are premeditated acts of lethal force employed by states in times of peace or during armed conflict to eliminate specific individuals outside their custody.[6]

The conduct of the lethal force to eliminate alleged terrorists or other enemies can vary widely. Methods of targeted killings are – *inter alia* – firing missiles from a Predator or Reaper drone (which is an unmanned, remote-controlled plane) or long-range sniper shooting. The U.S. targeted killings for example are, except for the special operation raid targeting Osama bin Laden, mostly done through drone

4 US President Barack Obama announced the death of Osama bin Laden live on television, full text of his speech see <http://www.spiegel.de/international/world/0,1518,760065,00.html> (04.10.2012). Former US President Bill Clinton confirmed this approach, in a statement released two days after the killing he announced: "I congratulate the president, the National Security team and the members of our armed forces on bringing Osama bin Laden to justice after more than a decade of murderous al-Qaida attacks." See <http://www.spiegel.de/international/world/0,1518,760025, 00.html> (04.10.2012).

5 See Jonathan Masters, Targeted Killings, Council on Foreign Relations, 29 August 2011, <http://www.cfr.org/intelligence/targeted-killings/p9627> (04.10.2012).

6 Report of the Special Rapporteur on extrajudicial, summary or arbitrary executions, Philip Alston, 28 May 2010, UN Doc. A/HRC/14/24/Add.6, para. 1.

strikes, directed against al-Qaeda and Taliban leadership networks in Afghanistan and the remote tribal regions of Pakistan.[7]

The following remarks will concentrate on two of the main questions arising when talking about the human rights aspects of targeted killings. First, it will be discussed whether Human Rights Law is the relevant legal regime for the evaluation of targeted killings. In doing so the issue will be addressed if it were not more appropriate to consider targeted killing as part of an international or non-international armed conflict and therefore to be judged according to International Humanitarian Law. Second, and after it has be proven that Human Rights Law is the suitable legal frame for the assessment of the legality of targeted killings, the crucial question to examine will be which obligations or rather which human rights treaties would be applicable. In this assessment the aspect of the extraterritorial application of human rights treaties will be examined.

Most of the targeted killings of alleged terrorists take place abroad, in countries often reputedly without effective state structure to prevent terrorist attacks. These killings have in common that they are not decided upon based on a previous trial or other judicial review but are either employed by a nation's intelligence or armed services decided by the executive branch.

Yet the circumstances of targeted killings generally vary from killings in the context of an on-going armed conflict or an occupation, for example in Afghanistan or Iraq.[8] To assess their legality, the framework of International Humanitarian Law as well as human rights treaties could be appropriate. But there are also targeted killings, which are carried out sporadically in disjointed parts of the world, aside from any conflict zones, for example the Yemen incident in 2002, where six persons inside a car driving through the desert were

7 See fn. 5.

8 See Targeted Killing is new U.S. Focus in Afghanistan, New York Times, 31 July 2010, <http://www.nytimes.com/2010/08/01/world/asia/01afghan.html?pagewanted=all> (04.10.2012).

killed in an attack by – allegedly – the USA/CIA.[9] As these killings take place outside an armed conflict, they are not covered by the scope of International Humanitarian Law.[10] Therefore, they have to be evaluated according to Human Rights Law only.[11] For this evaluation, the provisions of the European Convention on Human Rights (ECHR) and the International Covenant on Civil and Political Rights (ICCPR) are the most relevant legal frameworks, as most states engaging in a policy of targeted killings will be member to either one of them.

As stated above, the different circumstances of targeted killings result in the mix of applicable legal frameworks – Human Rights Law and International Humanitarian Law, which leads to the question whether International Humanitarian Law and Human Rights Law are both applicable at the same time.[12]

---

9 Latest example, taking place after the presentation of this paper, was the killing of Anwar al Awlaki in Yemen through a CIA operated drone attack on the 30 September 2011, its legal assessment being still controversial at the time of writing, see The Death of Jihad's English-Language Mouthpiece, <http://www.spiegel.de/international/world/0,1518,789427,00.html> (04.10.2012).

10 Especially the targeted killings of members of Al Qaeda in the Arabian Peninsula, based in Yemen, and the Somalia-based Shabab has heated up the discussion about a territorial restriction of the battlefield, e. g. by the State Department's lawyer Harold H. Koh, who had agreed that the armed conflict with Al Qaeda is not limited to the battlefield theater of Afghanistan and adjoining parts of Pakistan, see At White House, Weighing Limits of Terror Fight, New York Times, 15 September 2011, <http://www.nytimes.com/2011/09/16/us/white-house-weighs-limits-of-terror-fight.html?pagewanted=2&_r=1> (04.10.2012).

11 Apart from potentially relevant rules of national criminal law.

12 In both scenarios, the employment of the lethal force on foreign territory also constitutes a possible violation of the respective state sovereignty and the prohibition of force in international relations, which is a question concerning general public international law. If the affected state did not authorize the targeted killing, potential justifications as the right to self-defence and other aspects of the ius contra bellum have to be discussed. It would go beyond the scope of this paper to elaborate on this aspect as well.

To discuss the rather controversial relationship between International Humanitarian Law and Human Rights Law in-depth would go beyond the scope of this paper, as I am dealing primarily with the human rights aspects of targeted killing. However, I am of the opinion that the relationship between Human Rights Law and International Humanitarian Law is a complementary one. To put it in a nutshell, in times of armed conflict the more specific provisions of the International Humanitarian Law are more suitable for most of the occurring situations. But this does not prevent from also considering human rights standards when suitable or seen fit.

The compatibility between Human Rights Law and International Humanitarian Law can be seen based on the right to life in the ECHR, which actually cannot be derogated from.[13] The only exception is for killings resulting from lawful acts of war, these do not violate the right to life.[14] Although human rights virtually still apply, the legality of a targeted killing during armed conflict has still to be evaluated with the help of International Humanitarian Law provisions.

The same complementary approach is taken for the provisions of the ICCPR. This view is expressed by the Human Rights Committee, who is responsible for the implementation of the ICCPR, in General Comment No. 29[15] and confirmed in General Comment No. 31.[16]

---

13 Article 2 ECHR: "Everyone's right to life shall be protected by law. No one shall be deprived of his life intentionally save in the execution of a sentence of a court following his conviction of a crime for which this penalty is provided by law. [...]".

14 Article 15 ECHR: "In time of war or other public emergency threatening the life of the nation any High Contracting Party may take measures derogating from its obligations under this Convention to the extent strictly required by the exigencies of the situation, provided that such measures are not inconsistent with its other obligations under international law. No derogation from Article 2, except in respect of deaths resulting from lawful acts of war, or from Articles 3, 4 (paragraph 1) and 7 shall be made under this provision."

15 General Comment No. 29 on States of Emergencies, adopted on 24 July 2001, UN Doc. CCPR/C/21/Rev.1/Add.11, para. 3: "[...] During armed conflict, whether international or non-international, rules of international humanitarian law become applicable and help, in addition to the provisions in article 4 and

Furthermore, the International Court of Justice (ICJ) stated that the protection of the ICCPR does not cease in times of war, but the right to life, respectively the arbitrary deprivation of life can only be decided by reference to the law applicable in armed conflict.[17]

---

article 5, paragraph 1, of the Covenant, to prevent the abuse of a State's emergency powers. The Covenant requires that even during an armed conflict measures derogating from the Covenant are allowed only if and to the extent that the situation constitutes a threat to the life of the nation. [...]."

16 General Comment No. 31, The Nature of the General Legal Obligation Imposed on States Parties to the Covenant, adopted on 29 March 2004, UN Doc. CCPR/C/21/Rev.1/Add. 13, para.11: "As implied in General Comment 29, the Covenant applies also in situations of armed conflict to which the rules of international humanitarian law are applicable. While, in respect of certain Covenant rights, more specific rules of international humanitarian law may be specially relevant for the purposes of the interpretation of Covenant rights, both spheres of law are complementary, not mutually exclusive."

17 ICJ, *Legal Consequences of the Construction of a Wall in the Occupied Palestinian Territory*, Advisory Opinion, 9 July 2004, para. 106: "More generally, the Court considers that the protection offered by human rights conventions does not cease in case of armed conflict, save through the effect of provisions for derogation of the kind to be found in Article 4 of the International Covenant on Civil and Political Rights. As regards the relationship between international humanitarian law and human rights law, there are thus three possible situations: some rights may be exclusively matters of international humanitarian law; others may be exclusively matters of human rights law; yet others may be matters of both these branches of international law. In order to answer the question put to it, the Court will have to take into consideration both these branches of international law, namely human rights law and, as lex specialis, international humanitarian law"; ICJ, *Legality of the Threat or Use of Nuclear Weapons*, Advisory Opinion, 8 July 1996, para. 25: "The Court observes that the protection of the International Covenant of Civil and Political Rights does not cease in times of war, except by operation of Article 4 of the Covenant whereby certain provisions may be derogated from in a time of national emergency. Respect for the right to life is not, however, such a provision. In principle, the right not arbitrarily to be deprived of one's life applies also in hostilities. The test of what is an arbitrary deprivation of life, however, then falls to be determined by the applicable lex specialis, namely, the law applicable in armed conflict, which is designed to regulate the conduct of hostilities. Thus whether a particular loss of life, through the use of a certain weapon in warfare, is to be considered an arbitrary deprivation of life contrary to

These findings mean that targeted killings in the context of armed conflict do not necessarily violate human rights, in particular the right to life, when they are consistent with International Humanitarian Law.

As stated earlier, the circumstances of targeted killings can also lead to the exclusive application of Human Rights Law. As already mentioned, the most relevant human rights treaties in this context are the ICCPR and the ECHR, which the following considerations will be focussed on.

Targeted killings mostly take place on foreign territory. There is an on-going discussion if States – while acting extraterritorially – have to abide by their human rights obligations. This controversy is based on the contentious question of the exact meaning and scope of 'jurisdiction', as phrased in Art. 1 ECHR and Art. 2 ICCPR.[18]

Concerning the ICCPR, the Human Rights Committee takes the view that its provisions apply also extraterritorially. In the GC No. 31 it says that:

> [...] States Parties are required by article 2, paragraph 1, to respect and to ensure the Covenant rights to all persons who may be within their territory and to all persons subject to their jurisdiction. This means that a State party must respect and ensure the rights laid down in the Covenant to anyone within the power or effective control of that State Party, even if not situated within the territory of the State Party. [...][19]

Article 6 of the Covenant, can only be decided by reference to the law applicable in armed conflict and not deduced from the terms of the Covenant itself."

18 Article 1 ECHR: "The High Contracting Parties shall secure to everyone within their jurisdiction the rights and freedoms defined in Section I of this Convention"; Article 2 ICCPR: "Each State Party to the present Covenant undertakes to respect and to ensure to all individuals within its territory and subject to its jurisdiction the rights recognized in the present Covenant, without distinction of any kind, such as race, colour, sex, language, religion, political or other opinion, national or social origin, property, birth or other status [...]".

19 See fn. 16, para. 10.

Further it states that

> […] This principle also applies to those within the power or effective control of the forces of a State Party acting outside its territory, regardless of the circumstances in which such power or effective control was obtained, such as forces constituting a national contingent of a State Party assigned to an international peace-keeping or peace-enforcement operation.[20]

But this still does not clarify the actual application of the ICCPR for targeted killings on foreign territory, as the General Comments issued by the Human Rights Committee explain its interpretation of the ICCPR, but are not legally binding. In contrast, the US argues that the ICCPR does not apply extraterritorially, and therefore could accordingly not be applied, for example, to a targeted killing in Pakistan.[21]

From the jurisprudence of the ICJ, however, one can conclude that the Court acknowledges the extraterritorial obligations arising

---

20 See fn. 19.

21 Second and Third Reports of the United States of America to the Human Rights Committee, 21 October 2001, UN Doc. CCPR/C/USA/3 Annex I, p. 109: "The Vienna Convention on the Law of Treaties states the basic rules for the interpretation of treaties. In Article 31(1), it states that: A treaty shall be interpreted in good faith in accordance with the ordinary meaning to be given to the terms of the treaty in their context and in the light of its object and purpose. Resort to this fundamental rule of interpretation leads to the inescapable conclusion that the obligations assumed by a State Party to the International Covenant on Civil and Political Rights (Covenant) apply only within the territory of the State Party. Article 2(1) of the Covenant states that '[e] ach State Party to the present Covenant undertakes to respect and to ensure to all individuals within its territory and subject to its jurisdiction the rights recognized in the present Covenant, without distinction of any kind.' Hence, based on the plain and ordinary meaning of its text, this Article establishes that States Parties are required to ensure the rights in the Covenant only to individuals who are both within the territory of a State Party and subject to that State Party's sovereign authority." Also further confirmed in the follow-up response to the Committee's concluding observations, see Comments of the United States of America on the concluding observations on the Human Rights Committee, 1 November 2007, UN Doc. CCPR/C/USA/CO/3/Rev.1/Add.1, pp. 2-3.

from the ICCPR. The ICJ confirmed them referring to Israel and the Occupied Territories [22], and maybe more significant since less ambiguous with regard to status related questions, in the Case DRC v. Uganda.[23]

With regard to the European Convention on Human Rights, the question of its extraterritorial application is almost equally difficult to answer. There had been a controversial discussion over the past years.

The early case-law of the European Court of Human Rights (ECtHR) established the 'effective control of an area criteria', whereby states were obliged to respect their human rights treaties obligations when they – for example – occupied foreign territory and

---

22 ICJ, *Legal Consequences of the Construction of a Wall in the Occupied Palestinian Territory*, Advisory Opinion, 9 July 2004, para. 109: "The Court would observe that, while the jurisdiction of States is primarily territorial, it may sometimes be exercised outside the national territory. Considering the object and purpose of the International Covenant on Civil and Political Rights, it would seem natural that, even when such is the case, States parties to the Covenant should be bound to comply with its provisions […]"; para. 111: "In conclusion, the Court considers that the International Covenant on Civil and Political Rights is applicable in respect of acts done by a State in the exercise of its jurisdiction outside its own territory."

23 ICJ, *Armed activities in the territory of the Congo* (Democratic Republic of the Congo v. Uganda), Judgement, 19 December 2005, para. 216: "[...] The Court further concluded that international human rights instruments are applicable "in respect of acts done by a State in the exercise of its jurisdiction outside its own territory", particularly in occupied territories [...]." para. 217: "The Court considers that the following instruments in the fields of international humanitarian law and international human rights law are applicable, as relevant, in the present case: [...] International Covenant on Civil and Political Rights of 19 December 1966. The DRC (at the time Republic of Zaire) acceded to the Covenant on 1 November 1976; Uganda acceded on 21 June 1995; [...]." Para. 220: "The Court thus concludes that Uganda is internationally responsible for violations of international human rights law and international humanitarian law committed by the UPDF and by its members in the territory of the DRC and for failing to comply with its obligations as an occupying Power in Ituri in respect of violations of international human rights law and international humanitarian law in the occupied territory."

exercised effective control over it.[24] Furthermore there were the criteria of states agents' authority and control over persons or property.[25] Extraterritorial jurisdiction was assumed in situations where state agents, either through administrative powers or soldiers through military force, exercised authority over individuals, on state territory as well as on foreign territory. These two sets of criteria were used in several decisions and judgements of the ECtHR and the European Commission on Human Rights, with no obvious preference either way.[26]

It was only *Bankovic and others v. Belgium and 16 other contracting states*[27], a decision on the non-admissibility of an

---

24 ECtHR, *Loizidou v. Turkey* (Preliminary Objections), Judgment, 23 March 1995, para. 62.

25 ECommHR, *Cyprus v. Turkey* (Appl. No. 6780/74, 6950/75), 26 May 1975, para. 136: "The term 'within its jurisdiction' is not equivalent to or limited to the territory of the High Contracting party concerned. It is clear from the language, in particular from the French text, and the object of this Article, and from the purpose of the Convention as whole, that the High Contracting Parties are bound to secure the said rights and freedoms to all persons under the actual authority and responsibility, whether that authority is exercised on its own territory or abroad. [...] authorised agents of a State, including diplomatic or consular agents and armed forces, not only remain under its jurisdiction when abroad but bring any other persons or property 'within the jurisdiction' of that state, to the extent that they exercise authority over such persons or property [...]."

26 Although the personal approach to jurisdiction and the extraterritorial application of the ECHR was mainly promoted through the European Commission on Human Rights, it was later on confirmed and further used in the jurisprudence of the ECtHR as well, see *Xhavara and Others v. Italy and Albania*, (Appl. No. 39473/98), Decision on admissibility, 11 January 2001, para. 1: "[...] La Cour note d'emblée que le naufrage du Kater I Rades a été directement provoqué par le navire de guerre italien Sibilla. Par conséquent, toute doléance sur ce point doit être considérée comme étant dirigée exclusivement contre l'Italie. Le fait que l'Albanie est partie à la Convention italo-albanaise ne saurait, à lui seul, engager la responsabilité de cet Etat au regard de la Convention pour toute mesure adoptée par les autorités italiennes en exécution de l'accord international en question. [...]".

27 ECtHR, *Bankovic and others v. Belgium and 16 other contracting states*, (Appl. No. 52207/99), Decision on admissibility, 12 December 2001.

individual complaint rendered by the ECtHR, which heated up the discussion about the scope of extraterritorial application of the ECHR. Especially the discussion about the meaning of 'jurisdiction' in relation to obligations arising from human rights treaties was significant.[28] It concerned the question whether the bombing by State Parties to the European Convention on Human Rights of a territory that was not party to the Convention invoked responsibility under the Convention. The key question in that case was whether the victims of these bombings fell within the jurisdiction of the respondent States. The Court answered in the negative, seeing the jurisdiction as primarily territorial and none of the exceptions present.[29] The main arguments were that the respondent states did not have effective control over the territory which was bombed.[30] Furthermore the Court stated that the condition of the legal space was not given either, as the

28 See *Bankovic*, fn. 27, para. 36, 37, 46 - 53, 59 - 73.

29 See *Bankovic*, fn. 27, para. 59: "As to the "ordinary meaning" of the relevant term in Article 1 of the Convention, the Court is satisfied that, from the standpoint of public international law, the jurisdictional competence of a State is primarily territorial. While international law does not exclude a State's exercise of jurisdiction extra-territorially, the suggested bases of such jurisdiction (including nationality, flag, diplomatic and consular relations, effect, protection, passive personality and universality) are, as a general rule, defined and limited by the sovereign territorial rights of the other relevant States [...]." Para. 71: "In sum, the case-law of the Court demonstrates that its recognition of the exercise of extra-territorial jurisdiction by a Contracting State is exceptional: it has done so when the respondent State, through the effective control of the relevant territory and its inhabitants abroad as a consequence of military occupation or through the consent, invitation or acquiescence of the Government of that territory, exercises all or some of the public powers normally to be exercised by that Government [...]." Para. 82: "The Court is not therefore persuaded that there was any jurisdictional link between the persons who were victims of the act complained of and the respondent States. Accordingly, it is not satisfied that the applicants and their deceased relatives were capable of coming within the jurisdiction of the respondent States on account of the extra-territorial act in question [...]".

30 *Bankovic*, fn. 27, para. 70, 71, 74, 75.

State, whose territory was bombed, was not a Contracting State to the Convention.[31]

After this decision several questions remained unclear and were objects of a controversial debate.[32] Firstly it was disputed whether the effective control test was the only significant exception of extraterritorial jurisdiction. In addition, it was controversially discussed if the legal space aspect had to be seen as a general restriction to all recognised exceptions of extraterritorial jurisdiction.

When the ECtHR rendered its judgement in the case *Al-Skeini and others v. the United Kingdom*[33] in July 2011, those controversial questions experienced a certain clarification. In *Al-Skeini*, the Court ruled on the application of the ECHR to the conduct of British troops in Iraq. The case concerned six appellants, the first five of whom had been killed by UK 'patrols' in occupied Basra, for example while eating a family evening meal, during a raid on a family member's house or while driving a minibus. The sixth was tortured while in UK custody in Iraq.[34] The UK Government – in line with the highest UK

31 *Bankovic*, fn. 27, para. 80: "[…] In short, the Convention is a multi-lateral treaty operating, [...], in an essentially regional context and notably in the legal space (espace juridique) of the Contracting States. The Convention was not designed to be applied throughout the world, even in respect of the conduct of Contracting States. Accordingly, the desirability of avoiding a gap or vacuum in human rights' protection has so far been relied on by the Court in favour of establishing jurisdiction only when the territory in question was one that, but for the specific circumstances, would normally be covered by the Convention."

32 For an overview of the initiated (academic) discussion see *Rick Lawson*, Life after Bankovic: On the extraterritorial Application of the European Convention on Human Rights, in: *Fons Coomans/Menno Kamminga*, Extraterritorial Application of Human Rights Treaties, 2004, pp. 83 ff; *Michael O'Boyle*, The European Convention on Human Rights and Extraterritorial Jurisdiction: A Comment on 'Life after Bankovic', in: *Coomans/Kamminga*, Extraterritorial Application, pp. 125 ff.

33 ECtHR, *Al-Skeini and others v. The United Kingdom* (Appl. No. 55721/07), Judgement, 07 July 2011.

34 *Al-Skeini*, fn. 33, para. 33-71.

court, the House of Lords[35] – argued that the ECHR did indeed apply to persons in UK custody in Iraq but not to persons killed or injured on the streets of Basra.[36] The Court, however, rejected this opinion and decided that not only persons in custody of the UK in Iraq were subject to the jurisdiction of the UK but also individuals who were killed by British soldiers in Basra, Iraq.[37]

The ruling in *Al-Skeini* represents a progress of human rights protection by the ECHR. The Grand Chamber stated that the legal space aspect as discussed in the *Bankovic* decision must not necessarily be understood as excluding all (state) acts outside the convention legal space from the jurisdiction of Convention states.[38] This constitutes a significant turn for the future implementation of human rights guarantees given the fact that most of the targeted killings are not executed within the territory of one of the Convention states but nevertheless maybe sometimes executed by forces of the Convention states.

35 UK House of Lords, *Al-Skeini et al. v. Secretary of State for Defence* [2007], UKHL 26. Judgment of 13 June 2007.

36 *Al-Skeini*, fn. 33, para. 88, 109-118.

37 *Al-Skeini*, fn. 33, para. 149: "[...] the Court considers that the United Kingdom, through its soldiers engaged in security operations in Basrah during the period in question, exercised authority and control over individuals killed in the course of such security operations, so as to establish a jurisdictional link between the deceased and the United Kingdom for the purposes of Article 1 of the Convention."

38 *Al-Skeini*, fn. 33, para. 142: "The Court has emphasised that, where the territory of one of the Convention State is occupied by the armed forces of another, the occupying State should in principle be held accountable under the Convention for breaches of human rights within the occupied territory, because to hold otherwise would be to deprive the population of that territory of the rights and freedoms hitherto enjoyed and would result in a "vacuum" of protection within the "Convention legal space" [...]. However, the importance of establishing the occupying State's jurisdiction in such cases does not imply, a contrario, that jurisdiction under Article 1 of the Convention can never exist outside the territory covered by the Council of Europe Member States. The Court has not in its case-law applied any such restriction [...]".

Furthermore, regarding human rights protection against targeted killings, it is very significant whether the European Convention applies beyond situations of detention or other forms of custody. If restricted to detention scenarios, an individual's human rights protection would depend on whether his abusers were courteous enough to arrest him beforehand, or whether his abuse occurred inside or outside prison walls.

When applied to the specific circumstances of targeted killings it would imply a general non-application of human rights provisions. After all, the characteristics of targeted killings are precisely their remotely controlled execution, no physical contact or custody being one of their essential characteristics.

It remains to be seen whether this, in a way, novel approach by the European Court of Human Rights will be adopted elsewhere, especially as the US line of arguing in the academic debate sometimes holds that their view is supported by the *Bankovic* decision.[39]

Assuming the provisions of the ICCPR and the ECHR are applicable when targeted killings are carried out outside armed conflict, for example in Yemen, or Abbottabad, Pakistan,[40] the right to life, codified in all human rights treaties and accepted under customary law, is the guarantee of major importance.

Human rights treaties prohibit the arbitrary deprivation of life.[41] Most of them do not define what is meant by arbitrary. The European

---

39 See, i.e. *Dominic McGoldrick*, Extraterritorial Application of the International Covenant on Civil and Political Rights, in: *Coomans/Kamminga*, Extraterritorial Application, fn. 32, p. 41 f.

40 The author is aware of the ongoing discussion on whether the theatre of hostilities, i.e. the battlefield in the so-called war on terror has a broader scope than the territory on which the actual fighting takes place. In the view of the author, nevertheless, the surroundings of the compound in Abbottabad did not belong to the theatre of hostilities of a potential non-international armed conflict. A comprehensive evaluation of the relevant conditions would again go beyond the scope of this paper.

41 Article 6 ICCPR: "Every human being has the inherent right to life. This right shall be protected by law. No one shall be arbitrarily deprived of his life [...]";

Convention on Human Rights, however, illustrates in Art. 2 that the deprivation of life will – for example – not be deemed arbitrary when it results from the use of force that was absolutely necessary in defence of any person from unlawful violence.[42]

The requirement of absolute necessity can be seen as the relevant threshold for the legality of a targeted killing outside armed conflicts. Further information can be drawn from the case law of the European Court of Human Rights, where it ruled on killings outside armed conflicts. The Court has for example affirmed the lawfulness of killing a person, when the authorities thought that the person was about to detonate a bomb.[43] This will be seen as a case where it was absolutely necessary in defence of any person from unlawful violence.[44]

By and large, other universal and regional human rights bodies take the same approach. For example, according to the UN Basic Principles on the Use of Force and Firearms by Law Enforcement

---

Article 4 Banjul Charter: "Human beings are inviolable. Every human being shall be entitled to respect for his life and the integrity of his person. No one may be arbitrarily deprived of this right." Article 4 American Convention on Human Rights: "Every person has the right to have his life respected. This right shall be protected by law and, in general, from the moment of conception. No one shall be arbitrarily deprived of his life. [...]".

42 Article 2 ECHR: " [...] Deprivation of life shall not be regarded as inflicted in contravention of this article when it results from the use of force which is no more than absolutely necessary: in defence of any person from unlawful violence; in order to effect a lawful arrest or to prevent the escape of a person lawfully detained; in action lawfully taken for the purpose of quelling a riot or insurrection."

43 ECtHR, *McCann v. United Kingdom* (Application No. 18984/91), Judgement, 5 September 1995, para. 195, 200.

44 See *McCann v. United Kingdom*, fn. 43, para. 148: "[…] Paragraph 2 (art. 2-2) does not primarily define instances where it is permitted intentionally to kill an individual, but describes the situations where it is permitted to 'use force' which may result, as an unintended outcome, in the deprivation of life. The use of force, however, must be no more than 'absolutely necessary' for the achievement of one of the purposes set out in the sub-paragraphs […]".

Officials[45], intentional lethal use of firearms may only be made when strictly unavoidable in order to protect life.[46]

Considering these findings, some conclusions can be drawn concerning the meaning of arbitrary in the context of targeted killings outside an armed conflict:

An alleged terrorist can only be killed when his death is the only way of preventing his imminent attack to take place. Killing him is only absolutely necessary when he poses an immediate threat/danger to life or limb of other persons, which cannot be eliminated otherwise. The death itself has to be *ultima ratio*, which means that the targeting state has no choice but to execute a targeted killing to prevent the imminent attack.

Whenever a state uses drones for targeted killings it has to engage first in an assessment as to whether it would be possible to capture rather than kill the individual concerned. It must use lethal force only as a last resort.

Applying these requirements to the killing of Osama bin Laden, its legality is at best disputable. A the moment of his killing, he was said not to have been planning, preparing nor carrying out acts which could have been considered as immediate threat to other persons well being.[47]

---

45 The Human Rights Committee uses them as guidelines in its evaluation of State Reports, see i.e. Concluding Observations on the 5th State Report by Belgium, UN Doc. CCPR/C/BEL/CO/5, 16 November 2010, para. 14. They are also taking into considerations in the jurisprudence of the ECtHR, see *McCann v. United Kingdom*, fn. 43, para. 138, 139.

46 Principle 9, UN Basic Principles on the Use of Force and Firearms by Law Enforcement Officials, adopted by the 8th UN Congress on the Prevention of Crime and the Treatment of Offenders, Havana, Cuba, 27 August-07 September 1990, available at <http://www2.ohchr.org/english/law/firearms.htm> (08.10. 2012).

47 See New York Times, 9 May 2011, The Death of Osama bin Laden, <http://topics.nytimes.com/top/reference/timestopics/people/b/osama_bin_laden/index.html> (last visited on 04/10/2011).

Under the circumstances known so far the absolute necessity of his death is thus questionable. It might have been operationally too risky to capture Bin Laden alive, and that when all circumstances were assessed a kill order was appropriate. But it was certainly no *ultima ratio* action when he could have been arrested instead.

There have been rumours and allegations that the killing of bin Laden was a "blanket kill, don't detain policy."[48] Yet John Brennan, chief counterterrorism advisor to U.S. President Obama confirmed that it was a capture-or-kill operation in which surrender and capture were very much options, although it was assumed that capture might not be feasible.[49]

Although he was allegedly unarmed when the Navy Seals entered, and an arrest/capture could have been feasible under other circumstances, it is not clear without ambiguity that the killing was not absolutely necessary and therefore unlawful as the situation of the raid is said to have seemed too dangerous for an attempt to capture.[50]

In summary it can be said, that the human rights regime plays an important role in the evaluation of targeted killings. Its provisions have to be observed in the majority of the cases of targeted killings. States have to respect their human rights obligations when they conduct an extraterritorial targeted killing, either specified by International Humanitarian Law regulations in the context of armed conflict, or, outside armed conflict, determined broadly by the

48 See "U.S. team's mission was to kill bin Laden, not capture", Mark Hosenball/Matt Spetalnick (Reuters), 2 May 2011, <http://www.reuters.com/article/2011/05/02/us-binladen-kill-idUSTRE7413H220110502> (Last visited on 04/10/2011).

49 Cf. Mary Ellen O'Connell, The bin Laden aftermath: Abbottabad and international law, Foreign Policy, 4 May 2011, available at <http://afpak.foreignpolicy.com/posts/2011/05/04/the_bin_laden_aftermath_abbottabad_and_international_law> (Last visited on 04/10/2011).

50 The U.S. government stated that bin Laden was killed while he was resisting. According to CIA director Panetta he made "threatening moves", although he was unarmed. Furthermore the SEAL team had to fight their way into the room, see fn. 49.

requirements of the right to life. Based on human rights conditions, a targeted killing is either legitimate as a lawful act of war according to International Humanitarian Law or as an act of *ultima ratio* to prevent immediate threat/danger to life or limb of other persons.

Direct human rights obligations of non-state parties to armed conflicts: between positive international law and human rights aspirations

Olaf SEIRING*

The majority of today's armed conflicts do not arise between states, but between states and non-state parties.[1] Both sides commit equally grave acts of violence and limit individual freedoms.[2] At the same time, international human rights law continues to apply during armed conflicts.[3] This leads to the question whether non-state parties to armed conflicts are bound by human rights. In the meaning of common Article 3 of the Geneva Conventions of 1949 (GC), a non-state party to an armed conflict is an association of individuals which does not exercise public power in the sense of sovereignty. The party must be able to enforce discipline, which means that a minimum grade

---

* Maître en Droit (Université Paris Ouest Nanterre La Défense), PhD candidate (Universität Potsdam), LL.M. candidate (London School of Economics and Political Science).

1 Dieter Fleck, 'Humanitarian Protection Against Non-State Actors', in Jochen A. Frowein and others (eds), *Verhandeln für den Frieden: Liber Amicorum Tono Eitel* (Berlin: Springer, 2003), p. 69; Cedric Ryngaert, 'Human Rights Obligations of Armed Groups' (2008) XLI, Revue belge de droit international, pp. 355–81, p. 356.

2 Christian Tomuschat, 'The Applicability of Human Rights Law to Insurgent Movements', in Horst Fischer and others (eds), *Krisensicherung und Humanitärer Schutz – Crisis Management and Humanitarian Protection: Festschrift für Dieter Fleck* (Berlin: Berliner Wissenschaftsverlag, 2004), p. 576.

3 *Legality of the threat or use of nuclear weapons* (Advisory opinion), [1996] ICJ Rep 226, para 25; *Legal consequences of the construction of a wall in the occupied Palestinian territory* (Advisory opinion), [2004] ICJ Rep 136, para 106.

of internal organization is required.[4] These conditions are fulfilled by armed opposition groups as for example the Libyan insurgents in 2011 before they became the government of Libya. The 2nd Additional Protocol of 1977 (AP II) is more restrictive and contains a second condition in Article 1(1): a non-state party has to control a part of the state territory.[5] Traditionally, human rights law is limited to the protection of individuals against states; the protection against non-state actors was not anticipated.[6] But can it legally matter who commits the infringement when the effect on the protected individual is the same?

The purpose of this contribution is to provide an overview of the discussion on human rights obligations of armed groups and its recent developments.[7] It argues that even if positive human rights law barely contains legally binding direct obligations of non-state actors, it is both possible and desirable that such obligations exist in the case where armed groups are exercising quasi-governmental power. Lastly, the article addresses the question of which legal stance best supports the development of such obligations. For the sake of clarity, an attempt will be made to separate the discussion of arguments relating to the law as it is and as it should be, even if it might not always be possible to make this distinction.

Consequently, the first part of the paper will focus on the state of affairs of positive human rights law and demonstrate that the existence

---

4 Sylvain Vite, 'Typology of armed conflicts in international humanitarian law: legal concepts and actual situations' (2009) 91, IRRC, pp. 69–94, p. 77, see also Jean S. Pictet (ed), *The Geneva Conventions of 12 August 1949, Commentary: 1st Geneva convention for the amelioration of the condition of the wounded and sick in armed forces in the field* (Geneva: International Committee of the Red Cross, 1952), p. 49.

5 Under Article 3 GC, territorial control is not mandatory, Vite (n 4), pp. 77, 79; This paper will not discuss the question of international organizations, since their members are not private persons but states. Moreover, the question of private security firms will be excluded. Being enterprises with a commercial aim, they are representing a case on their own.

6 Tomuschat (n 2), p. 573.

7 Ryngaert (n 1) for a comprehensive analysis.

of direct human rights obligations under today's positive law is problematic, but possible (I.). Neither human rights law nor analogies to international humanitarian law provide sufficient legal grounds for direct obligations (I.A. and I.B.). Nevertheless, human rights provide enough legal space for the creation of direct obligations. (I.C.). In the second part, attention will be drawn to aspirations for direct human rights obligations of non-state parties (II.). From a legal policy point of view, direct human rights obligations are desirable (II.A.). But which legal position is appropriate to support their development? Do intermediary positions based on soft-law help? (II.B.).

I. The existence of direct human rights obligations under today's positive law is problematic, but possible

A. The legal basis offered by human rights is very scant

It is difficult to ascertain direct human rights obligations under today's positive law. The legal basis in human rights law is very scant. This point will be demonstrated by looking briefly at several human rights conventions and at the present situation in international customary law.[8]

1. Human rights conventions

Article 31 and 32 of the Vienna Convention on the Law of Treaties (VCLT) stipulate that treaties governed by international law have to be interpreted according to their wording, object and context. Their *travaux préparatoires* can be used as a supplementary mean of interpretation. Already the interpretation of the wording of the relevant conventions leads to the conclusion that they exclude direct

8 Ibid, pp. 363ff, 366ff, providing a detailed overview.

obligations of non-state actors.[9] The conventions explicitly mention the state parties as the entities having to respect the conventions. In Article 2(1) the International Covenant on Civil and Political Rights (ICCPR) states that "each State Party to the present Covenant undertakes to respect […] the rights recognized in the present Covenant".[10] According to Article 1 and 59(1) of the European Convention on Human Rights (ECHR) and Article 4 of the Statute of the Council of Europe, only Members of the Council, *ergo* only states, are bound to respect the ECHR.[11] The UN Convention against Torture (CAT) speaks in Article 1 of "a public official or other person acting in an official capacity", which aims at the state parties acting via their agents.[12] The American Convention on Human Rights (ACHR) leads to an equal result in Article 1(1).[13] The same conclusion can be drawn by looking at the object, context and *travaux préparatoires* of the conventions. Traditionally, human rights protect private individuals exclusively against the state.[14] Finally, there is general consent that the conventions have no direct effect on third parties.[15]

2. *International customary law*

Customary law consists of state practice and *opinio juris*.[16] The states are very reluctant to affirm direct human rights obligations of non-state actors, because governments fear to politically legitimize their non-state opponent.[17] Since the 1990s, the UN Security Council and

---

9 Tomuschat (n 2), p. 574; Ryngaert (n 1), pp. 363ff.

10 Ryngaert (n 1), p. 363.

11 Tomuschat (n 2), p. 573.

12 Ryngaert (n 1), p. 363.

13 Liesbeth Zegveld, *Accountability of Armed Opposition Groups in International Law* (Cambridge: Cambridge University Press, 2002), p 41 for further reasons.

14 Ibid, p 41 concerning the ACHR.

15 Tomuschat (n 2), p. 574 for more references concerning the ICCPR and ECHR.

16 Article 38(1)(b) Statute ICJ.

17 UNCHR, 'Report of the Special Rapporteur on extrajudicial, summary or arbitrary executions', Mission to Sri Lanka (27 March 2006) UN Doc E/CN.4/2006/53/Add.5, para 26.

the General Assembly are, nevertheless, constantly condemning human rights violations of armed opposition groups.[18] This was, among others, the case concerning conflicts in Afghanistan, Angola, Congo, Ivory Coast, Liberia, Sierra Leone, Somalia, Sudan and Yugoslavia.[19] The practice of international organizations is considered to be relevant for the development of customary law.[20] But as there is a lack of direct state practice, because states are generally not willing to acknowledge direct obligations at all, it is difficult to confirm a rule of customary international law.[21]

B. *An analogy to international humanitarian law is not promising*

Another argument which arises is that for over 60 years, international humanitarian law has been recognizing direct obligations of armed groups.[22] The Geneva Conventions from 1949 state in Article 3: "each Party to the conflict shall be bound to apply". Today nearly nobody disputes the fact that international humanitarian law is binding on non-state parties.[23] But can the same point be made for human rights? This can only be the case if humanitarian law itself provides good legal arguments for direct obligations.[24] Otherwise, the analogy would be rather weak.

---

18 Tomuschat (n 2), pp. 577ff.

19 Ibid., pp. 577ff.

20 Ian Brownlie, *Principles of Public International Law*, 7th edn (New York: Oxford University Press, 2008), pp. 6f.

21 Bruno Simma and Philip Alston, 'The Sources of Human Rights Law: Custom, Jus Cogens, and General Principles' (1988-1989) 12, Australian Yearbook of International Law, pp. 82–108, p. 97, see Ryngaert (n 1), p. 367, stressing the political and less legal character of UN organs, and p. 374 referring to Simma and Alston, see also Tomuschat (n. 2), p. 585, underlining the legal character.

22 Fleck (n 1), p. 79, see Ryngaert (n. 1), p. 357, who seems to be skeptical about humanitarian law analogies.

23 Zegveld (n. 13), pp. 10ff; Tomuschat (n. 2), p. 587; Ryngaert (n. 1), p. 357.

24 Ryngaert (n. 1), p. 357, for a review of the IHL arguments presented below.

Non-state actors are not parties to the Geneva Conventions; they did not negotiate or sign them. But it is argued that it was the will of the state parties to the conventions to create direct obligations for non-state actors.[25] If non-state actors are thought to bear obligations under an international treaty, it seems natural to apply the rules of the VCLT which repeats custom.[26] Article 34-36 VCLT state that if a treaty shall apply to a third party two conditions have to be met: intention of the treaty parties and consent of the third party.[27] In the case of Article 3 GC, the intention of state parties can be deduced from the wording "each Party to the conflict shall be bound". In the case of AP II this is more complicated. The formulation "the parties to the conflict" was expressly deleted during the drafting process because there was no consent concerning direct obligations of armed groups.[28] There are other ways to deduce this intention from the wording of AP II.[29] Still, one element is certainly lacking: the consent of armed groups who never agreed or disagreed to an effect on third parties.[30] Another line of argument is that non-state actors are exercising de-facto governmental authority. They are representing the state in the same way as the government does.[31] Nevertheless, this observation does not explain the reason why armed groups are bound by Article 3 GC. Contrary to AP II, territorial control is no condition for its application.[32] As a consequence of the deficit in reasoning[33], the

25 Antonio Cassese, 'The Status of Rebels Under the 1977 Geneva Protocol on Non-International Armed Conflict' (1981) 30, International & Comparative Law Quarterly, pp. 416–39, p. 421.

26 Lindsay Moir, *The Law of Internal Armed Conflict* (Cambridge: Cambridge University Press, 2002), p. 53.

27 Cassese (n. 25), p. 423; Moir (n. 26), p. 53.

28 Cassese (n. 25), p. 421.

29 Cassese (n. 25), pp. 424ff; Andrew Clapham, 'Human rights obligations of non-state actors in conflict situations' (2006) 88, International Review of the Red Cross, pp. 491–523, p. 498.

30 Moir (n. 26), p. 53.

31 Tomuschat (n. 2), p. 587; Ryngaert (n. 1), p. 356, referring to the quasi-government argument in Human Rights, see I.C.

32 Ryngaert (n. 1), p. 358, for further references.

argument proposing an analogy to international humanitarian law turns out to lack solidity.

C. Human rights provide enough legal space for development

It has been shown that it is not possible to affirm with certainty direct obligations under positive law. Despite this fact there is enough legal space for development, so that there may be a direct obligation in the future. This is the case when armed groups are exercising quasi-governmental power, which makes them compatible with the conception of human rights. Moreover, it is possible to identify tendencies which indicate that human rights law has already accepted obligations of private actors as an issue located within its scope.

1. Quasi-governmental power is equivalent to state action

The only relevant difference between a state and an armed opposition group is that only states have territorial sovereignty.[34] But what if the rebels exercise effective control over a territory and if they are running their own administrative and judicial institutions? De facto, the rebels would exercise quasi-governmental power, which would enable them to comply with human rights obligations.[35] Examples for that are the FARC in Colombia and the LTTE in Sri Lanka.[36] In these territories, the state is absent whereas the rebels exercise a complete control. Then the difference between the state and the private actors is only a formal one. Conceptually, it would be in accordance with human rights to speak of a direct obligation in this situation.[37] Moreover, without direct obligations under human rights there would be a space without legal protection, because the regime normally protecting

33 Clapham (n. 29), p. 498.
34 Ryngaert (n. 1), p. 369.
35 Ibid, pp. 369, 371.
36 Ryngaert (n. 1), p. 370; UNCHR, Report Sri Lanka (n. 17), para. 26.
37 Ryngaert (n. 1), p. 369, for further references.

individuals, the national criminal law, cannot be enforced.[38] This situation would not respect the principles of human rights.[39] The lack of structural differences between a state and a quasi-governmental entity is illustrated by the recent case law of the Committee against Torture under the CAT.[40] In several decisions, the Committee had to deal with the question if the conditions of the rule of *non-refoulement* in Article 3(1) CAT are fulfilled when the menace of torturous acts derives from a private group. As indicated above, in the meaning of the CAT "torture" implies acts committed by "a public official or other person acting in an official capacity".[41] The Committee first set out the general rule that acts committed "by a non-governmental entity, without the consent or acquiescence of the Government" do not constitute torture.[42] In a following decision concerning a *refoulement* to Somalia, the Committee formulated an exception. It noticed that "Somalia has been without a central government" and "that some of the factions operating in Mogadishu have set up quasi-governmental institutions and are negotiating the establishment of a common administration".[43] In that case, non-state actors fall under the wording "other person acting in an official capacity" of the definition of torture. In a later decision, the Committee merged these two views to form a single rule and emphasized the significance of territorial control for a quasi-government:

---

38 Ibid., p. 369.

39 Ibid., p. 369, quoting the preamble of the Universal Declaration of Human Rights, "the inherent dignity and of the equal and inalienable rights of all members of the human family".

40 For a comprehensive study of the relevant cases see Maral Kashgar, 'Art. 3 im Rahmen des Individualbeschwerdeverfahrens gemäß Art. 22 des Übereinkommens gegen Folter und andere grausame, unmenschliche oder erniedrigende Behandlung oder Strafe: Teil 2 des Berichts über die Arbeitsweise des Ausschusses gegen Folter' (2011), MenschenRechtsMagazin, pp. 52–73, pp. 61ff.

41 Article 1(1) CAT.

42 *G.R.B. v Sweden,* Communication No 120/1998 UN Doc CAT/C/20/D/83/1997, para 6.5; Kashgar (n. 40), p. 61.

43 *Elmi v Australien,* Communication No 120/1998 UN Doc CAT/C/22/D/120/1998, para 6.5; Kashgar (n. 40), p. 63.

> pain or suffering inflicted by a non-governmental entity, without the consent or acquiescence of the Government, falls outside the scope of Article 3 of the Convention, unless the non-governmental entity occupies and exercises quasi-governmental authority over the territory to which the complainant would be returned.[44]

Of course, the Committee did not discuss direct obligations of a non-state actor under the convention. It only interpreted the scope of the obligation of *non-refoulement* of a state party. But still the Committee clearly recognized that human rights violations by governments and quasi-governmental powers have the same legal relevance. The formal quality of the perpetrator does not matter as long as it is equivalent to a state. In this sense, it contributes to the discussion about human rights obligations of non-state actors. But it is not only the structural resemblance of these groups which would facilitate their integration into the conception of human rights. Moreover, the latter is already preoccupied with actors other than the state.

2. *Human rights law no longer ignores non-state actors*

It is difficult to maintain any longer that human rights are blind to the idea that some private actors bear duties under human rights law.[45] Firstly, international criminal law sanctions human rights violations by private individuals.[46] Even if it only incriminates acts committed by individuals and does not address groups, it shows that already now the focus of human rights reaches beyond the state. Secondly, even below the extreme threshold of international criminal law, states have already addressed human rights violations by non-state actors with

44 *S.S. v The Netherlands,* Communication No 191/2001 UN Doc CAT/C/30/D/191/2001, para. 6.4; Kashgar (n. 40), p. 65.

45 Andrew Clapham, *Human rights obligations of non-state actors*, The collected courses of the Academy of European Law (New York: Oxford University Press, 2006), XV/1, pp. 15ff.

46 Andrew Clapham, 'The Rights and Responsibilities of Armed Non-State Actors: The Legal Landscape & Issues Surrounding Engagement', Draft for Comment February 2010, <http://www.adh-geneva.ch/RULAC/application_of_international_law_to_non_State_armed_groups.php> (18 May 2012), para. 4.

regard to terrorism.[47] While doing so, they did not limit themselves to individual responsibility, but referred also to violations perpetrated by groups.[48]

Even if this tendency has probably not resulted in direct obligations under customary international law (see above), it might show that the preoccupation with non-state actors is no longer foreign to the conception of human rights law.[49]

It can be concluded that direct human rights obligations of armed groups are far from being a well-established principle in international law. Nevertheless, there is legal space for development in the future. A condition for direct obligations would be the exercise of quasi-governmental power by the armed group.

II. Direct obligations from a legal policy perspective

Apart from the fact that direct human rights obligations of non-state parties are legally possible, they are also desirable from a legal policy perspective because they assure legal protection.[50] Another complex issue is the question which legal standpoint would be appropriate to support these aspirations. An interesting example is the approach developed by Philip Alston as Special Rapporteur of the UN Human Rights Commission on extrajudicial, summary or arbitrary executions.[51]

47 See the statements of Argentina, India, Cuba and Kuwait in Clapham (n. 45), p. 40.

48 Ibid., p. 40.

49 Ibid., p. 41.

50 Ryngaert (n. 1), pp. 368, 378, providing an overview of the main arguments.

51 UNCHR, Report Sri Lanka (n. 17); Clapham (n 29), p. 505; Ryngaert (n. 1), pp. 371ff, focusing more on the respect of positive law than on the impact on the future legal development.

A. Direct human rights obligations of non-state parties are desirable

In armed conflicts, human rights obligations of non-state parties would increase the protection of individuals in domains that are not covered by international humanitarian law or international criminal law.[52] Humanitarian law protects only an essential core of rights, as the right to life or the prohibition of torture.[53] International criminal law protects merely against crimes of an extreme gravity as war crimes or genocide.[54] In contrast, the protection offered by human rights is more comprehensive, since it contains rights as the liberty of movement, the right to freedom of expression or the right to political participation.[55] If a rebel group controls a territory for a longer period of time and sets up a rudimentary administration, those rights are needed.[56] From a legal policy point of view, obligations tend to be more effective when there is a possibility for legal remedy.[57] Performing that task would be very difficult for the existing human rights bodies. Bodies like the Human Rights Committee or the ECtHR are bound by the scope of their conventions, which is limited to infringements committed by states.[58] But there are other mechanisms at hand, which are reportedly effective. One important mechanism is making the violations public, the "naming and shaming".[59] Particularly non-state actors seeking for international recognition may be sensitive in this context.[60] This task could be fulfilled by Special Rapporteurs of the UN Human Rights Council and local offices of the

52 Ryngaert (n. 1), p. 378, the problem of ineffectiveness of the national criminal law has been pointed out above.

53 Article 4(2)(a)-(h) AP II.

54 See Article 5(1) Statute of the International Criminal Court.

55 Tomuschat (n. 2), p. 589; Clapham (n. 29), p. 506, referring to UNCHR, Report Sri Lanka (n. 17), para. 85; Ryngaert (n. 1), p. 378.

56 Ryngaert (n. 1), p. 370.

57 Tomuschat (n. 2), p. 590.

58 Ibid, p. 590, concering the HRC.

59 Ryngaert (n. 1), p. 380.

60 Clapham (n. 29), p. 511.

High Commissioner for Human Rights.[61] NGOs are also playing a vital role in this area.[62] Another method already used by NGOs is the negotiation of human rights declarations with non-state actors in combination with a compliance monitoring.[63] Finally, the danger that direct obligations of non-state actors are providing a justification for states to breach human rights obligations themselves is minimized by the limitation to non-state parties which are exercising quasi-governmental power.[64] Today, human rights may be mostly of rhetoric relevance for non-state parties.[65] Nevertheless, a creation of competent treaty bodies is still possible, even if this might happen only in the distant future.[66] In addition, naming and shaming may be more effective if it is founded on legally binding obligations than on unbinding expectations.[67]

B. *Which legal standpoint to promote legally binding obligations?*

Having explained the need for direct obligations, at least one question remains: which standpoint could be taken to promote the development of such rules? This very complex issue goes beyond the scope of this article. Consequently, only some questions can be raised and one example be given.

The standpoint probably depends on who is advancing it and in which environment, for instance state representatives in or outside the UN, state parties to non-international armed conflicts, UN treaty bodies, UN Special Rapporteurs or NGOs. On the substantial level, it

---

61 Ibid., pp. 505, 507, for practical examples.

62 Ibid., pp. 511f.

63 Ibid., p. 512.

64 Ryngaert (n. 1), p. 376.

65 Ibid., p. 375, for further references.

66 Martin Scheinin, 'Towards a World Court of Human Rights', Research report within the framework of the Swiss Initiative to commemorate the 60th anniversary of the Universal Declaration of Human Rights (2009), <http://www.udhr60.ch/report/hrCourt_scheinin0609.pdf> (30 April 2012).

67 See below.

can be asked whether it is better to just claim the existence of legally binding obligations under treaty law, customary law or even universal standards or to take an intermediate stance by speaking of non-binding standards.[68] It can be imagined that this question is particularly delicate with regard to human rights monitoring based on a mandate agreed by states. There might be a dilemma between promoting direct obligations and keeping the states on board.[69]

An interesting example is the position of Philip Alston, in his function as Special Rapporteur of the UN Human Rights Commission.[70] His report about extrajudicial, summary or arbitrary executions in Sri Lanka advances the following idea. Human rights can function on three levels, as rights of the individual, as obligations of states and, finally, as legitimate expectations of the international community.[71] According to Alston, without consent, private persons are not directly bound by human rights. Nevertheless, the international community can legitimately expect that they too respect the latter.[72] This is deduced from the preamble of the Universal Declaration of Human Rights from 1948:

> [...] [t]he General Assembly [p]roclaims this Universal Declaration of Human Rights *as a common standard of achievement for all peoples and all nations, to the end that every individual and every organ of society*, keeping this Declaration constantly in mind, *shall strive* by teaching and education to promote respect for these rights and freedoms and *by progressive measures, national and international, to secure their universal and effective recognition*

68 Clapham (n. 45), p. 99; Clapham, Draft for Comment February 2010 (n. 46), for "universal standards" and the work of UN Special Rapporteurs and NGOs.

69 UNCHR, 'Report of the Special Rapporteur on extrajudicial, summary or arbitrary executions', Interim Report (16 August 2007) UN Doc A/62/265, para. 37ff, giving an account of the diplomatic sensibilities.

70 UNCHR, Report Sri Lanka (n. 17); Clapham (n. 29), p. 505; Ryngaert (n. 1), pp. 371ff.

71 UNCHR, Report Sri Lanka (n 17), para. 25.

72 Ibid, para. 25.

and observance, both among the peoples of Member States themselves and among the peoples of territories under their jurisdiction.[73]

According to Alston, only two conditions have to be met: effective territorial control and identifiable political institutions.[74] In his report about the Philippines he added that non-state parties can only bear human rights obligations if they assent to the latter.[75] The view expressed in the Sri Lanka report has several important advantages. It respects today's positive law, since it does not refer to direct obligations of armed groups.[76] The states do not have to fear to legitimize their opponents because both are not put on a same level.[77] At the same time, it pushes forward the discourse about direct obligations, because it permits states from now on to condemn human rights violations by non-state actors.[78] As a consequence, the Special Rapporteur's position should be taken as a possible intermediate stance which may contribute to the creation of direct human rights obligations of non-state parties. It is difficult to ascertain if the Special Rapporteur had this aim in mind, and it is probably too early to assess the report's impact. It would also be beyond the scope of this contribution to discuss eventual alternatives or the position's appropriateness for other actors.[79]

---

73 Emphasis added, ibid, para. 25, 27, referring to the "common standard of achievement" and that "every organ of society respect and promote human rights", Ryngaert (n. 1), p. 372.

74 UNCHR, Report Sri Lanka (n. 17), para. 25.

75 UNHRC, 'Report of the Special Rapporteur on extrajudicial, summary or arbitrary executions', Mission to Philippines (16 April 2008) UN Doc A/HRC/8/3/Add.2, para. 5; Ryngaert (n. 1), p. 372.

76 Ryngaert (n. 1), p. 377.

77 Ibid., p. 377.

78 Ibid., p. 380, focussing more on the possibility of monitoring as such than on its impact on the future legal development.

79 Clapham, Draft for Comment February 2010 (n. 46), providing examples of how NGOs are addressing this question.

III. Conclusion

It has been shown above that under today's positive human rights law a confirmation of direct obligations of non-state parties in armed conflicts is very problematic or may be even lacking. However, direct obligations would be compatible with the nature of human rights law, if the non-state party is structurally equivalent to its state counterpart. This condition is fulfilled when it exercises quasi-governmental power. Moreover, it is no longer possible to assert that human rights law is ignoring non-state actors. Given the numerous advantages of direct obligations from a perspective of human rights policy, the door to legally binding human rights obligations must not be closed prematurely. The question of an adequate stance to promote direct obligations is very complex and needs further clarification. The position of the Special Rapporteur on extrajudicial, summary or arbitrary executions, which is promoting the existence of legitimate expectations of the international community, could be conceived as a tool and an intermediate step towards the recognition of legally binding direct obligations of non-state parties.

Human rights and criminal law and enforcement

Droits de l'Homme, droit pénal et procédure pénale
Menschenrechte, Strafrecht und Strafvollzug

Der Beitrag des ICTY und ICTR zur Entwicklung des Völkerstrafrechts zu sexueller Gewalt

Eliette MIRAU-GONDOIN*

Im Sommer 2010 wurden innerhalb von drei Tagen 387 Menschen Opfer einer Massenvergewaltigung im Ostkongo[1]. Im Abschlussbericht des „Bureau conjoint des Nations Unies aux droits de l'Homme" (BCNUDH) über diese Ereignisse in Nord-Kivu wurde festgestellt, dass die Vergewaltigungen als Kriegswaffe eingesetzt wurden, um die Zivilbevölkerung zu terrorisieren und zu unterwerfen[2]. Darüber hinaus wurden die Angriffe vorausgeplant und systematisch und zielgerichtet begangen, was eine Bestrafung der Taten als Verbrechen gegen die Menschlichkeit und Kriegsverbrechen sowohl nach kongolesischem

* LL.M. Doktorandin und wissenschaftliche Hilfskraft an der juristischen Fakultät der Universität Potsdam.

1 Vom 30. Juli bis zum 2. August 2010 haben geschätzte 200 Kämpfer der Demokratischen Kräfte zur Befreiung Rwandas (FDLR) und der Mai-Mai Milizen in 13 Dörfern nach offiziellen Angaben 387 Menschen (200 Frauen, aber auch 23 Männer, 55 Mädchen und 9 Jungen) vergewaltigt, 116 entführt und 965 Häuser und Läden geplündert. Es ist jedoch davon auszugehen, dass die Zahl der Vergewaltigungen deutlich höher liegt, denn viele Opfer schwiegen aus Angst um ihre Sicherheit oder um nicht stigmatisiert zu werden. Vgl. Rapport final des missions d'enquête du Bureau Conjoint des Nations Unies aux Droits de l'Homme (BCNUDH) sur les viols massifs et autres violations des droits de l'Homme commis par une coalition de groupes armés sur l'axe Kibua-Mpofi, en territoire de Walikale, Province du Nord-Kivu, du 30 juillet au 2 août 2010 § 25; § 30. Abrufbar unter: <http://www.ohchr.org/Documents/Countries/ZR/BCNUDHRapportViolsMassifsKibuaMpofi_fr.pdf> (25.04.2012).

2 Rapport final des missions d'enquête du BCNUDH (oben Fn. 1), § 34.

Recht [3] als auch nach Art. 7 und 8 des Römischen Statuts auf internationaler Ebene ermöglichen würde[4].

Dieses Beispiel veranschaulicht den Stand des heutigen Völkerstrafrechts zu sexueller Gewalt. Es hat aber lange Zeit gedauert bis vergewaltigte Opfer ihre Peiniger vor einem internationalen Strafgericht sehen konnten. Vor der Rechtsprechung der internationalen Strafgerichtshöfe für das ehemalige Jugoslawien (ICTY) beziehungsweise Ruanda (ICTR), war demnach lange unklar, ob Vergewaltigungen und andere Formen von sexueller Gewalt in bewaffneten Konflikten eine individuelle strafrechtliche Verantwortlichkeit auf internationaler Ebene mit sich zieht. Die Urteile des ICTY und ICTR stellen daher einen Wendepunkt in der Bestrafung sexueller Gewalt auf internationaler Ebene dar und haben maßgeblich zur Weiterentwicklung des humanitären Völkerrechts in diesem Bereich beigetragen.

Nach einer kurzen Einführung zum Stand des Völkerstrafrechts bezüglich sexueller Gewalt vor der Errichtung der Strafgerichtshöfe werden wichtige Urteile des ITCY und ICTR zu dem Thema erörtert (I). Zum Schluss wird anhand des Römischen Statuts festgestellt, dass der Schutz vor sexueller Gewalt ein vollwertiger Tatbestand des humanitären Völkerrechts geworden ist, der den Frauen auf internationaler Ebene umfassenden rechtlichen Schutz bietet[5] (II).

---

3 Art. 170 der gesetztesvertretenden Verordnung Nr. 06/018 vom 20.07.2006 zur Änderung und Ergänzung des kongolesischen Strafgesetzbuchs vom 30. Januar 1940.

4 Rapport final des missions d'enquête du BCNUDH (oben Fn. 1), § 35.

5 Wie oft im Völkerrecht weicht der rechtliche Schutz der Frauen oft von dem tatsächlichen Schutz vor Ort ab, wie die wiederholten Vergewaltigungen im Ostkongo zeigen. Die These der Verfasserin ist, dass der Schutz vor sexueller Gewalt am effektivsten durch die Verbindung repressiver Maßnahmen mit präventiven Maßnahmen erreicht werden kann. Vertieft wird dies im Promotionsvorhaben zu dem Thema: „Protection, Prevention, Prosecution: die Vereinten Nationen und der Schutz der Frauen vor sexueller Gewalt im Rahmen bewaffneter Konflikten", Fertigstellung voraussichtlich 2014.

I. Stand des Völkerstrafrechts vor der Errichtung des ICTY und ICTR

A. Die ersten gescheiterten Versuche einer Bestrafung sexueller Verbrechen auf internationaler Ebene

Bereits 1474 wurde ein Kommandant im Rahmen des ersten in der Rechtsgeschichte bekannten internationalen Kriegsverbrecherprozesses[6] wegen durch seine Untergebenen begangener Vergewaltigungen zu Tode verurteilt. Allerdings wurde der Ritter Peter von Hagenbach nur deshalb bestraft, weil diese Taten im Rahmen eines unerklärten Kriegs stattgefunden haben. Wäre der Krieg ordnungsgemäß erklärt worden, wären die Vergewaltigungen erlaubt gewesen[7].

1919 hatte sich das humanitäre Völkerrecht soweit entwickelt, dass Kriegsvergewaltigungen verboten waren. Der 1863 erlassene Lieber Code, der als die bedeutendste Grundlage für die spätere Ausarbeitung des Kriegsrechts auf internationaler Ebene gilt, listete in Art. 44 Vergewaltigung als Kapitalverbrechen auf und die Landkriegsordnung als Anlage des IV. Haager Abkommens betreffend der Gesetze und Gebräuche des Landkrieges vom 18. Oktober 1907 ordnete in Art. 46 an, „die Ehre und die Rechte der Familie zu achten", was nach zeitgenössischer Auffassung zu Beginn des Jahrhunderts sexuelle Angriffe auf die Frau einschließlich Vergewaltigung verbot[8].

---

6 Das Gericht bestand aus 28 Richtern aus alliierten Staaten des heiligen römischen Reichs.

7 Kelly D. Askin, *War Crimes against Women*, Den Haag 1997, S. 29.

8 Kelly D. Askin, *Women and international humanitarian Law*, S. 41 (51), in: Kelly D. Askin, Dorean M. Koenig (Hrsg.), *Women and International Human Rights Law*, Vol.1, New York 1999, Dies wird dadurch bestätigt, dass der IKRK-Kommentar zu Art. 27 der vierten Genfer Konvention vom 12. August 1949 zum Schutz von Zivilpersonen in Kriegszeiten, der in seinem zweiten Absatz ein klares Vergewaltigungsverbot beinhaltet, bei der Auslegung des ersten Absatzes und der Achtung der Familienrechte auf Art. 46 HLKO verweist

Während des ersten Weltkriegs wurde sexuelle Gewalt als Terrormittel gegen die Zivilbevölkerung eingesetzt. Auch wenn das Ausmaß der Gewalttaten sich durch den Propagandamissbrauch nur schlecht ermitteln ließ[9], konnte die nach dem ersten Weltkrieg eingerichtete Untersuchungskommission genug Beweise über Vergewaltigung belgischer und französischer Frauen durch deutschen Soldaten sammeln, um in seinem Kriegsverbrechenkatalog „Notzucht" und „die Verschleppung von jungen Mädchen und Frauen, um sie der Prostitution auszuliefern" aufzunehmen[10].

Nach Art. 227 und 228 des Friedensvertrags von Versailles vom 28. Juni 1919 sollten Kaiser Wilhelm II. und weitere Personen, die gegen Gesetze und Gebräuche des Krieges sowie Gesetze der Menschlichkeit verstoßen hatten, vor einem internationalen Gerichtshof angeklagt werden. Doch die Verweigerung der Niederlande, Wilhelm II. auszuliefern und die ablehnende Haltung der Vereinigten Staaten gegenüber einem internationalen Gerichtshof setzte der Hoffnung einer erstmaligen Strafverfolgung und Verurteilung von sexuellen Gewaltverbrechen auf internationaler Ebene ein Ende[11]. Die Straflosigkeit sexueller Kriegsverbrechen bestand nach der Einrichtung der Militärgerichtshöfe von Nürnberg (IMT) und Tokio (IMTFE) nach dem zweiten Weltkrieg fort. Sexuelle Gewalt fand während des zweiten Weltkriegs in unterschiedlichen Formen und Ausmaßen statt: von den brutalen Massenvergewaltigungen der russischen Armee und der japanischen Soldaten über die vereinzelten Vergewaltigungen der Alliierten während ihres Vormarsches nach Berlin bis hin zur sexuellen Versklavung der Frauen im asiatisch-

---

und ausdrücklich betont, „Respect for family life is also covered by the clause prohibiting rape and other attacks on women's honour as stated in the next paragraph." (Jean S. Pictet, *The Geneva Conventions of 12 August 1949, Commentary, Vol. IV*, Genf 1958, S. 202).

9 Siehe dazu Gabriela Mischkowski, Sexualisierte Gewalt im Krieg, eine Chronik, *in*: Medica mondiale e.V. (Hrsg.), *Sexualisierte Kriegsgewalt und ihre Folgen*, Frankfurt am Main 2004, S. 17 (21-23).

10 Christina Möller, Sexuelle Gewalt im Krieg, *in*: Hasse/Müller/Schneider (Hrsg.), *Humanitäres Völkerrecht*, Baden-Baden 2001, S. 280 (285).

11 Askin (oben Fn. 8), S. 44.

pazifischen Raum und Zwangsprostitution in den Wehrmachtsbordellen und in den Konzentrationslagern; alle Parteien des Konflikts waren an sexuellen Verbrechen beteiligt[12]. Doch in einer Zeit, wo die Welt um über 15 Millionen zivile Kriegsopfer trauerte, sind diese Taten in den Hintergrund gerückt. Während in Nürnberg trotz vorhandener unmissverständlicher Beweise [13] kein sexuelles Verbrechen zur Anklage kam, befasst sich das internationale Militärtribunal in Tokio mit den Vergewaltigungen während der Eroberung von Nanking. Das Gericht verurteilte die Vergewaltigungen von 20 000 Frauen und Mädchen als „unmenschliche Behandlung“, „Misshandlung“ und „Nichtbeachtung der Rechte und Ehre der Familie“ und verhing gegen einen General der japanischen Armee und den zur Tatzeit regierenden japanischen Außenminister Koki Hirota, unter anderen für diese Taten, die Todesstrafe[14]. Die Vernachlässigung der sexuellen Verbrechen in den Statuten und Urteilen der internationalen Militärtribunale erklärt sich damit, dass der Fokus ihrer Arbeit auf der Verfolgung der Verbrechen gegen den Frieden und Verbrechen gegen die Menschlichkeit an den Juden lag. Doch die internationale Gemeinschaft hatte die Taten zur Kenntnis genommen und ihnen zumindest bei der Ausarbeitung der Genfer Konventionen Rechnung getragen[15].

B. Sexuelle Gewalt in den Genfer Konventionen von 1949

1949 ist zu dem sog. Haager Recht, das die Methoden der Kriegsführung regelt, das sog. Genfer Recht hinzugestoßen.

---

12 Vgl. dazu Mischkowski (oben Fn. 9), S. 23-31.

13 Für eine Auflistung der dem Gericht vorgelegten Beweistücke s. Askin (oben Fn. 8), S. 53, Fn. 183.

14 Gabriela Mischkowski, Strafverfolgung und Wahrheitsfindung, *in*: Medica mondiale e.V. (Hrsg.), *Sexualisierte Kriegsgewalt und ihre Folgen*, Frankfurt am Main 2004, S. 94 (94).

15 Pictet (oben Fn. 8), S. 205.

Bestehend aus 4 Konventionen[16] und 3 ergänzenden Protokollen[17], befasst sich das Genfer Recht mit dem Verhalten der Parteien gegenüber nicht oder nicht mehr am Kampf beteiligten Personen. Lediglich einzelne Vorschriften des Genfer Rechts verbieten ausdrücklich ausgewählte Formen von sexueller Gewalt. Explizite Hinweise zu sexueller Gewalt finden sich in:

Art. 27 Abs. 2 der vierten Konvention:

> Die Frauen sollen besonders vor jedem Angriff auf ihre Ehre und namentlich vor Vergewaltigung, Nötigung zur Prostitution und jeder unzüchtigen Handlung geschützt werden.

Art. 75 Abs. 2 lit. b ZP I:

> Folgende Handlungen sind und bleiben jederzeit und überall verboten, gleichviel ob sie durch zivile Bedienstete oder durch Militärpersonen begangen werden: [...]
> b) Beeinträchtigung der persönlichen Würde, insbesondere entwürdigende und erniedrigende Behandlung, Nötigung zur Prostitution und unzüchtige Handlungen jeder Art, [...]

---

16 I. Genfer Abkommen vom 12. August 1949 zur Verbesserung des Loses der Verwundeten und Kranken der Streitkräfte im Felde (GK I); II. Genfer Abkommen vom 12. August 1949 zur Verbesserung des Loses der Verwundeten, Kranken und Schiffbrüchigen der Streitkräfte zur See (GK II); III. Genfer Abkommen vom 12. August 1949 über die Behandlung der Kriegsgefangenen (GK III); IV. Genfer Abkommen z vom 12. August 1949 um Schutz von Zivilpersonen in Kriegszeiten (GK IV); Online abrufbar unter <http://www.icrc.org/eng/war-and-law/treaties-customary-law/geneva-conventions /index.jsp> (27.07.2011).

17 Zusatzprotokoll vom 8. Juni 1977 zu den Genfer Abkommen vom 12. August 1949 über den Schutz der Opfer internationaler bewaffneter Konflikte (ZP I); Zusatzprotokoll vom 8. Juni 1977 zu den Genfer Abkommen vom 12. August 1949 über den Schutz der Opfer nichtinternationaler bewaffneter Konflikte (ZP II).

Art. 76 Abs. 1 ZP I:

> Frauen werden besonders geschont; sie werden namentlich vor Vergewaltigung, Nötigung zur Prostitution und jeder anderen unzüchtigen Handlung geschützt.

Und Art. 4 Abs. 2 lit. e) ZP II, für nicht-internationale Konflikte:

> Unbeschadet der allgemeinen Gültigkeit der vorstehenden Bestimmungen sind und bleiben in Bezug auf die in Absatz 1 genannten Personen jederzeit und überall verboten […]
> e) Beeinträchtigung der persönlichen Würde, insbesondere entwürdigende und erniedrigende Behandlung, Vergewaltigung, Nötigung zur Prostitution und unzüchtige Handlungen jeder Art; [...]

Allerdings gehören diese Verbote nicht zu den in den Genfer Konventionen und dem ersten Protokoll (u.a. Art. 147 GK IV und Art. 85 ZP I) aufgezählten schweren Verletzungen der Genfer Konventionen, welche dem Weltrechtsprinzip unterliegen. Demnach können sie nicht überall und jederzeit von der Völkergemeinschaft verfolgt und bestraft werden, unabhängig davon wo, von wem oder gegen wen die Taten begangen worden sind. Dies änderte sich in den 1990er Jahren mit der Errichtung der internationalen Strafgerichtshöfe für das ehemalige Jugoslawien[18] und Ruanda[19] durch den UN- Sicherheitsrat.

---

18 UN Docs. S/Res/808 vom 22.02.1993 und S/Res/827 vom 25.05.1993. In der letzteren Resolution erklärte sich der Sicherheitsrat höchst beunruhigt „angesichts der fortgesetzten Berichte über weitverbreitete und flagrante Verstöße gegen das humanitäre Völkerrecht im Hoheitsgebiet des ehemaligen Jugoslawien […] [und] der Berichte über massenhafte Tötungen, die massive, organisierte und systematische Internierung und Vergewaltigung von Frauen […].“

19 UN Doc. S/Res/ 955 vom 8.11.1994.

II. Die Entwicklung des Völkerstrafrechts zu sexueller Gewalt

Das ICTY und ICTR verurteilten in mehreren Prozessen sexuelle Verbrechen als Kriegsverbrechen, als schwere Verletzung der Genfer Konventionen, als Verbrechen gegen die Menschlichkeit und sogar als Genozide und dies, obwohl die Statuten beider Gerichte lediglich Vergewaltigung als Verbrechen gegen die Menschlichkeit auflisteten (Art. 5 lit. g ICTY-Statut, Art. 3 lit. g ICTR-Statut)[20]. Durch eine erweiterte Auslegung der Straftatbestände seitens der Anklagebehörde und die Interpretation der Statuten unter Einbeziehung neuer Rechtsauffassungen seitens der Richter konnten sexuelle Verbrechen erstmals in der Geschichte als schwerste Gewaltverbrechen angeklagt und verurteilt werden. Dabei hat die Rechtsprechung der Gerichtshöfe den Weg zu einer völligen Neufassung der Tatbestände zu sexueller Gewalt im ICC-Statut geebnet.

A. Erweiterte Auslegung der Strafbestände

Da das ICTY-Statut explizit keine Verurteilung von sexueller Gewalt als schwere Verletzung der Genfer Konventionen (Art. 2), als Verstoß gegen die Gesetze oder Gebräuche des Kriegs oder Völkermord (Art. 4) zuließ, ohne gegen den Legitimitätsgrundsatz „*nuella poena sine lege*" zu verstoßen, musste die Anklagebehörde, um eine vollumfängliche Verfolgung von sexueller Gewalt zu ermöglichen, die Gewalttaten auch unter diejenigen Vorschriften des Statuts subsumieren, die geschlechtsspezifische Verbrechen nicht explizit aufführten[21].

20 In Art. 4 lit. e ICTR-Statut wird zudem Zwangsprostitution als Verstoß gegen den gemeinsamen Artikel 3 der Genfer Abkommen und gegen deren Zusatzprotokoll II benannt.

21 Kathrin Greve, *Vergewaltigung als Völkermord*, Baden-Baden 2008, S. 154.

Besonders schwierig erwies sich die Anklage als Kriegsverbrechen unter Art. 2 und 3 des ICTY-Statuts, denn wie erwähnt gehörte Vergewaltigung nicht zu den schweren Verletzungen der Genfer Konventionen. Die Anklagebehörde half sich deshalb zunächst mit Auffangtatbeständen wie unmenschliche Behandlung, grausame Behandlung und Beeinträchtigung der persönlichen Würde oder verfolgte sexuelle Gewalt als Element anderer Tatbestände insbesondere Folter[22].

Erst 1999, nachdem das Gericht im Fall Delalic feststellte, dass es keinen Zweifel an einem ausdrücklichen Verbot von Vergewaltigung im humanitären Völkerrecht gebe[23] und im Fall Furundjiža erklärte, „*it is indisputable, that rape and other serious assaults in armed conflicts entail the criminal liability of the perpetrators*“[24] wurden Vergewaltigung und sexuelle Gewalt als Kriegsverbrechen nach Art. 3 des ICTY-Statuts ohne Rekurs auf kodifizierte Auffangtatbestände angeklagt. Die Verurteilung von sexueller Gewalt war nur deshalb erfolgreich, weil die Richter keine Anklage zurückwiesen, welche sexuelle Gewalt unter Tatbestände subsumierte, die dies nicht ausdrücklich vorsahen.

B. Grundlegende Urteile des ICTY und ICTR

Bestimmte Urteile des ICTY und ICTR gelten als Meilensteine in der Bestrafung sexueller Gewalt auf internationaler Ebene[25]. Die vier

---

22 Nicolas Lamp, Der Beitrag der Vereinten Nationen zur Entwicklung des Völkerstrafrechts zu sexueller Gewalt, *in*: Sabine von Schorlemer (Hrsg.), *Die Vereinten Nationen und neuere Entwicklungen der Frauenrechte*, Frankfurt am Main 2007, S. 369 (381).

23 ICTY, Prosecutor vs. Delalic, Mucic, Delic, Landzo, Judgment, 16.11.1998, IT-96-21-T, § 476.

24 ICTY, Prosecutor vs. Furundjiža, Judgment, 10.12.1998, IT-95-17-1, § 169.

25 Für eine ausführliche Darstellung der Urteile zu sexueller Gewalt von ICTY, ICTR und SCL bis März 2009 siehe: Review of the sexual violence elements of the judgments of the former Yugoslavia, the International Criminal Tribunal for

unten dargelegten Fälle stellen Präzedenzfälle dar und haben demnach eine große Bedeutung für die nachfolgenden Prozesse gehabt.

Die *Akayesu*-Entscheidung[26] vom 2. September 1998 ist in vielen Hinsicht bedeutsam und dies obwohl Vergewaltigung am Anfang gar nicht als Anklagepunkt aufgelistet worden war. Erst als eine Zeugin im Lauf des Prozesses die Vergewaltigung ihrer Tochter erwähnte, wurde dieser Tatbestand in die Anklageschrift aufgenommen. Jean-Paul Akayesu war Bürgermeister der Kommune von Taba in Ruanda. Er wird schuldig befunden, sexuelle Gewalttaten gegen Tutsi-Frauen unterstützt (indem er keine Maßnahmen ergriff, um die Taten zu verhindern oder um die Täter zu bestrafen) und zu diesen angestiftet zu haben.

Zum einen wurde für das erste Mal in der Geschichte des Völkerstrafrechts Vergewaltigung als Verbrechen gegen die Menschlichkeit abgeurteilt. Zum anderen musste sich die Kammer als erste mit der Definition des Tatbestands der Vergewaltigung auseinandersetzen, denn trotz ausdrücklichen Verbots fehlte eine Definition. Die Kammer stützte sich auf ein konzeptionelle Verständnis und definiert Vergewaltigung als

> a physical invasion of a sexual nature, committed on a person under circumstances which are coercive. Sexual violence which includes rape, is considered to be any act of a sexual nature which is committed on a person under circumstances which are coercive.

Dabei unterstrich sie, dass

> coercive circumstances need not be evidenced by a show of physical force. Threats, intimidation, extortion and other forms of duress which prey on fear or desperation may constitute coercion.[27]

Rwanda, and the Special Court of Sierra Leone in the light of Security Council resolution 1820, UN Department of Peacekeeping Operations, 2010.

26 ICTR, Prosecutor vs. Akayesu, Judgment, 2.9.1998, ICTR 96-4.

27 Ebenda, §§ 598, 688.

Schließlich ist das Urteil deswegen wichtig, weil es anerkennt, dass Vergewaltigung und andere Formen von sexueller Gewalt, wenn sie mit der Absicht begangen werden, eine nationale, ethnische, rassische oder religiöse Gruppe als solche ganz oder teilweise zu zerstören, den Tatbestand des Völkermords erfüllen können. Somit stellt sexuelle Gewalt einen integralen Bestandteil der Zerstörung im Rahmen des Völkermords dar. Im Rahmen des Völkermords in Ruanda wurde es gezielt zur Zerstörung der Volksgruppe der Tutsi eingesetzt.[28] Diese Bewertung wurde im Laufe der Arbeit des ICTR bestätigt, wie der *Musema*-Fall zeigt[29].

Das sog. Čelibići-Urteil vom 16. November 1998 [30] im Fall *Delalic und al.* führt vor dem ICTY zu der ersten Verurteilung wegen Vergewaltigung.

Čelibići war ein Internierungslager in Bosnien-Herzegowina, wo die Inhaftierten unter einer permanenten Atmosphäre des Terrors lebten und andauernd misshandelt wurden, unter anderen wurden Frauen wiederholt vergewaltigt. Da die Vergewaltigungen im Rahmen von Verhören stattgefunden hatten, mit dem Ziel, andere Häftlinge zu terrorisieren und zu Informationen bezüglich des Ehemanns des Opfers zu gelangen, kam die Kammer zu dem Schluss, dass die Vergewaltigungen den Tatbestand der Folter erfüllen und demnach eine schwere Verletzung der Genfer Konventionen darstellen [31]. Hiermit wurde das Universalitätsprinzip für die Verfolgung von Vergewaltigung als Kriegsverbrechen eröffnet. Im ersten Urteil des ICTY zu sexueller Gewalt wurde die Vergewaltigungsdefinition aus dem Akayesu-Urteil übernommen.

Das *Furundjiža*-Urteil [32] vom 10. Dezember 1998 beschäftigte sich ausschließlich mit einem einzigen Fall sexueller Gewalt. Furundjiža war anwesend, als einer Frau bei ihrer Vernehmung

---

28 Ebenda, § 731.

29 ICTR, Prosecutor vs. Musema, Judgment, 27.01.2000, ICTR 96-13-T.

30 ICTY, Prosecutor vs. Delalic, Mucic, Delic, Landzo, Judgment, 16.11.1998, IT-96-21-T.

31 Ebenda, § 496.

32 ICTY, Prosecutor vs. Furundjiža, Judgment, 10.12.1998, IT-95-17/1-T.

gedroht wurde, ihr ein Messer in die Vagina zu stoßen, während sie danach von einem Dritten oral und vaginal vergewaltigt wurde.

Das *Furundjiža*-Urteil ist deshalb wichtig, weil die Kammer einen anderen, „mechanischeren" Ansatz nahm, um den Tatbestand der Vergewaltigung zu definieren. Um dem auch im Völkerstrafrecht geltenden Bestimmtheitsgrundsatz zu genügen, müsse Vergewaltigung aus den folgenden objektiven Elementen bestehen:

> (i) the sexual penetration, however slight:
> (a) of the vagina or anus of the victim by the penis of the perpetrator or any other object used by the perpetrator; or
> (b) of the mouth of the victim by the penis of the perpetrator;
> (ii) by coercion or force or threat of force against the victim or a third person.33

Außerdem stellte die Kammer fest, dass der Tatbestand der sexuellen Gewalt sich hauptsächlich darin von der Vergewaltigung unterscheidet, dass kein Eindringen stattfinde[34].

Zum Schluss sollte man das *Kunarac*-Urteil[35] vom 22. Februar 2001 aus dem Foca-Prozess in Erinnerung behalten. Der Foca-Prozess ist einmalig, weil dort explizit, zusätzlich zu massiven Vergewaltigungen, sexuelle Versklavung zum Gegenstand gemacht wurde. Da aber sexuelle Versklavung nicht im ICTY-Statut vorgesehen ist, wurden Vergewaltigung und Versklavung als getrennte Straftaten angeklagt und verurteilt. Für die Definition von Vergewaltigung nahm die Kammer diejenige aus dem Furundjiža-Fall als Ausgangspunkt, betonte aber stärker das fehlende Einverständnis des Opfers[36].

Die Rechtsprechung der internationalen Strafgerichthöfe hat vor allem eins erreicht: sie hat der Straflosigkeit von sexuellen Verbrechen auf internationaler Ebene ein Ende gesetzt und maßgeblich zur Ächtung dieser Gewalttaten im humanitären Völkerrecht beigetragen.

---

33 Ebenda, § 185.

34 Ebenda, § 186.

35 ICTY, Prosecutor vs. Kunarac, Kovac, Vukovic, Judgement, 22.02.2001, IT-96-23 und IT-96-23/1.

36 Ebenda, § 460.

III. Ein umfassender Schutz vor sexueller Gewalt im Römischen Statut

Das Statut des Internationalen Strafgerichtshofs kodifiziert die Rechtsprechung der Strafgerichtshöfe und ergänzt sie um neue, präzisere Tatbestände. Die Kodifikation der Rechtsprechung zeigt sich in der Definition des Tatbestands der Vergewaltigung. Diese Definition ist in den im Art. 9 des Statuts vorgesehenen Verbrechenelementen enthalten. Sie ist ein Kompromiss zwischen den beiden oben dargestellten Ansätzen mit einer leichten Hervorhebung des mechanischen Ansatzes[37]. Nach Art. 7 und 8 des Römischen Statuts kann aber nicht nur Vergewaltigung, sondern auch sexuelle Sklaverei, Nötigung zur Prostitution, erzwungene Schwangerschaft, Zwangssterilisation oder jede andere Form sexueller Gewalt von vergleichbarer Schwere als Kriegsverbrechen – im Rahmen internationaler bewaffneter Konflikte und nicht-internationaler bewaffneter Konflikte – und Verbrechen gegen die Menschlichkeit vor dem Internationalen Strafgerichtshof verfolgt werden. Demnach sind die Tatbestände der „erzwungenen Schwangerschaft, Zwangssterilisation", der „sexuellen Sklaverei" und der Auffangtatbestand „sexuelle Gewalt" Neuschöpfungen der Vertragsparteien des Internationalen Strafgerichtshofs. Diese Auflistung der einzelnen Tatbestände ermöglicht in Zukunft eine Aburteilung sexueller Gewalt als solche und nicht mehr unter Rückgriff auf Auffangtatbestände, was eine Verfolgung dieser Verbrechen eindeutig erleichtern wird. Von den 25 anhängigen Anklagen vor dem IStGH beinhalten 12 Anklagepunkte betreffend sexuelle Gewalt. Den meisten Angeklagten wird Vergewaltigung vorgeworfen, drei davon stehen auch wegen sexueller Sklaverei vor Gericht. In drei laufenden Prozessen werden Sachverhalte sexueller Gewalt behandelt. Diese Repression sexueller Gewalttaten ist wichtig, aber nicht ausreichend. Die Frauen müssen im Voraus im Rahmen von Präventionsprogrammen geschützt werden. Eine grundlegende

37 Knut Dörmann, Elements of crime, 2004, S. 327.

Voraussetzung für den Schutz der Frauen vor sexueller Gewalt wäre das Ende der Diskriminierungen aufgrund des Geschlechts.

Die Sicherungsverwahrung vor dem EGMR, dem Bundesverfassungsgericht und dem *Conseil Constitutionnel* – Rechtsvergleich und Ausblick

Rieke ARENDT*

Mit seinem Urteil vom 17. Dezember 2009 sprach der Europäische Gerichtshof für Menschenrechte (EGMR) eine harsche Kritik an der Praxis der Sicherungsverwahrung in Deutschland aus.[1] Er verurteilte Deutschland wegen Verletzung von Art. 5 und 7 der Europäischen Menschenrechtskonvention (EMRK) und widersprach damit der Einschätzung des deutschen Bundesverfassungsgerichts (BVerfG) vom 5. Februar 2004[2], in welcher dieses die Sicherungsverwahrung für mit den Grund- und Menschenrechten vereinbar erklärte. Obwohl das Urteil des EGMR nicht dahingehend interpretiert werden kann, dass die Straßburger Richter das Prinzip der Sicherungsverwahrung an sich als mit der Europäischen Menschenrechtskonvention unvereinbar sehen[3], entfaltet das Urteil nichtsdestotrotz eine Relevanz für die anderen Mitgliedsstaaten des Europarates.

Momentan haben – neben Deutschland – acht europäische Staaten das Institut der Sicherungsverwahrung eingeführt: Österreich[4], Dänemark[5], Italien[6], Liechtenstein[7], San Marino[8], die Slowakei[9], die

---

* Doktorandin an der Universität Potsdam.

1 EMGR, Nr. 19359/04 „M. v. Germany" – Urteil v. 17.12.2009.

2 BVerfG, 2 BvR 2029/01 – Urteil v. 05.02.2004, BVerfGE 109, 133.

3 S. die Folgeurteile: EGMR, Nr. 30493/04 „Schmitz v. Germany" – Urteil v. 09.06.2011; EGMR, Nr. 31047/04 und Nr. 43386/08 „Mork v. Germany" – Urteil v. 09.06.2011.

4 Vgl. §§ 23 ff, 47 ff österreichisches Strafgesetzbuch und §§ 435 ff österreichische Strafprozessordnung.

5 §§ 70 ff Straffeloven.

6 Art. 199 ff des italienischen Codice Penale.

Schweiz[10] und Frankreich[11]. Frankreich war hierbei das letzte Land, welches die Sicherungsverwahrung eingeführt hat – die französischen Regelungen traten erst 2008 in Kraft[12]. Eine weitere Verurteilung von Seitens Straßburgs ist nicht ausgeschlossen, sofern nationale Regelungen Mängel aufweisen, die eine Verletzung der europäischen Menschenrechtskonvention darstellen.

Der folgende Artikel untersucht, welche möglichen Lehren aus dem Urteil des EGMR für die französischen Regelungen der Sicherungsverwahrung gezogen werden können und soll eine Prognose wagen, ob auch Frankreich demnächst mit einer Verurteilung von Seiten Straßburgs zu rechnen hat.

Hierfür wird zunächst die Rechtslage in Deutschland (I) sowie ihre Bewertung im Urteil des EGMR (II) dargestellt, und anschließend auf mögliche Folgen des Urteils für die französischen Regelungen eingegangen (III).

Ein besonderer Schwerpunkt der Studie liegt auf der Darstellung der Natur der Sicherungsverwahrung, welche vom BVerfG, vom EGMR und vom französischen Verfassungsrat (*Conseil Constitutionnel*) jeweils unterschiedlich qualifiziert wird.

---

7 §§ 23ff, 47 ff Strafgesetzbuch Liechtenstein und § 345 ff Strafprozessordnung Liechtenstein.

8 Art. 121 ff des Codice Penale San Marino.

9 §§ 81, 82 trestný zákon.

10 Art. 56 ff Schweizer Strafgesetzbuch.

11 Art. Art. 706-53-13 Code de la procédure pénale.

12 Loi relative à la rétention de sûreté et à la déclaration d'irresponsabilité pénale pour cause de trouble mental, L. n°2008-174 vom 25.02.2008, Journal Officiel 26. Februar 2008, p. 3266.

I. Die Sicherungsverwahrung in Deutschland – Rechtslage und Entwicklung einer Maßregel der Besserung und Sicherung

Die Sicherungsverwahrung wurde in Deutschland im Jahr 1933 mit dem „Gesetz gegen gefährliche Gewohnheitsverbrecher und über Maßregeln der Besserung und Sicherung“[13] eingeführt. Dieses Gesetz führte erstmals eine Trennung zwischen Strafen und „Maßregeln der Besserung und Sicherung“, als präventive Maßnahmen, im deutschen Strafrecht ein. Diese Unterscheidung ist bis zum heutigen Tag beibehalten worden. Die Sicherungsverwahrung ist gem. § 61 Nr. 3 Strafgesetzbuch[14] (StGB) eine Maßregel der Besserung und Sicherung und damit nach der gesetzlichen Definition keine Strafe.

Materielle Voraussetzung für die Sicherungsverwahrung ist, dass der Betroffene wegen der Begehung einer vorsätzlichen Straftat aus einem abschließenden Katalog zu einer Freiheitsstrafe von mindestens zwei Jahren verurteilt wurde, er bereits früher wegen Begehung einer solchen Tat mindestens zweimal zu einer Strafe von mindestens einem Jahr verurteilt wurde und er wegen einer oder mehrerer dieser Taten mindestens zwei Jahre Freiheitsstrafe verbüßt oder sich im Vollzug einer Maßnahme der Besserung und Sicherung befunden hat. Überdies muss eine Gesamtwürdigung des Täters und seiner Taten ergeben, dass er in Folge eines Hanges zu erheblichen Straftaten, namentlich zu solchen, durch welche die Opfer seelisch oder körperlich schwer geschädigt werden, zum Zeitpunkt der Verurteilung für die Allgemeinheit gefährlich ist.[15] Von diesem Grundfall gibt es

---

13 Gesetz gegen gefährliche Gewohnheitsverbrecher und über Maßregeln der Besserung und Sicherung vom 24.11.1933, (RGBl I S. 995).

14 Strafgesetzbuch in der Fassung der Bekanntmachung vom 13.11.1998 (BGBl. I S. 3322), das zuletzt durch Artikel 4 des Gesetzes vom 23.06.2011 (BGBl. I S. 1266) geändert worden ist.

15 Vgl. § 66 Abs. 1 Nr. 1 StGB.

verschiedene Abweichungen bezüglich der Anzahl der früheren Verurteilungen und Freiheitsentziehungen[16].

Es gibt drei mögliche Zeitpunkte, zu denen die Sicherungsverwahrung verhängt werden kann. Grundsätzlich muss sie vom erkennenden Gericht im Zeitpunkt des Ausspruchs der Freiheitsstrafe angeordnet werden[17]. Ausnahmsweise kann sich das Gericht im Urteil aber auch vorbehalten, zu einem späteren Zeitpunkt über eine Sicherheitsverwahrung zu entscheiden. Dies muss jedoch spätestens bis zur vollständigen Vollstreckung der Freiheitsstrafe geschehen.[18] Voraussetzung hierfür ist, dass alle Merkmale des § 66 StGB vorliegen, aber es zum Zeitpunkt der Verurteilung noch nicht mit Sicherheit feststellbar – jedoch wahrscheinlich – ist, ob der Täter eine Gefahr für die Allgemeinheit darstellt.

Des Weiteren ist in Ausnahmefällen eine nachträgliche Verhängung der Sicherungsverwahrung möglich. Voraussetzung hierfür ist, dass eine Unterbringung in einem psychiatrischen Krankenhaus gem. § 67 d Abs. 6 StGB für erledigt erklärt wird, welche auf Grund der Begehung mehrerer der in § 66 Abs. 3 S. 1 StGB aufgeführten Taten verhängt wurde, bzw. der Betroffene wegen der Begehung einer dieser Taten schon einmal zu einer Freiheitsstrafe von mindestens drei Jahren verurteilt oder in einem psychiatrischen Krankenhaus untergebracht wurde und eine Gesamtwürdigung ergibt, dass der Täter erneut erhebliche Straftaten begehen wird, durch welche er die Opfer schwer zu schädigen droht.[19]

Was die mögliche Dauer der Sicherungsverwahrung anbelangt, so unterlagen die Regelungen verschiedenen Gesetzesänderungen. Im Jahr 1933, als die Sicherungsverwahrung zum ersten Mal eingeführt wurde, konnte sie noch unbegrenzt verhängt werden. Im Jahr 1969

16 Vgl. § 66 Abs. 2, 3 und 4 StGB.
17 Vgl. § 66 Abs. 1 StGB.
18 Vgl. § 66 a StGB.
19 § 66 b StGB.

wurde dann ein Reformgesetz verabschiedet, welches ihre Dauer im Fall einer erstmaligen Anordnung auf maximal zehn Jahren begrenzte.[20] Diese Beschränkung wurde im Jahr 1998, wiederum durch ein Reformgesetz,[21] aufgehoben. Seit 1998 ist damit theoretisch die Verhängung einer zeitlich unbegrenzte Sicherungsverwahrung wieder möglich. Die Neuregelung besagt, dass das zuständige Gericht eine Sicherungsverwahrung nach zehn Jahren für erledigt erklärt, es sei denn, die Richter befinden, dass der Betroffene weiterhin eine Gefahr für die Allgemeinheit darstellt.[22] Im Anschluss muss das zuständige Gericht die Sicherungsverwahrung im Abstand von höchstens zwei Jahren überprüfen.[23]

Durch ein zweites Urteil des Bundesverfassungsgerichts zur Sicherungsverwahrung vom Mai diesen Jahres[24] wurden fast alle, die Sicherungsverwahrung betreffenden Regelungen außer Kraft gesetzt. Das Bundesverfassungsgericht trug damit dem Urteil des EGMR Rechnung. Aus diesem Grund fehlt es momentan an gültigen Regelungen zur Länge der Sicherungsverwahrung. Ein baldiges Tätigwerden des Gesetzgebers ist wünschenswert. Eine erste Gesetzesinitiative hierzu wurde auf einer Sonder-Justizministerkonferenz im September 2011 vorgelegt.[25]

Problematisch an der Gesetzesänderung von 1998 war, dass sie auf Grund bestimmter strafrechtlicher Vorschriften einen rückwirkenden Effekt entfaltete. § 2 Abs. 6 StGB legt fest, „dass über Maßregeln der Besserung und Sicherung nach dem Gesetz entschieden wird, das zur Zeit der Entscheidung gilt". Dies hat zur Folge, dass bei Maßregeln der Besserung und Sicherung – zu welchen

---

20 Zweites Gesetz zur *Reform* des Strafrechts vom 04.06.*1969, (*BGBl I S. 717).

21 Gesetz zur Bekämpfung von Sexualdelikten und anderen gefährlichen Straftaten vom 26.01.1998, (BGBl I S. 160).

22 § 67d Abs. 3 StGB.

23 § 67 e Abs. 2 StGB.

24 BVerfG, 2 BvR 2365/09 – Urteil v. 04.05.2011, BVerfGE 128, 326.

25 Heribert Prantl, „Auch Täter haben Rechte", SZ vom 22.09.2011, abrufbar unter <http://www.sueddeutsche.de/politik/neuregelung-der-sicherungsverwahrung-auch-taeter-haben-rechte-1.1147218> (12.10.2011).

die Sicherungsverwahrung zählt – nicht auf die Gesetzeslage zum Zeitpunkt der Erfüllung des Tatbestandes, sondern auf die Gesetzeslage zum Zeitpunkt der gerichtlichen Entscheidung abgestellt wird. Da es sich um präventive Maßnahmen handelt, stellt dies keinen Verstoß gegen das Rückwirkungsverbot aus Art. 103 Abs. 2 Grundgesetz (GG) dar. Auf Grund der Gesetzesänderung konnten auch Personen, deren Sicherungsverwahrung noch vor 1998 verhängt wurde, über die Zehn-Jahres-Grenze hinaus in Haft behalten werden. Dies führte zu folgendem Fall vor dem EGMR:

Kläger vor dem EGMR war M. 1957 geboren, befand er sich fast sein gesamtes Erwachsenenleben im Gefängnis, jeweils unterbrochen durch ein paar Wochen in Freiheit. Im Jahr 1986 wurde er vom Landgericht Marburg wegen versuchten Mordes in Tateinheit mit Raub zu einer Freiheitsstrafe von 5 Jahren verurteilt. Zusätzlich ordnete das Landgericht Marburg daneben seinen Verbleib in Sicherungsverwahrung an. M verbüßte seine Freiheitsstrafe bis August 1991 und trat dann die angeordnete Sicherungsverwahrung an. Am 8.9.2001 war die – zum Zeitpunkt seiner Verurteilung noch geltende – 10-Jahres-Grenze der Sicherungsverwahrung erreicht und er stellte vor dem Landgericht Marburg den Antrag auf seine Entlassung. In einem Beschluss stellte dieses jedoch eine weiterhin von M ausgehende Gefahr fest und ordnete einen weiteren Verbleib von M in Sicherungsverwahrung über den 8. September an.[26] Das Oberlandesgericht Frankfurt bestätigte diesen Beschluss.[27] Am 26. November 2001 erhob M gegen die beiden Entscheidungen der ersten und zweiten Instanz Verfassungsbeschwerde vor dem BVerfG, welche dieses am 5. Februar 2004 als unbegründet abgewiesen hat.[28] In seiner Verfassungsbeschwerde rügte M, dass die Vorschriften zur Sicherungsverwahrung gegen das absolute Rückwirkungsverbot bei Strafen aus Art. 103 Abs. 2 GG, das Rechtsstaatsprinzip aus Art. 20

26 Landgericht Marburg, 7 StVK 50/01 und 7 StVK 51/01, Beschl. v. 10.04.2001.

27 Oberlandesgericht Frankfurt a.M., 3 Ws 543 und 544/01, Beschl. v. 26.10.2001.

28 BVerfG, Urteil v. 05.02.2004 (oben Fn. 2).

Abs. 3 GG, sein Grundrecht auf Freiheit nach Art. 2 Abs. 2 S. 2 GG und die Garantie der Menschenwürde aus Art. 1 Abs 1 GG verstießen.

Das BVerfG folgte Ms Argumentation nicht. Aus Platzgründen soll im Folgenden lediglich auf die Verletzung des Rückwirkungsverbots aus Art. 103 Abs. 2 GG eingegangen werden.

Das BVerfG hat einen Verstoß gegen das Rückwirkungsverbot mit dem Argument verneint, dass es sich bei Maßregeln der Besserung und Sicherung nicht um Strafen iSd Art. 103 Abs. 2 GG handele und sie demzufolge auch nicht vom Schutzbereich des Art. 103 Abs. 2 GG erfasst seien. Eine Strafe diene primär dem Schuldausgleich, wohingegen eine Maßnahme der Besserung und Sicherung präventiven Charakter habe.[29] Maßnahmen der Besserung und Sicherung sollen außerdem, im Gegensatz zur Strafe, nicht begangenes Unrecht sühnen, sondern vielmehr die Allgemeinheit vor dem Täter schützen[30]. Laut Argumentation des BVerfG, genüge auch die Tatsache, dass die Sicherungsverwahrung an ein rechtswidriges Verhalten anknüpfe nicht, um sie als Strafe zu qualifizieren[31].

Der EGMR folgte dieser Wertung des BVerfG in seiner Einschätzung der Sicherungsverwahrung nicht.

II. Das Urteil des EGMR – Unvereinbarkeit einer Maßnahme mit Strafcharakter

In seinem Urteil vom 17. Dezember 2009 stellte der EGMR fest, dass die deutschen Vorschriften zur Sicherungsverwahrung das Rückwirkungsverbots aus Art. 7 Abs. 1 S. 1 EMRK, sowie eine Verletzung des Rechts auf Freiheit aus Art. 5 Abs. 1 EMRK darstellen.

29 Ebenda, Rn. 144 ff.

30 Ebenda, Rn. 148.

31 Ebenda, Rn. 129.

Das Rückwirkungsverbot aus Art. 7 Abs. 1 S. 1 EMRK legt fest, dass niemand wegen einer Handlung oder Unterlassung verurteilt werden darf, die zur Zeit ihrer Begehung weder nach innerstaatlichem noch nach internationalem Recht strafbar war. Dies verbietet insbesondere die rückwirkende Anwendung von Strafgesetzen zu Lasten eines Täters.[32] Der Begriff der „Strafe" sei hierbei als autonomer Strafbegriff iSd europäischen Menschenrechtskonvention zu verstehen.[33] Er wird vom EGMR dabei sehr weitgehend ausgelegt. Um den Charakter einer Maßnahme als Strafe zu verstehen, greift der EGMR auf ein Bündel an Kriterien zurück:

Erstes Kriterium ist, ob die Maßnahme auf Grund der Begehung einer Straftat verhängt wurde.[34] Dies bejaht der Gerichtshof im Fall der deutschen Sicherungsverwahrung, da diese im Zusammenhang mit einer strafrechtlichen Verurteilung verhängt wird. Zweites Kriterium ist die Charakterisierung der Maßnahme im nationalen Recht. Die Tatsache, dass die Sicherungsverwahrung im deutschen Recht gerade keine Strafe ist, vermag das Ergebnis des EGMR jedoch nicht zu beeinflussen – die Richter stellen lediglich fest, dass die Charakterisierung nach nationalem Recht zwar ein möglicher Faktor, jedoch kein bestimmender sei.[35] Drittes Kriterium ist die Art und Weise des Vollzugs der Maßnahme. Der EGMR kritisiert, dass kein oder nur ein geringer Unterschied zwischen dem Vollzug einer Sicherungsverwahrung und dem einer Gefängnisstrafe zu erkennen sei. Beide Maßnahmen resultierten in einem Freiheitsentzug der betroffenen Person, wobei beide Maßnahmen häufig nacheinander im selben Gefängnis vollzogen würden.[36] Viertes Kriterium ist der Zweck der Maßnahme. Nach Ansicht des EGMR, der damit direkt dem BVerfG widerspricht, haben die Sicherungsverwahrung und eine Gefängnisstrafe denselben Zweck: beide dienten dazu, die

32 EGMR, Nr. 14307/88 „Kokkinakis v. Greece" – Urteil v. 25.5.1993, Series A no. 260-A, Rn. 52.

33 EGMR, „M. v. Germany" (oben Fn. 1), Rn. 120.

34 Ebenda, Rn. 124.

35 Ebenda, Rn. 126.

36 Ebenda, Rn. 127.

Öffentlichkeit vor dem Täter zu schützen und den Täter auf sein späteres Leben in Freiheit vorzubereiten.[37]

Insgesamt kommt der EGMR damit zu dem Ergebnis, dass die deutsche Sicherungsverwahrung als Strafe iSv Art. 7 EMRK zu qualifizieren sei. Da es zweifellos zu einer rückwirkenden Anwendung der Gesetze über die Sicherungsverwahrung gekommen ist, liegt damit eine Verletzung des Rückwirkungsverbots aus Art. 7 Abs. 1 EMRK vor.

Daneben stellt das Gericht ebenfalls eine Verletzung des Rechts auf Freiheit und Sicherheit gem. Art. 5 Abs. 1 S. 1 EMRK fest. Art. 5 Abs. 1 S. 1 EMRK legt fest, dass einer Person die Freiheit nur dann entzogen werden darf, wenn einer der in Art. 7 Abs. 1 S. 2 EMRK enumerativ aufgezählten Gründe vorliegt, andere Gründe sind nicht ausreichend.[38] Vorliegend verneinte das Gericht den Rechtfertigungsgrund einer rechtmäßigen Verurteilung durch ein zuständiges Gericht, Art. 5 Abs. 1 S. 2 lit. a) EMRK, da keine ausreichende Kausalbeziehung zwischen der (rechtmäßigen) Verurteilung von M im Jahr 1986 und der Verlängerung der Sicherungsverwahrungsanordnung im Jahr 2001 bestünde. Vielmehr stelle die Gesetzesänderung im Jahr 1998 den eigentlichen kausalen Grund für die Verlängerung der Sicherungsverwahrung dar.[39] Der Rechtfertigungsgrund des Art. 5 Abs. 1 S. 1 lit. c, 2. HS – begründeter Anlass zu der Annahme, dass vom Täter zukünftig Straftaten begangen werden könnten – wurde vom Gerichtshof ebenfalls abgelehnt, da die Begehung dieser zukünftigen Taten noch nicht hinreichend bestimmt sei.[40]

Insgesamt kann man aus dem Urteil des EGMR nicht ableiten, dass die Praxis der Sicherungsverwahrung für den Gerichtshof generell einen Verstoß gegen die EMRK darstellt. Kritikpunkt und Grund für die Verurteilung Deutschlands war vielmehr allein die Tatsache der rückwirkenden Anwendung zu Lasten der Straftäter.

37 Ebenda, Rn. 130.

38 EGMR, Nr. 7367/76 „Guzzardi v. Italy“ – Urteil v. 6. 11. 1980, Serie A Nr. 39, Rn. 96.

39 EGMR, „M. v. Germany“ (oben Fn. 1), Rn. 100.

40 Ebenda, Rn. 102.

Andere Länder, in denen es keine rückwirkende Anwendung von Sicherungsverwahrungsgesetzen gibt, scheinen demnach zunächst keine Verurteilung aus Straßburg zu fürchten haben.

Der Gerichtshof bestätigt diese Annahme in zwei weiteren Urteilen vom 9. Juli 2011, in denen er feststellt, dass die primäre Sicherungsverwahrung keinen Verstoß gegen die EMRK darstelle.[41] Fraglich ist aber, ob der EGMR, sofern er über die Sicherungsverwahrungsvorschriften eines anderen Landes zu urteilen hat, die Qualifizierung der Sicherungsverwahrung als Strafe aufrechterhalten würde. In seinem Urteil hat der Gerichtshof ausdrücklich festgestellt, dass ein- und dieselbe Maßnahme in einem Staat eine Strafe und in einem anderen Staat lediglich eine präventive Maßnahme darstellen könne[42]. Damit hat er sich die Möglichkeit eines Richtungswechsel in zukünftigen Urteilen offen gehalten. Er hat damit den anderen Mitgliedsstaaten der EMRK allerdings auch keine verbindliche Basis geliefert auf Grund derer diese ihre Vorschriften zur Sicherungsverwahrung überprüfen können.

III. Die *rétention de sûreté* in Frankreich – *„ni une peine, ni une sanction ayant le caractère d'une punition"*

Im Folgenden soll untersucht werden, welche Schlussfolgerungen aus dem Urteil des EGMR in Bezug auf die Vereinbarkeit der *rétention de sûreté* mit der EMRK gezogen werden können.

Die Regelungen zur *rétention de sûreté* finden sich in den Artikeln 706-53-13 ff des *Code de procédure pénale* (CPP). Materielle Voraussetzung einer *rétention de sûreté* ist die Verurteilung zu einer Gefängnisstrafe von mindestens 15 Jahren für die Begehung

41 EGMR, „Schmitz v. Germany" (oben Fn. 3), Rn. 3 und EGMR „Mork v. Germany" (oben Fn. 3), Rn. 3.

42 EGMR, „M. v. Germany" (oben Fn. 1), Rn. 126.

eines in einer limitativen Liste aufgezählten Verbrechens. Der betroffene Straftäter muss außerdem auf Grund einer schweren Persönlichkeitsstörung eine besondere Gefahr für die Allgemeinheit darstellen und eine besonders hohe Rückfallgefahr aufweisen.[43] Die materiellen Voraussetzungen ähneln damit denen der deutschen Sicherungsverwahrung, wobei die Anforderungen an die Länge der vorherigen Verurteilung in Frankreich signifikant höher ist – in Deutschland ist lediglich eine Verurteilung zu einer zweijährigen Gefängnisstrafe erforderlich. Zuständig für die Verhängung der *rétention de sûreté* ist ein spezielles Gericht, welches aus einem Kammervorsitzenden und zwei Beratern des örtlich zuständigen Berufungsgerichts (*Cour d'appel)* gebildet wird. Es wird vom Oberstaatsanwalt (*procureur général*) angerufen, welcher wiederum auf Antrag einer pluridisziplinär besetzten Kommission (*commission pluridisciplinaire des mesures de sûreté*) tätig wird.[44] Bevor es zu diesem Antrag kommt, stellt die Kommission den Straftäter unter eine sechswöchige besondere medizinische Beobachtung zweier Experten, um seine Gefährlichkeit zu bewerten.[45]

Wie in Deutschland muss die Anordnung der *rétention de sûreté* schon im Strafurteil vorbehalten sein.[46] Eine nachträgliche Sicherungsverwahrung ist im Gesetz nicht vorgesehen. Ein Jahr vor der anstehenden Entlassung des Straftäters wird dann von der pluridisziplinär besetzten Kommission untersucht, ob der konkrete Fall die Verhängung einer *rétention de sûreté* erforderlich macht[47].

Liegen die Voraussetzungen einer *rétention de sûreté* nach Einschätzung der Kommission nicht vor, erscheint ihr der Strafgefangene aber nichtsdestotrotz gefährlich, verweist sie den Fall an den Haftrichter zurück, welcher dann über die Verhängung der

---

43 Art. 706-53-13 al. 1 Code de la procédure pénale (CPP).

44 Art. 706-53-15 al. 1 CPP.

45 Art. 706-53-14 al. 2 CPP.

46 Art. 706-53-13 al. 3 CPP.

47 Art. 706-53-14 al. 1 CPP.

nächstschwächeren Maßnahme, der Sicherungsüberwachung (*surveillance de sécurité)* entscheiden kann.[48]

Signifikanter Unterschied zu den deutschen Vorschriften ist die Dauer der *rétention de sûreté.* Ein entsprechender Beschluss des zuständigen Gerichts gilt jeweils nur für ein Jahr, nach dessen Ablauf die Maßnahme automatisch ausläuft und der Betroffene entlassen werden muss. Stellt der Straftäter nach Ansicht der pluridisziplinär besetzten Kommission weiterhin eine Gefahr für die Allgemeinheit dar, so muss sie erneut Verfahrensschritte zur Verhängung der *rétention de sûreté* ergreifen. Auch die Verlängerung gilt jedoch wiederum nur für ein Jahr.[49] Aus diesem Grund kann sich zwar ebenfalls – wie in Deutschland – die Möglichkeit ergeben, dass ein Betroffener lebenslang in Sicherungsverwahrung bleibt, allerdings muss seine Gefährlichkeit jedes Jahr erneut positiv festgestellt werden. Diese Vorschriften sind für den Betroffenen deutlich günstiger als die deutschen, welche eine anfängliche Dauer von 10 Jahren gestatten und im Weiteren nur eine Überprüfung der Sicherungsverwahrung im Zweijahresabstand vorsehen. Dies könnte bei einem zukünftigen Urteil einen Grund für den EGMR sein, die *rétention de sûreté* für weniger schwerwiegend als die deutsche Sicherungsverwahrung einzustufen.

Auch der Vollzug der *rétention de sûreté* unterscheidet sich deutlich von dem deutschen Vollzug. So wird die *rétention de sûreté* nicht in einem normalen Gefängnis, sondern in speziell geschaffenen Anstalten, den *centres socio-médico-judicaires*[50] vollzogen. Damit entspricht die französische Regelung in weitem Sinne dem vom EGMR ausgesprochenen Abstandsgebot und erfüllt damit nicht das dritte Kriterium, welches der EGMR für die Qualifizierung der Sicherungsverwahrung als Strafe angewandt hat – die Art und Weise des Vollzugs der Maßnahme. Interessant ist ebenfalls eine nähere Untersuchung des zweiten Kriteriums – der Qualifizierung der

48 Art. 706-53-14 al. 4 CPP.

49 Art. 706-53-16 CPP.

50 Art. 706-53-13 al. 4 CPP.

Maßnahme im nationalen Recht – auch wenn dies für den EGMR nicht das bestimmende Kriterium ist. Während das deutsche BVerfG die Sicherungsverwahrung als präventive Maßnahme qualifiziert hat und auch in seinem Urteil vom Mai 2011 seiner früheren Wertung nicht ausdrücklich widerspricht[51] und der EGMR die Sicherungsverwahrung als Strafe qualifiziert hat, ist die französische Einordnung der *rétention de sûreté* ambivalent.

Aus dem Gesetzestext selber kann keine Qualifizierung der Maßnahme abgeleitet werden. Die Vorschriften zur *rétention de sûreté* enthalten keine ausdrückliche Qualifizierung als Strafe oder Präventivmaßnahme und befinden sich in einem Gesetzesabschnitt, welcher neutral mit dem Titel „verschiedene Maßnahmen" (*de quelques procédures particulières*) überschrieben ist. Der Gesetzestext lässt die genaue Natur der Maßnahme damit (bewusst?) offen. Eine Einordnung der *rétention de sûreté* kann aber der Rechtsprechung des französischen Verfassungsrates (*Conseil Constitutionnel*) entnommen werden. Im Zuge einer Vorabanfrage hat dieser zur Vereinbarkeit des Gesetzesentwurfs zur rétention de sûreté mit der französischen Verfassung Stellung genommen.[52] In ihrem Gutachten stellten die Richter ausdrücklich fest, dass die *rétention de sûreté* im französischen Recht weder eine Strafe noch eine strafähnliche Sanktion darstelle (*„ni une peine, ni une sanction ayant le caractère d'une puniton"*[53]). Sie erklärten jedoch gleichzeitig auf Grund der besonderen Schwere der *rétention de sûreté* das – eigentlich nur für Strafen geltende – Rückwirkungsverbot für anwendbar und zensierten den Gesetzesentwurf dahingehend[54]. Die *rétention de sûreté* als Präventivmaßnahme mit Rückwirkungsverbot? Dieser Ansatz des *Conseil Constitutionnel* ist entweder ein dritter Weg zwischen der Qualifizierung als Präventivmaßnahme, so wie er vom BVerfG beschritten wurde und der Qualifizierung als Strafe, so wie es der

51 BVerfG, Urteil vom 04.05.2011 (oben Fn. 24).

52 *Conseil constitutionnel*, Nr. 2008-562-DC, Beschluss vom 21.02.2008, Journal officiel 26.02.2008, S. 3272.

53 Ebenda, Rn. 9.

54 Ebenda, Rn. 5.

EGMR vertritt – oder juristisch unsauber. Durch seinen Kunstgriff scheint der *Conseil Constitutionnel* jedoch geschickt eine Verurteilung des EGMR zu vermeiden, da eine rückwirkende Anwendung der *rétention de sûreté* in Frankreich – Grund für die deutsche Verurteilung – nun in Frankreich ausgeschlossen scheint. Insgesamt spricht also vieles dafür, dass Frankreich in Zukunft keine Verurteilung durch den EGMR zu fürchten hat[55].

Nichtsdestotrotz haben die französischen Verfassungsrichter in ihrem Urteil einen Fall der rückwirkenden Anwendung der *rétention de sûreté* übersehen. Auf die schwächere Maßnahme der *surveillance de sécurité*[56] erstreckt sich das Rückwirkungsverbot nicht. Wenn nun ein französisches Gericht eine Maßnahme der *surveillance de sûreté* anordnet und die unter *surveillance de sécurité* stehende Person ihren Auflagen nicht nachkommt ist die Sanktion – die Einweisung in ein *centre socio-médico-judiciaire de sûreté*. Die *rétention de sûreté* kann also auch als Folge der Verletzung von Auflagen im Rahmen der *surveillance de sûreté* verhängt werden.

Es ist damit also durchaus möglich, dass es bereits vor 2023 zu einer *rétention de sûreté* kommt. Eine erste *surveillance de sûreté* wurde im Jahr 2009 bereits verhängt[57].

Es bleibt spannend, wie der EGMR bei einer entsprechenden Beschwerde entscheiden wird.

---

55 So auch: Ludivine Grégoire, Fernand Boulan, „La détention de sûreté est une peine! Qualifications et conséquences“, Droit pénal n°5, Mai 2010, étude 9.

56 Art. 706-53-19 CPP.

57 *Juridiction régionale de rétention de sûreté Paris*, Nr. 09-02963 vom 06.04. 2009.

Human rights and private actors

Droits de l'Homme et acteurs privés
Menschenrechte und private Akteure

Human rights and public policy exception in private international law

Raphaël CALLSEN*

In a private legal dispute, a national court may be required to apply foreign law by virtue of its private international law. But what recourse is there if that application amounts to a violation of the forum state's binding human rights? The traditional response, adhered to by German law, is to use the public policy exception. In France, however, there has recently been a discussion about the immediate application of international human rights without utilizing the traditional mechanisms of private international law. As Georgia is a party to the European Convention on Human Rights (ECHR) and its statute "Concerning International Private Law" has in part been modelled after German private international law, the evolutions in France and Germany could give an impetus to legal discussion. In such a tri-national perspective we first need a common understanding of private international law (*Internationales Privatrecht* in German; *droit international privé* in French) (I). This will then allow us to analyze the function and contents of the so-called public policy exception (II). Finally, it will be possible to show that the inclusion of human rights within the public policy exception and an adaptation of the latter are preferable to an immediate application of human rights (III).

---

* Master en Droit, PhD candidate at the universities of Göttingen (Germany) and Paris Ouest Nanterre La Défense (France), research assistant at the Institute for Labor Law of the university of Göttingen. This text is a revised version of a presentation given on 9 September 2011 in Tbilisi, Georgia.

I. Private international law

A. Choice of law

In Germany, France and Georgia, private international law is aimed to encompass, at a minimum, the rules governing choice of law. These rules determine for example the law applicable to an international contract or to a marriage between persons of different nationality.

In the EU, an important part of choice of law rules is now contained in three regulations concerning contractual obligations, non-contractual obligations and divorce – the so-called Rome I[1], Rome II[2] and Rome III[3] Regulations. The Rome I Regulation replaces the 1980 Rome Convention,[4] which entered into force, inter alia, for France and Germany on 1 April 1991. Previously, the major part of choice of law rules was established by each state. In Germany and France, this area of law had been left for a long time to the judges. The first comprehensive codification in Germany was the reform of the Introductory Act to the German Civil Code (EGBGB) in 1986, which transposed the Rome Convention into national law even before its entry into force.[5] In France, except the areas covered by the Rome Convention or the Rome Regulations, the situation resembles the one in Germany before 1986, i.e. French private international law is basically case law. While there exist some choice of law rules in the

---

1 Regulation (EC) No. 593/2008 of the European Parliament and of the Council of 17 June 2008 on the law applicable to contractual obligations (Rome I), OJ L 177, 4.7.2008, pp. 6–16.

2 Regulation (EC) No. 864/2007 of the European Parliament and of the Council of 11 July 2007 on the law applicable to non-contractual obligations (Rome II), OJ L 199, 31.7.2007, pp. 40–49.

3 Council Regulation (EU) No. 1259/2010 of 20 December 2010 implementing enhanced cooperation in the area of the law applicable to divorce and legal separation, OJ L 343, 29.12.2010, pp. 10–16.

4 Convention on the law applicable to contractual obligations opened for signature in Rome on 19 June 1980, 80/934/EEC, OJ L 266, 9.10.1980, pp. 1–19.

5 Infra note 19.

Code civil, there is no comprehensive codification.[6] Georgia, by contrast, has in place a systematic statute "Concerning the International Private Law" of 29 April 1998,[7] entered into force on 1 October 1998, which includes choice of law rules for all areas. To this regulation of material aspects of private international relations may be added procedural rules.

B. International jurisdiction, recognition of foreign judgments

In Germany, the expression *Internationales Privatrecht* is limited to the choice of law rules.[8] The procedural aspects including international jurisdiction and recognition and enforcement of foreign judgments are generally addressed as international civil procedure *(Internationales Zivilprozessrecht)*. By contrast, in the French academic tradition the expression *droit international privé* not only includes these procedural aspects but also, in an even broader understanding, the law of nationality and the laws governing the status of foreigners. In other words, it pertains to all laws that in some way regulate the effects state frontiers have on private relations.[9] Georgian lawmakers opted for the middle ground. The statute concerning the international private law of 1998 governs international jurisdiction, choice of law and, finally, the recognition and enforcement of foreign judgments.

However, since an important part of international civil procedure between EU member states is regulated by specific instruments which

---

6 Marie-Laure Niboyet & Géraud de Geouffre de la Pradelle, *Droit international privé* (Paris: L.G.D.J. 2007) at para. VIII.

7 For an English list of Georgian statutes see <http://www.parliament.ge/index.php?lang_id=ENG&sec_id=69>; for a German translation see <http://www.gtz.de/de/dokumente/gtz2010-de-geo-gesetz-int-privatrecht.pdf> (last visited on 29.5.2012; this applies to all internet sources).

8 See Article 3 EGBGB.

9 Niboyet & de Geouffre de la Pradelle, supra note 6 at para. III.

restrict the intervention of the public policy exception,[10] this paper will focus on choice of law issues which are governed by similar principles in Georgia, Germany and France. All four systems of private international law, including the European one, recognize the mechanism known as the public policy exception (*exception d'ordre public* in French; *Vorbehalt der öffentlichen Ordnung* in German).

II. Public policy exception

A. Function

The public policy exception is characteristically defensive and negative in its function.[11] It empowers the judge to avoid the application of a foreign law if the result is deemed contrary to fundamental principles of the forum state. This is provided for by Article 18 of the Rome Convention and Article 21 of the Rome I Regulation, Article 6 of the German Introductory Act to the Civil Code, Article 5 of the Georgian statute concerning international private law and French case law.[12] The judge consequently first applies the law determined by the choice of law rules. He then looks at the result. If, in the specific circumstances, he finds the result to be

10 See Article 34(1) of the Brussels I Regulation; cf. also Article 68(2g) of the Georgian law concerning the international private law of 1998.

11 See e.g. Hans Jürgen Sonnenberger, "Art. 6 EGBGB Öffentliche Ordnung" in Franz Jürgen Säcker & Roland Rixecker, eds., *Münchener Kommentar zum Bürgerlichen Gesetzbuch. Band 10: Internationales Privatrecht*, 5th ed., München: Beck 2010, 1508 at para. 3; Paul Lagarde, "Chapter 11: Public Policy" in Kurt Lipstein, ed., *International Encyclopedia of Comparative Law. Volume III: Private International Law* (Tübingen; Dordrecht: Mohr; Martinus Nijhoff 1994) at 2; but see, speaking also of a positive effect regarding the substitution of the evinced foreign law by domestic law: Niboyet & de Geouffre de la Pradelle, supra note 6 at para. 230.

12 See Niboyet & de Geouffre de la Pradelle, supra note 6 at para. 305.

unacceptable according to national values, the *ordre public* clause enables him to discard the foreign rules.[13]

In modern conflicts law, this concept of public policy has to be distinguished from overriding mandatory norms, which apply regardless of the law determined by the choice of law rules and thus fulfil a positive function. Although this functional distinction has recently been challenged by some authors,[14] for the purposes of this paper it shall be sufficient to observe that the distinction results from legislative choices which have been translated into different normative provisions for public policy and overriding mandatory provisions (*lois de police* in French; *Eingriffsnormen* in German).[15]

B. Contents

1. EU: Rome I Regulation

It must be stressed that none of the norms cited above contains a comprehensive definition of public policy. For example, Article 21 of the Rome I Regulation reads:

> Article 21
> Public policy of the forum
> The application of a provision of the law of any country specified by this Regulation may be refused only if such application is manifestly incompatible with the public policy (ordre public) of the forum.

---

13 Lagarde, supra note 11.

14 See especially, with differing argumentation: Andrea Bonomi, *Le norme imperative nel diritto internazionale privato* (Zürich: Schulthess Polygraph. Verl. 1998); Benjamin Remy, *Exception d'ordre public et mécanisme des lois de police en droit international privé* (Paris: Dalloz 2006); Mathias Forteau, "L'ordre public 'transnational' ou 'réellement international'. L'ordre public international face à l'enchevêtrement croissant du droit international privé et du droit international public" (2011) 138 Journal du Droit International 3–49.

15 At EU-level: Article 9 and 21 Rome I Regulation, replacing Article 7 and 18 Rome Convention; in Germany Article 6 and former Article 34 EGBGB; in Georgia: Article 5 and 6 of the statute concerning international private law.

The wording reveals a restrictive tendency ("only if", "manifestly"), which is confirmed by recital no. 37. However, the determination of what principles are constitutive of public policy is expressly left to the forum state.

2. France

French private international law lacks a statutory definition of public policy. According to French legal literature the following contents of public policy may be derived from case law: fundamental principles of morals and objective justice, including human rights, on the one hand, and the political and social foundations of the French civilization or certain legislatives policies, on the other.[16] The first aspect can be traced back to a classic decision of the French *Cour de cassation* from 25 May 1948 in the Lautour case.[17] The court stated that French international public policy was constituted by "principles of universal justice which are considered, in French opinion, to be endued with absolute international value".[18]

3. Germany

In Germany, a statutory circumscription of the concept of public policy referring to "fundamental principles of German law" and especially fundamental rights has been part of Article 6 EGBGB, the Introductory Act to the Civil Code, since the reform of 1986:[19]

---

16 Dominique Bureau & Horatia Muir Watt, *Droit international privé. Tome I - Partie générale*, 2nd rev. ed. (Paris: Presses Universitaires de France 2010) at paras. 465-466; Bernard Audit & Louis d'Avout, *Droit international privé*, 6th éd. (Paris: Economica 2010) at paras. 312-313.

17 In: Bertrand Ancel & Yves Lequette, *Les grands arrêts de la jurisprudence française de droit international privé*, 5th ed (Paris: Dalloz 2006) at 164.

18 The translation is mine; the original expression is: "principes de justice universelle considérés dans l'opinion française comme doués de valeur internationale absolue".

19 Gesetz zur Neuregelung des Internationalen Privatrechts (IntPRNRG) of 25 July 1986, entered into force on 1 September 1986, Bundesgesetzblatt (BGBl.) I 1986, p. 1142.

> Article 6
> Public policy (ordre public)
> A provision of the law of another country shall not be applied where its application would lead to a result which is manifestly incompatible with the fundamental principles of German law. In particular, inapplicability ensues, if its application would be incompatible with civil rights. [20]

The explanations in the bill presented to the German Parliament stated that the expression "in particular" is intended to underline that the fundamental principles not only include constitutional rights, but also those deriving from international human rights treaties.[21]

4. Georgia

The Georgian public policy clause in Article 5 of the statute concerning the international private law is similar to the German one, but more succinct:

> Article 5
> Public policy (Ordre public)
> Provisions of the law of another country shall not be applied in Georgia if this is incompatible with the fundamental principles of Georgian law. [22]

The similarity to the German text is not accidental since the Georgian lawmakers had consulted with the former German Society for Technical Cooperation (GTZ, now GIZ) in drafting the law. Models for the Georgian statute included the German, Swiss and Italian statutes on private international law as well as several international agreements including the Rome Convention.[23] But three differences

---

20 English translation by Juliana Mörsdorf-Schulte, published online at <http://www.gesetze-im-internet.de/englisch_bgbeg/index.html>.

21 Bundestagsdrucksache 10/504 at 44.

22 My translation on the basis of the German version provided for by the GTZ, supra note 7.

23 Sulchan Gamkrelidze, "The Law of Georgia on Private International Law - Principles and Review" [1998, Second/Third Quarter] Georgian Law Review 20, online: <http://www.geplac.ge/publicat/law/archives/glr98q2q3e.pdf>.

can be observed in the Georgian law. First, no "manifest" incompatibility is required; second, the emphasis on the incompatibility of the result of the foreign law's application is lacking; third, there is no reference to fundamental rights – the wording only refers to fundamental principles of Georgian law. However, the latter difference should not be interpreted as somehow excluding human rights from the public policy exception, since fundamental rights have a prominent place in Article 7 as well as in the second part of the Georgian constitution.[24]

III. Human rights within the public policy exception

For the purpose of this paper, the term "human rights" is defined as the rights of individuals and groups that are recognized in national and international law.[25] The issue as to whether, how and which human rights play a role in private international law depends to a large extent on their source and thus their rank in the hierarchy of norms, as well as the remedies available for their enforcement. The German and French experiences reveal a different focus on constitutional and international human rights. These discussions on how to give effect to human rights in private international law seem to be somewhat outdated in the actual context of EU law.

---

24 The Constitution of Georgia, adopted on 24 August 1995; English translation available online: <http://www.parliament.ge/index.php?lang_id=ENG&sec_id= 68>; see for a more recent German translation: <http://www.gtz.de/de/dokumente/giz2011-de-geo-verfassung.pdf>.

25 Cf., focusing on international human rights: Thomas Buergenthal, "Human Rights", in Rüdiger Wolfrum, ed., *The Max Planck Encyclopedia of Public International Law* (Oxford University Press, 2008-), online edition: <www.mpepil.com>, at para. 1.

A. International human rights and domestic law

1. Status of international human rights in domestic legal orders

The French constitution[26] states that international treaties take precedence over ordinary domestic laws (Article 55). In Germany, only the general rules of international law take precedence over domestic laws (Article 25 of the German Basic Law [*Grundgesetz – GG*][27]). International, even human rights, treaties have the same formal value as the law on ratification, i.e. as a federal statute (cf. Article 59 GG). Nonetheless, according to the interpretation given by the German Constitutional Court *(Bundesverfassungsgericht – BVerfG)*, several constitutional provisions show a special commitment to international law *(Völkerrechtsfreundlichkeit)*. This principle requires courts to interpret domestic law, including the provisions of the Basic Law, in a manner that is open to international law in order to give effect to rights deriving from international treaties. In particular, this concerns regional human rights treaties like the European Convention on Human Rights (ECHR) including the case law of the European Court of Human Rights (ECtHR).[28]

In this respect, the solution of the Georgian constitution is similar to the French one, as Article 6(2) confers superiority to international treaties:[29]

---

26 Constitution of France of 4 October 1958, online: <http://legifrance.gouv.fr/Droit-francais/Constitution; English translation: <http://www.conseil-constitutionnel.fr/conseil-constitutionnel/root/bank_mm/anglais/constiution_anglais_oct2009. pdf>.

27 Basic Law for the Federal Republic of Germany of 23 May 1949; online: <http://www.gesetze-im-internet.de/gg/index.html>; English translation: <http://www.gesetze-im-internet.de/englisch_gg/englisch_gg.html>.

28 See e.g. Bundesverfassungsgericht, Order of 14 October 2004 – 2 BvR 1481/04, Entscheidungen des Bundesverfassungsgerichts (BVerfGE) 111, 307 at paras. 30-37, online (English translation): <www.bverfg.de/entscheidungen/rs20041014_2bvr148104en.html>; Judgment of 4 May 2011 – 2 BvR 2333/08, BVerfGE 128, 326 at paras. 86-94, see in English press release no. 31/2011 online at <http://www.bverfg.de/en/press/bvg11-031en.html>.

29 Translations by Georgian Parliament, supra note 7.

> [...] 2. The legislation of Georgia shall correspond to universally recognised principles and rules of international law. An international treaty or agreement of Georgia unless it contradicts the Constitution of Georgia, the Constitutional Agreement, shall take precedence over domestic normative acts.

Article 7 of the constitution adds:

> The state shall recognise and protect universally recognised human rights and freedoms as eternal and supreme human values. While exercising authority, the people and the state shall be bound by these rights and freedoms as directly acting law.

This precedence given to international human rights treaties over ordinary domestic statutes (but not, however, over constitutional provisions) has led to a discussion, especially in France, about whether they could be given effect regardless of the rules of private international law (see below B.1).

2. Institutional background and remedies

In German case law concerning private international law, there seem to be few references to the human rights guaranteed by international treaties, especially those guaranteed by the ECHR.[30] The fundamental rights guaranteed by the Basic Law are deemed to be adequate and more specific, above all due to the case law of the Constitutional Court.[31] In France, by contrast, it is precisely the fundamental rights enshrined in the constitution that do not receive special consideration in private international law.[32] It has been opined from a French perspective that the attention paid in Germany to these constitutional rights was primarily due to the existence of effective constitutional

30 Ioanna Thoma, *Die Europäisierung und die Vergemeinschaftung des nationalen ordre public* (Tübingen: Mohr Siebeck 2007) at 83.

31 Hans Jürgen Sonnenberger, "Einleitung IPR" in Franz Jürgen Säcker & Roland Rixecker (eds.): *Münchener Kommentar zum Bürgerlichen Gesetzbuch. Band 10: Internationales Privatrecht*, 5th ed., München: Beck 2010, 5 at para. 345; Thoma, supra note 30 at 83.

32 Mayer, infra note 42 at 660.

remedies after the promulgation of a law.[33] Besides an abstract control exercised by the Constitutional Court upon the request of the federal or state governments or a quarter of the members of the German Bundestag (Article 93[1][2] GG), other courts can ask for preliminary rulings on the constitutionality of norms which are relevant for their decision (Article 101[1] GG) and any individual may file complaints arguing that his or her constitutional rights have been infringed on by a public authority (Article 93[1][4a] GG).

Such a mechanism was in fact unknown in French law until the entry into force of the so-called priority preliminary ruling on the issue of constitutionality *(question prioritaire de constitutionnalité – QPC)* on 1 March 2010. Only afterwards could an individual argue at any stage of the procedure that a statutory provision infringes on constitutional rights.[34] Of course, French statutes had to respect the constitution prior to this reform. But the ability to seize the French Constitutional Council *(Conseil constitutionnel)* was restricted to the Republic's president, the prime minister, the presidents of the parliamentary assemblies or groups of 60 members of parliament, and this could only be done before the promulgation of the statute (Article 61 of the French constitution). If this was not done and even if the statute raised serious doubts, it was virtually impossible to challenge the constitutionality once the statute had entered into force.[35] The conformity of a statute to international treaties, by contrast, can be controlled by civil and administrative courts, which may decide not to apply a domestic statute if it infringes on rights derived from international treaties.[36] These differences in the

33 Ibid. at 664.

34 Article 61-1 and 62 Constitution of France, supra note 26, introduced by constitutional reform of 23 July 2008, and implemented by Constitutional Law 2009-1523 of 10 December 2009; all relevant texts including procedural rules and decisions of the French Constitutional Council are available, in part with English translation, online: <http://www.conseil-constitutionnel.fr/conseil-constitutionnel/english/homepage.14.html>.

35 Pierre Pactet & Ferdinand Mélin-Soucramanien, *Droit constitutionnel*, 29th rev. ed. (Paris: Sirey 2010) at 507.

36 Ibid. at 569-573.

institutional settings explain well the special impact of the ECHR on French law[37] and the different focus in the German and French debates.

B. Inclusion in the public policy exception vs. immediate application

The influence of human rights on private international relations is discussed from various angles. In fact, two types of argumentation can be distinguished. The first focuses on the question of whether human rights oblige a state to recognize a situation legally constituted in a foreign country according to foreign laws, even if the latter could be, at first glance, deemed contrary to national public policy. Some speak of a "method of recognition".[38] This implies a positive, offensive attitude with regard to human rights in the context of private international law. The second attitude of human rights discussed here is a negative, defensive one. The question concerns how human rights may intervene in order to discard a foreign solution determined by the choice of law rules. In reference to this latter defensive attitude, two approaches may again be distinguished. The first argues for an immediate application of human rights, while the second advocates an inclusion of human rights into the public policy exception (as already illustrated by Article 6 EGBGB).

1. France: immediate application of ECHR rights?

The most cited example in France for an immediate application of human rights, without regard to the normal choice of law rationale, is

37 See ibid. at 579-581.

38 See on this aspect the article by Romuald Di Noto in this volume; cf. also Sonnenberger, supra note 31 at para. 331; this discussion is similar to that one in EU-law concerning "mutual recognition" or "principle of origin", see, generally, Pierre Mayer "Les méthodes de la reconnaissance en droit international privé" in: Pierre Mayer & Marie-Noëlle Jobard-Bachellier, eds., *Le droit international privé: esprit et méthodes. Mélanges en l'honneur de Paul Lagarde* (Paris: Dalloz 2005) at 547.

a decision made by the Paris Appeals Court on 14 June 1994.[39] In that case, an Argentine transsexual demanded his sex to be changed from male to female. The Argentine law governing his personal status did not permit the change. The Paris Appeals Court, however, inferred the right to such a change directly from Article 8 ECHR without regard to the law governing the personal status. Two arguments were submitted in support of this solution. The first refers to the formal superiority of human rights to ordinary laws.[40] Nevertheless, as we have seen above (III.A.), this can only be argued in France and Georgia because in these countries the constituent power chose to give superiority to international treaties over domestic laws. The second argument underlines the material superiority of human rights: they are absolute values which cannot be relativized.[41] Critics, however, underline that human rights are too general to be applied directly[42] and that such an approach would put into question the whole system of private international law, reducing the predictability of solutions.[43] Furthermore, an immediate application would exceed the aim of preventing violations of national values, because not every fundamental right would necessarily require application to every international situation.[44] An indirect application within the public policy exception as expressly stated by Article 6 of the German EGBGB is therefore preferable.

39 Cour d'appel de Paris, Judgment of 14 June 1994, (1995) 84 Revue critique de droit international privé 308, with annotation by Yves Lequette.

40 Cf. Petra Hammje, "Droits fondamentaux et ordre public" (1997) 86 Revue critique de droit international privé 1 at 8.

41 Cf. ibid.

42 Pierre Mayer, "La Convention Européenne des droits de l'homme et l'application des normes étrangères" (1991) 80 Revue critique de droit international privé 651 at 663; Hammje, supra note 40 at 9.

43 Yves Lequette, "Le droit international privé et les droits fondamentaux" in Rémy Cabrillac, Marie-Anne Frison-Roche & Thierry Revet, eds., *Libertés et droits fondamentaux*, 14th ed. (Paris: Dalloz 2008) 99 at 121; Thoma, supra note 30 at 71.

44 Hammje, supra note 40 at 9.

This also seems to be the position of the French Court of Cassation *(Cour de cassation)*. The First Civil Chamber, which usually decides private international law cases, gives effect to human rights within the public policy exception.[45] However, in a case of domestic slavery, the Social Chamber recently stated – without referring to concrete international norms, but generically to conditions that infringed on the liberty of the worker[46] – that the *ordre public international* barred the employer from relying on rules on international jurisdiction and choice of law in order to elude the application of French (labor) law.[47] The wording refers to the public policy exception in its traditional understanding, but the way the Court argues seems incompatible with the functioning of the public policy clause, giving the impression of an immediate application of that concept.[48] Nonetheless, this shortcut in the reasoning might be explained by the fact that the violation of human rights in that case was blatant.

2. Germany: constitutional rights included in the public policy clause

Several decades ago, the inclusion of human rights in the public policy exception had also been contested in Germany. In the 1960s, the German Federal Court of Justice *(Bundesgerichtshof – BGH)* and some legal literature took a very restrictive position, stating that, in general, the fundamental rights enshrined in the Basic Law should not have a direct effect on the application of foreign law. But the German Constitutional Court, in its famous "Spaniard decision" of 1971, held the opposite view, essentially on the grounds that according to Articles

---

45 E.g. Cour de cassation,1ère chambre civile, Judgment of 17 February 2004 – 01-11549, Bulletin 2004 I N° 47 p. 38 (explicitly); Judgment of 26 October 2011 – 09-71369 (implicitly; see Elisa Viganotti, Actualité Juridique Famille 2012, 50).

46 See for an overview of the instruments prohibiting forced labor: Etienne Pataut & Petra Hammje, "De l'ordre public universel et de l'esclavage domestique" (2006) 95 Revue critique de droit international privé 856 sub I.A.

47 Cour de cassation, chambre sociale, Judgment of 10.05.2006 – 03-46593, Bulletin V N° 168 p. 163.

48 Pataut & Hammje, supra note 46.

1(3) and 20(3) of the Basic Law constitutional rights bind the judiciary as directly applicable law, and applying a foreign law is an act of the judiciary.[49] It observed, without expressing a clear preference, that constitutional rights must be given effect either by an immediate application, independent from the choice of law reasoning, or through the public policy exception.[50] Some of the legal literature indeed advocated special choice of law rules for constitutional rights.[51] The main argument raised against this position was the lack of clear connecting factors. If those advocating special choice of law rules called instead for a link within the ambit of the constitution, this resulted in nothing more than the general requirement for the application of the public policy exception, i.e. some connection to the forum.[52] Finally, the German legislature opted for the second approach by expressly including fundamental rights into the public policy exception in its 1986 reform of private international law.

3. Incompatibility of immediate application with EU law

In the context of EU law, the discussions about an immediate application of human rights enshrined in national constitutions or international treaties are to some extent obsolete. The reference to a higher rank of human rights in the domestic hierarchy of norms only works in the following cases: (a) the human right is enshrined in the constitution and choice of law rules have a lower rank, i.e. are contained in domestic statute or law or in an international treaty; (b) the human right is enshrined in an international treaty and the choice of law rules have a lower rank, i.e. are contained in domestic statute or

49 Bundesverfassungsgericht, Judgment of 4 May 1971 – 1 BvR 636/68, BVerfGE 31, 58 at paras. 38-47 with references.

50 Ibid., para. 67.

51 See especially Wilhelm Wengler, Annotation of BGH, 29 June 1964 – IV ZR 93/63, (1965) 20 Juristenzeitung 100 at 101.

52 Hans Jürgen Sonnenberger "Einleitung IPR" in Kurt Rebmann & Roland Rixecker, eds., *Münchener Kommentar zum Bürgerlichen Gesetzbuch. Band 7: Einführungsgesetz zum Bürgerlichen Gesetzbuche*, 1st ed. (München: Beck 1983) 5 at paras. 177-178.

law. Nonetheless, in the latter case, if the choice of law rules also derive from an international treaty, they formally have the same rank.

The whole configuration changes if choice of law rules are established by EU law, especially the Rome I or II Regulations. European Union law has primacy over national law, even over constitutional provisions.[53] The formal superiority argument could then only be used with respect to the EU hierarchy of norms, referring thus to human rights having the same rank as primary EU law, e.g. the EU Charter of Fundamental Rights (Article 6[1] EU Treaty), or being at least superior to secondary EU law (as will be the case for the ECHR after the ratification of the accession agreement [Article 216(2) Treaty on the Functioning of the EU]). However, there is no doubt that human rights guaranteed by national constitutions still belong to the fundamental principles of domestic law, whose application is expressly reserved, for example, by Article 21 of the Rome I Regulation. This again shows that an immediate application – regardless of the rules of private international law based alone on formal superiority – would lead to random results.

Within the European choice of law system, an immediate application of mainly national human rights could only be reached if they were considered to be overriding mandatory norms in the sense of Article 9 of the Rome I Regulation. On the other hand, only well-defined statutory provisions have traditionally been qualified and applied as overriding mandatory norms.[54] Of course, certain statutory norms may be seen as a concrete expression of human rights, but this should be distinguished from an immediate application of a human right as such.

53 ECJ, Judgment of 17 December 1970, *Internationale Handelsgesellschaft*, 11-70, ECR 1970, 1125 at para. 3; ECJ, Judgment of 2 July 1996, *Commission v. Luxemburg*, C-473/93, ECR I-03207 at para. 38.

54 See for examples in labor law: Raphaël Callsen, *L'influence croissante du droit de l'Union européenne en droit du travail international – l'exemple des lois de police* (Nanterre: Université Paris Ouest 2011) at 34-40 and 48-49.

C. Adaptation of the public policy exception

The inclusion of human rights in the public policy exception nonetheless raises new questions about an adaptation of its functioning. In the German debate, it had been objected that inclusion would mean subordinating constitutional rights to ordinary legislative choices, especially to the general condition of connections to the forum state (*Inlandsbeziehung* in German; in France there is a similar, but less systematic concept referred to as *ordre public de proximité*[55]). This objection had been invalidated by the German Constitutional Court in 1971. It argued that, because of the formal superiority of constitutional rights, the determination of the necessity (or lack thereof) of connections to the forum, and which ones, should be made according to the interpretation of the relevant fundamental right.[56]

The same is advocated for the human rights enshrined in the ECHR. Arguing from a German perspective – where the formal superiority argument does not apply – the application of foreign law which is constitutive of a violation of the Convention would lead to a condemnation of the state by the ECtHR.[57] To prevent this, the requirement of a connection to the forum state needs to be adapted. Some want to align the necessity of a connection to the forum with the Convention's area of application. However, the conclusions drawn of this assertion are contradictory. One is restrictive. Their supporters argue that opposing ECHR rights to the law of a state that is not a party to the Convention would be imperialistic. They should thus only intervene if the applicable law belongs to a state party.[58] In this view, ECHR rights would be applied as part of the public policy exception, essentially as a kind of sanction in the case of a state party's non-fulfilment of its obligations under the Convention. Nevertheless, this

55 See Niboyet & de Geouffre de la Pradelle, supra note 6 at para. 314; Audit & d'Avout, supra note 16 at para. 315.

56 Supra note 49 at para. 46

57 Sonnenberger, supra note 31 at para. 345.

58 Mayer, supra note 42 at 662; Forteau, supra note 14 at 20, para. 40; Thoma, supra note 30 at 116-117.

opinion disregards the fact that the question is not about extending ECHR rights to third states. It concerns rather the violation of those rights by courts of a state party through an application of foreign law, whether or not that law belongs to a state party.[59] Moreover, the function of the public policy exception is precisely to enable states to assert their own fundamental values if there are no common values.

According to a second opinion, aligning the connection requirement with the Convention's area of application would mean to broaden it. Instead of a connection specifically to the forum state, a connection to any state party to the ECHR should be sufficient.[60] This seems to be more in line with the function of the public policy exception. Nonetheless, it is doubtful that this criterion is really helpful. In the end, human rights are not to be applied schematically. The question remains whether in a concrete case the application of a foreign law by a domestic court would result in a violation of the ECHR.[61] This would mean specifically that in such a case the international jurisdiction of domestic courts would be a sufficient link to the forum state.[62] An interpretation of the relevant fundamental right will then be indispensable for assessing precisely whether the application of foreign law will result in a violation. It is therefore preferable to deduce the necessity and type of connection directly

---

59 Christian von Bar, "Menschenrechte im Kollisionsrecht" in Walter Kälin, Eibe Riedel & Wolfram Karl, eds., *Aktuelle Probleme des Menschenrechtsschutzes. Referate und Thesen mit Diskussion ; [23. Tagung der Deutschen Gesellschaft für Völkerrecht in Wien, Mai 1993]* (Heidelberg: Müller 1994) 191 at 208, 211; Bureau & Muir Watt, supra note 16 at para. 471.

60 See e.g. Hammje, supra note 40 at17.

61 See, although concerning recognition of judgments, for an obligation to check the conformity to the ECHR and its admissibility according to EU law, respectively: ECtHR, Judgment of 20 July 2001, *Pellegrini v. Italy*, no. 30882/96, ECHR 2001-VIII; ECJ, Judgment of 28 March 2000, *Krombach v. Bamberski*, C-7/98, ECR I-1956.

62 Sonnenberger, supra note 31 at para. 345; a recent decision of the French *Cour de cassation* may be interpreted in this sense, see Viganotti, supra note 45.

from the fundamental right.[63] This view also avoids lacunas and thus renders unnecessary the creation of a new subsidiary "human rights exception" recently proposed by one French author.[64]

IV. Conclusions

1. The choice of law rules in Germany, Georgia and France provide for a public policy exception, i.e. the possibility for the judge to discard a foreign law if its results are contrary to fundamental principles of domestic law. The Georgian norm was modelled, inter alia, after the German one.

2. Human rights laid down in international agreements, especially the ECHR, form part of Georgian, German and French domestic law. They can thus impede the application of a foreign law if this law would amount to a violation of a human right.

3. International treaties may have a different rank in the hierarchy of norms, depending on constitutional choices. A formal superiority to ordinary domestic law exists in France and Georgia, but not in Germany. Additionally, the enforcement of human rights enshrined in international treaties and national constitutions depends on procedural specificities and may lead to higher practical relevance of either constitutional (Germany) or international human rights (France).

4. The inclusion of human rights in the public policy exception has the advantage of giving effect to human rights of different sources, whether or not they are formally superior to choice of law rules. The argument of formal superiority which is often used to justify an

---

63 See Markus Voltz, *Menschenrechte und ordre public im internationalen Privatrecht* (Frankfurt am Main: Lang 2002) at 307-308.

64 Louis d'Avout, "Droits fondamentaux et coordination des ordres juridiques en droit privé" in Edouard Dubout & Sébastian Touzé, eds., *Les droits fondamentaux: charnières entre ordres et systèmes juridiques* (Paris: Pedone 2010) 165 at 197-198.

immediate application of human rights in choice of law is not applicable to human rights with respect to all legal sources or legal orders. Moreover, human rights generally do not contain clear connecting factors.

5. State obligations under public international law and/or formal superiority of human rights in the relevant legal order make it necessary to adapt the circumstances of intervention of the public policy exception. The required connection to the forum state will be deduced directly from the relevant human right.

Le droit au respect de la vie privée et familiale, nouveau paradigme en droit international privé des personnes ?

Romuald DI NOTO*

Le droit international privé (DIP) est le lieu par excellence de manifestation du pluralisme. Ce phénomène remarquable a notamment fait l'objet, en 2005, d'un cours donné par le Professeur Gaudemet-Tallon à l'Académie de Droit International de La Haye intitulé « Le pluralisme en droit international privé, richesses et faiblesses (le funambule et l'arc-en-ciel) »[1]. S'il y était avant tout question du pluralisme des sources et des objectifs du DIP, la métaphore du « funambule » illustre également la démarche que le juge doit adopter lorsqu'il se trouve confronté à la diversité des droits matériels nationaux, notamment en matière de droits fondamentaux. Cette pluralité de conceptions peut donner lieu à un « conflit » entre la conception qu'ont de ceux-ci les droits des Etats occidentaux et celle défendue par d'autres Etats.

Jusqu'à une époque récente, ces « conflits de civilisations »[2] apparaissaient principalement dans le cadre de relations privées internationales impliquant des personnes originaires de pays dont les traditions juridiques, en particulier en droit de la famille, sont

---

* Doctorant contractuel en droit international privé à l'Université Paris Ouest Nanterre La Défense, membre du CEDIN.

1 GAUDEMET-TALLON Hélène, « Le pluralisme en droit international privé, richesses et faiblesses (le funambule et l'arc-en-ciel) », *RCADI* 2005, tome 312.

2 V. en particulier les thèses de ZAHER Khalid, *Conflit de civilisations et droit international privé*, Paris, L'Harmattan, Collection Logiques juridiques, 2009 ; NAJM Marie-Claude, *Principes directeurs du droit international privé et conflit de civilisations : relations systèmes laïques et systèmes religieux,* Paris, Dalloz-Sirey, Collection Nouvelle Bibliothèque des Thèses, 2005.

sensiblement différentes de celles des Etats européens[3]. Cependant, depuis une dizaine d'années, ces divergences se manifestent également au sein de groupes d'Etats traditionnellement liés par une communauté de droit, notamment au sein de l'Union Européenne et du Conseil de l'Europe. Cet état de fait peut se révéler problématique, dans la mesure où, selon l'enseignement de Savigny, fondateur de la méthode des conflits de lois, une telle communauté de droit[4] constitue un élément essentiel au bon fonctionnement de la règle de conflit bilatérale[5]. Malgré les nombreuses entorses dont il a souffert, ce postulat reposant sur la fongibilité des droits nationaux constitue, encore aujourd'hui, un principe fondamental du DIP des Etats européens.

Le constat de ce pluralisme acquiert une résonnance particulière en droit de la famille. En effet, depuis le début des années 1990, certains Etats européens se sont, par la création d'unions nouvelles, ponctuellement éloignés de la communauté de droit qui les unissait aux autres. Parmi ces innovations figurent les « partenariats enregistrés », qui ont le plus souvent été mis à la disposition des couples composés de deux personnes de même sexe (Allemagne, France, Royaume-Uni, etc.) et le mariage homosexuel (Espagne, Portugal, Suède, Belgique, Pays-Bas, etc.)[6].

---

3 Pour les « conflits » impliquant les conceptions nord-africaines en droit de la famille, v. les thèses citées *supra* note 2. Les divergences de conceptions avec ces droits portent essentiellement sur le mariage (la polygamie), la dissolution du mariage (la répudiation) et la filiation.

4 Une telle communauté de droit se révèle dans une « équivalence des lois [...] des divers Etats de la planète » (NIBOYET Marie-Laure, DE GEOUFFRE DE LA PRADELLE Géraud, *Droit international privé,* Paris, L.G.D.J, 2011, 3e éd., n°7).

5 SAVIGNY Friedrich Carl von, *Traité de droit romain*, t. VIII, pp. 34-37 et 128-131.

6 Pour le détail des législations étrangères, et plus particulièrement européennes, v. WAALDIJK Kees, FASSIN Eric, *Droit conjugal et unions de même sexe. Mariage, partenariat et concubinage dans neuf pays européens*, Paris, PUF, 2008 ; GRANET-LAMBRECHTS Frédérique, « La diversité des modes de conjugalité : panorama de droit comparé », *in* FULCHIRON Hugues (dir.),

Dans ce contexte, notre contribution se propose d'examiner la question de la validité internationale des situations créées à l'étranger en matière de statut personnel sous l'angle du droit au respect de la vie privée et familiale, garanti par l'article 8 de la Convention européenne de sauvegarde des Droits de l'Homme et des Libertés fondamentales (CESDH). Cette problématique peut être illustrée par l'exemple suivant :

1. Une situation juridique (par exemple, un mariage entre deux hommes résidant en Espagne, dans le cadre duquel le premier, Giacomo, est de nationalité italienne, et le second, Alejandro, de nationalité espagnole) est créée par le droit d'un Etat A (par exemple, le droit espagnol), conformément à ses règles matérielles et, éventuellement, à ses règles de conflit de lois.

2. A la suite de leur déplacement physique de l'Etat A vers un Etat B (par exemple, de l'Espagne vers la France) où ils établissent leur domicile, les sujets de droit (en l'espèce, notre couple marié) se prévalent de cette situation devant les tribunaux ou autorités de l'Etat B (dans notre exemple, la France), afin que ceux-ci reconnaissent la validité de leur union célébrée dans l'Etat A (ici, en Espagne), et de pouvoir jouir des droits en découlant (successions, fiscalité, etc.). En l'état actuel du DIP, le juge français procédera à l'appréciation de la validité de cette situation à l'aune de ses propres règles de conflit de lois[7]. De ce contrôle résultera la nullité, du point de vue de l'ordre

---

Mariage-conjugalité, parenté-parentalité, Paris, Dalloz, Collection Thèmes et commentaires, 2009, p. 3.

7 Sur la méthode actuelle de contrôle de la validité des situations créées à l'étranger, v. NIBOYET Marie-Laure, DE GEOUFFRE DE LA PRADELLE Géraud, *Droit international privé*, *op. cit.,* n° 155 et 273 et s. Pour un regard critique, v. BUCHER Andreas, *La dimension sociale du droit international privé*, Leiden/Boston : M. Nijhoff, Les livres de poche de l'Académie de droit international de la Haye, 2011, pp. 296 et s. En matière de mariage entre personnes de même sexe célébré à l'étranger, cette méthode est explicitée par les réponses ministérielles des 26 juillet 2005 (Rép. min. n°41533, *JOAN* du 26 juillet 2005), 9 mars 2006 (Rép. min. n°20257, *JO du Sénat* du 9 mars 2006), 24 janvier 2008 (Rép. min. n°00886, *JO du Sénat* du 24 janvier 2008) et 19 janvier 2011 (Rép. min. n°1127S, *JO du Sénat* du 19 janvier 2011).

juridique français, du mariage célébré en Espagne, dans la mesure où la loi italienne (loi nationale de Giacomo) cumulativement désignée avec la loi espagnole par la règle de conflit française (loi nationale d'Alejandro), ne permet pas la formation valide d'une telle union[8]. Cette union sera donc considérée comme valide en Espagne, où les époux pourront jouir de tous les droits en résultant, mais comme nulle en France (« mariage boiteux »).

Outre qu'elle contrevient potentiellement à la liberté de circulation des personnes garantie par les traités fondateurs de l'Union européenne[9], cette solution consacrant une discontinuité internationale dans le statut familial du couple pourrait être contraire à l'article 8 CESDH, selon lequel « toute personne a droit au respect de sa vie privée et familiale ». Interprétant cette disposition, la Cour Européenne des Droits de l'Homme (CEDH) a énoncé que les Etats parties sont tenus de permettre aux personnes de mener une vie familiale normale et d'avoir accès à un régime juridique approprié reflétant cette relation familiale[10].

Après avoir examiné la question de la possible non-conformité à ce droit fondamental de la non-reconnaissance de situations créées à

---

8 En ce qui concerne la condition d'altérité des sexes, lorsque les futurs époux sont de nationalités différentes, les lois nationales de chacun d'entre eux sont cumulativement applicables, ce qui revient à se ranger aux exigences de la loi la plus sévère. Pour l'exposé détaillé des règles de conflit de lois applicables à la formation du mariage, v. MAYER Pierre, HEUZE Vincent, *Droit international privé*, Paris, Montchrestien, 2010, 10e éd., n°548 et s.

9 Nous n'aborderons pas ce débat dans la présente contribution. Sur cette question, v. DI NOTO Romuald, *Les conflits de qualification en matière de mariage entre personnes de même sexe et de partenariat enregistré dans le cadre européen, Etude de droit international privé de la famille français, allemand, belge et européen*, mémoire de Master II (dir. NIBOYET Marie-Laure), Université Paris Ouest Nanterre La Défense, Master 2 Contentieux international et européen, 2011, p. 73 et s., disponible en ligne : <http://www.village-justice.com/articles/conflits-qualifications-matiere-mariage ,11001.html> (consulté le 08/06/2012).

10 A titre d'exemple, v. CEDH, *Marckx c. Belgique*, arrêt du 13 juin 1979, § 31 ; *Johnston et autres c. Irlande*, arrêt du 18 décembre 1986, § 55 et 72-75.

l'étranger et touchant le statut personnel des personnes physiques (I), nous nous interrogerons sur les orientations méthodologiques qui pourraient être prises par le DIP afin de garantir au mieux le respect du droit au respect de la vie privée et familiale (II).

I. La non-reconnaissance des situations créées à l'étranger, une violation du droit à la vie privée et familiale ?

Dans certains de ses arrêts, la CEDH a fait obligation aux Etats parties de s'abstraire des solutions retenues par leurs règles de conflits de lois et, par conséquent, de reconnaître de plein droit la validité des statuts personnels créés par les autorités d'un Etat étranger (A.). La question de l'éventuelle extension du raisonnement retenu dans ces arrêts par la Cour de Strasbourg à l'ensemble des statuts personnels se pose donc (B.). Elle s'inscrit dans le cadre d'un mouvement de réflexion plus général conduisant certains auteurs à voir émerger un droit fondamental à l'identité, qui aurait vocation à intervenir dans les situations impliquant deux ou plusieurs ordres juridiques nationaux (C.).

A. La reconnaissance des situations créées à l'étranger dans la jurisprudence de la Cour Européenne des Droits de l'Homme

L'article 8 CESDH impose t-il aux Etats contractants « dans lesquels le rapport juridique familial tend à déployer ses effets » [11] de reconnaître des statuts familiaux constitués à l'étranger ? Selon le Professeur Bucher, une première manifestation d'une telle obligation devrait être recherchée dans l'arrêt *Abdulaziz, Cabales et Balkandali*

11 BUCHER Andreas, *Le couple en droit international privé*, Bâle/Genève/Munich/Paris, Helbing & Lichtenbahn, 2004, p. 10.

c. Royaume-Uni, rendu le 28 mai 1985[12]. Dans cette affaire, était en cause la validité d'un mariage célébré aux Philippines. Les autorités du pays d'immigration, le Royaume-Uni, s'appuyaient sur la prétendue nullité du mariage au regard du droit philippin pour refuser la délivrance d'un permis de séjour sur le territoire britannique au prétendu conjoint. Cette situation pouvait receler une atteinte à la vie privée et familiale du couple. Au lieu de s'intéresser à la question de la validité de ce mariage au regard du droit philippin, la CEDH se contente de constater que les époux « se croyaient mariés et souhaitaient sincèrement cohabiter et mener une vie familiale normale, comme ils n'ont pas manqué de le faire par la suite »[13]. Les relations nouées *de facto* entre les époux suffisaient donc à constituer une vie familiale au sens de l'article 8 CESDH, de telle façon que le respect de celle-ci faisait peser sur les autorités britanniques l'obligation de délivrer le permis de séjour au prétendu conjoint[14], indépendamment de la question de savoir si le mariage était valide du point de vue du droit philippin[15]. Selon le Professeur Bucher, cet arrêt amorce une évolution tendant à « assurer, dans le champ de l'article 8 CESDH, la reconnaissance de décisions ou actes étrangers protégeant la vie familiale au sens de cette disposition, nonobstant les règles plus restrictives du droit national »[16]. Toutefois, à aucun moment la CEDH ne fait mention d'une obligation de l'Etat partie de reconnaître la validité du mariage en tant que telle. Elle constate seulement que les relations développées entre les protagonistes sur la base de ce qu'ils croyaient être un mariage valide sont constitutives d'une vie familiale digne d'être protégée par l'article 8 CESDH, ce dont il résulte que

12 CEDH, *Abdulaziz, Cabales et Balkandali c. Royaume-Uni*, arrêt du 28 mai 1985.

13 *Ibid.*, § 63.

14 Les règles applicables s'agissant du titre de séjour étaient ici celles de l'*Immigration Act* de 1971 du *Statement of Change of Immigration Rules* de 1980. Elles ne permettaient de délivrer un titre de séjour au (prétendu) conjoint que dans la mesure où un mariage existait, ce qui supposait la validité de celui-ci.

15 BUCHER Andreas, *Le couple en droit international privé*, *op.cit.*, p. 11.

16 BUCHER Andreas, « La famille en droit international privé », *RCADI* 2000, n°58.

l'entrée et le séjour sur le territoire britannique ne sauraient être refusés au prétendu conjoint. Il est donc possible de soutenir une autre interprétation de cet arrêt, selon laquelle celui-ci ne fait aucunement obligation à l'Etat défendeur d'octroyer au couple l'ensemble des droits qui résulteraient d'un mariage valablement célébré.

L'arrêt *Wagner c. Luxembourg*, rendu le 28 juin 2007[17], constitue le point névralgique de la jurisprudence de la CEDH en matière de reconnaissance des situations créées à l'étranger. Les faits de l'espèce étaient les suivants : une personne célibataire de nationalité luxembourgeoise avait adopté un enfant au Pérou. Les autorités luxembourgeoises avaient refusé de conférer l'exequatur au jugement péruvien d'adoption car, selon la loi désignée par la règle de conflit de lois luxembourgeoise, c'est-à-dire la loi nationale de l'adoptante, les conditions de fond de l'adoption n'étaient pas réunies[18]. Les juges de Strasbourg ont considéré que le refus des autorités luxembourgeoises de reconnaître l'adoption prononcée au Pérou constituait une ingérence dans le droit au respect de la vie privée et familiale des requérantes[19]. Ils ont estimé qu'une vie familiale était née du « *statut juridique créé à l'étranger* » et qu'elle reposait sur le jugement péruvien d'adoption[20]. Alors que les autorités luxembourgeoises tentaient de justifier la non-reconnaissance du jugement péruvien d'adoption au nom de l'intérêt de l'enfant, la Cour a objecté que

> la décision de refus d'exequatur omet de tenir compte de la réalité sociale de la situation. Aussi, dès lors que les juridictions luxembourgeoises n'ont pas admis officiellement l'existence juridique des liens familiaux créés par l'adoption plénière péruvienne, ceux-ci ne déploient pas pleinement leurs effets au Luxembourg. Les requérantes en subissent les conséquences dans leur vie

---

17 CEDH, *Wagner et J.M.W.L. c. Luxembourg*, arrêt du 28 juin 2007.

18 La loi luxembourgeoise n'admettant pas, à l'époque, l'adoption par les personnes célibataires.

19 CEDH, *Wagner et J.M.W.L. c. Luxembourg*, *op. cit.*, § 123.

20 *Ibid.*, § 133.

> quotidienne et l'enfant ne se voit pas accorder une protection juridique rendant possible son intégration complète dans la famille adoptive[21].

Se fondant en particulier sur l'intérêt supérieur de l'enfant adopté,

> la Cour estime que les juges luxembourgeois ne pouvaient raisonnablement passer outre au statut juridique créé valablement à l'étranger et correspondant à une vie familiale au sens de l'article 8[22].

Obligation était donc faite à l'Etat défendeur de reconnaître la situation juridique créée à l'étranger et de la laisser déployer ses pleins effets sur le territoire luxembourgeois, nonobstant la solution matérielle contraire résultant de la mise en œuvre de la règle de conflit de lois du for[23]. Ainsi, on observe que ce n'est pas la règle de conflit de lois luxembourgeoise en tant que telle que l'arrêt *Wagner* condamne, mais uniquement ses conséquences concrètes sur le cas d'espèce[24]. La CEDH met donc à la charge de l'Etat défendeur l'obligation « d'adopter (ou de refouler) les mécanismes de droit international privé dont la mise en œuvre aboutit à un résultat conforme (ou contraire) à la Convention »[25]. Dans cette perspective, la méconnaissance d'une « réalité sociale » constituée à l'étranger telle que celle de la présente espèce aboutirait à un résultat contraire à l'esprit de la Convention[26].

---

21 *Ibid.,* § 132.

22 *Ibid.,* § 133.

23 A cet égard, Louis d'AVOUT relève que la solution adoptée par la CEDH revient à exiger de l'Etat défendeur que celui-ci « transforme la famille de fait en une famille de droit, et ce contrairement aux prescriptions de son ordre juridique » (D'AVOUT Louis, « Commentaire de l'arrêt *Wagner et J.M.W.L. c. Luxembourg* », *JDI* 2008, n°1, comm. 5).

24 KINSCH Philippe, « Commentaire de l'arrêt *Wagner et J.M.W.L. c. Luxembourg*, req. n°76240/01 », *Rev. crit. DIP* 2007, p. 807, spéc. p. 817-818.

25 NIBOYET Marie-Laure, « Le droit à une vie familiale au service de la reconnaissance des situations juridiques créées à l'étranger », *Gaz. pal.* 22 mars 2008, n°82, p. 31.

26 MARCHADIER Fabien, « La protection européenne des situations constituées à l'étranger », *D.* 2007, p. 2700, spéc. p. 2702.

B. La question de la généralisation de la démarche de la Cour Européenne des Droits de l'Homme

Eu égard au caractère très évolutif du droit de la famille, une certaine retenue s'impose. Si la démarche adoptée par la Cour dans l'arrêt *Wagner* présente des similitudes avec la méthode dite « de la reconnaissance »[27], il faut garder à l'esprit le caractère circonstancié de l'espèce. On peut néanmoins se demander si ce raisonnement a vocation à s'appliquer à « toutes les conditions du contrôle de l'exequatur » de la décision judiciaire étrangère ou de la validité de la situation constituée à l'étranger sans intervention d'une autorité judiciaire, uniquement à « celle du contrôle de la compétence de la loi appliquée par le jugement étranger » [28], ou si elle tient aux circonstances très particulières de l'espèce[29]. En outre, l'arrêt *Wagner* fait référence au « stade avancé d'harmonisation en Europe » s'agissant de l'adoption par des personnes célibataires[30]. Faut-il y voir un indice selon lequel à défaut d'une telle communauté juridique, l'Etat défendeur n'aurait pas été dans l'obligation de reconnaître l'adoption prononcée par le jugement péruvien ? Doit-on prendre en compte cette considération pour déterminer si une obligation de reconnaissance des statuts personnels (qu'il s'agisse de mariages, partenariats, adoptions ou autres) créés à l'étranger pèse sur les Etats parties ? Dans l'affirmative, de sérieux doutes pourraient être exprimés quant à une obligation de reconnaissance d'un mariage entre personnes de même sexe comme celui de notre exemple introductif,

27 NIBOYET Marie-Laure, « Le droit à une vie familiale au service de la reconnaissance des situations juridiques créées à l'étranger », *op. cit.*, p. 31.

28 *Idem.*

29 Groupe européen de droit international privé (GEDIP), dix-septième réunion (Hambourg, 2007, site officiel : <http://www.gedip-egpil.eu/reunionstravail/gedip-reunions-17t-fr.html> (consulté le 08/06/2012)). Ces circonstances particulières étaient les suivantes : la bonne foi de la requérante et une pratique administrative antérieure tendant à conférer systématiquement l'exequatur aux jugements d'adoption péruviens ayant fait naître des espérances légitimes, ainsi que l'interruption brutale de cette pratique.

30 CEDH, *Wagner et J.M.W.L. c. Luxembourg*, *op. cit.*, § 129.

car l'institution est encore peu répandue parmi les Etats du Conseil de l'Europe. De même, bien qu'il ait davantage essaimé, le partenariat enregistré est encore loin de constituer un standard.

La doctrine est partagée quant aux leçons à tirer de l'arrêt *Wagner*. Selon certains commentateurs, la solution adoptée par la CEDH pourrait être utilisée afin de contraindre les Etats parties à la CESDH à reconnaître les situations constituées à l'étranger sans l'intervention d'une juridiction ou d'un autre organe décisionnel en vertu d'une loi autre que celle désignée par les règles de conflits de for de reconnaissance[31]. Pour d'autres, les circonstances de l'espèce sont prépondérantes, de telle façon qu'une telle obligation générale de reconnaissance ne saurait être déduite de cet arrêt[32]. Ainsi, selon le Professeur d'Avout, il serait plus opportun de s'orienter vers un mécanisme « d'exception de reconnaissance de la situation constituée à l'étranger » auquel le recours serait permis en cas de « contrariété incontestable à un droit de l'homme garanti »[33] par la CESDH. La délimitation des cas dans lesquels une telle « contrariété incontestable » serait avérée constitue cependant une question extrêmement délicate, qui ne pourrait être tranchée avec certitude qu'en cas de condamnation d'un Etat par la CEDH.

Enfin, il faut relever que, dans une décision d'irrecevabilité rendue le 6 juillet 2010 et portant sur la reconnaissance d'un mariage polygamique[34], la Cour considère qu'un équilibre doit être recherché entre les droits de l'individu et les intérêts de l'Etat défendeur à la non-reconnaissance de l'union au titre de la justification de l'atteinte à

---

31 Au contraire, certains membres du GEDIP interprètent l'arrêt *Wagner* en ce sens qu'il ferait « simplement application d'une règle (non spécifique aux affaires de droit international privé) selon laquelle l'application d'une nouvelle pratique administrative ne pourrait pas se faire rétroactivement au détriment des attentes constituées sur la base de la pratique ancienne » (GEDIP, dix-septième réunion (Hambourg, 2007), *op. cit.*).

32 D'AVOUT Louis, « Commentaire de l'arrêt *Wagner et J.M.W.L. c. Luxembourg* », *op.cit.*, comm. 5.

33 *Idem.*

34 CEDH, *Mary Green et Arad Farhat c. Malte*, décision d'irrecevabilité du 6 juillet 2010.

la vie privée et familiale au sens de l'article 8 CESDH. A cet égard, elle considère qu'un Etat n'outrepasse pas la marge d'appréciation dont il dispose en recourant à son ordre public pour refuser de reconnaître un second mariage d'une femme dont le premier mariage n'a pas été dissous[35]. Cette solution pourrait amener l'interprète à considérer que la recherche d'un équilibre entre l'intérêt des individus à la reconnaissance de leur élément de statut personnel créé à l'étranger et celui des Etats à préserver leurs conceptions de droit de la famille peut déboucher sur un refus justifié de la reconnaissance de certains statuts personnels, comme les unions homosexuelles dans les Etats ne prévoyant aucune institution de ce type. Une certaine marge d'appréciation serait donc conférée aux autorités nationales, à tout le moins au stade du contrôle de la conformité de la situation à l'ordre public international du for de reconnaissance.

C. Vers un droit fondamental à l'identité ?

Selon le Professeur Bucher, « un droit fondamental de la personne à connaître et à affirmer son identité » fondé sur « la liberté de s'épanouir dans tout système social, économique et juridique faisant partie d'un ensemble d'Etats » serait en train d'émerger[36]. Celui-ci serait concrétisé par un droit subjectif de chaque individu à être placé dans une situation juridique unique en dépit du contexte international dans lequel il évolue[37]. Ce droit représenterait donc un obstacle aux « statuts boiteux » : un couple considéré comme marié dans un Etat A devrait, sauf exception, l'être également dans un Etat B. Pour ce faire,

---

35 Cette décision d'irrecevabilité, qui tend à préserver la « *public policy* » de l'Etat défendeur, peut être rapprochée de l'arrêt *Princesse de Bauffremont*, qui concernait un cas de fraude à la loi (Groupe européen de DIP, vingtième réunion, Copenhague, 2010, site officiel : <http://www.gedip-egpil.eu/reunionstravail/gedip-reunions-20-fr.htm> (consulté le 08/06/2012)).

36 BUCHER Andreas, *Le couple en droit international privé, op. cit.*, p. 8.

37 BUCHER Andreas, *La dimension sociale du droit international privé, op.cit.*, n°67.

devrait être retenue par chaque système national de conflit de lois une solution permettant d'atteindre cet objectif. Au stade des conflits de lois relatifs à des éléments du statut personnel créés à l'étranger comme le mariage d'Alejandro et de Giacomo, la règle de conflit attributive devrait ainsi s'effacer au profit d'une règle de reconnaissance (ou règle de conflit réceptive) « lorsqu'elle aboutit à une solution différente de celle d'un ou plusieurs autres systèmes concernés »[38]. A l'échelle européenne, ce droit fondamental à l'identité aurait pour assise à la fois l'article 8 CESDH et les libertés de circulation consacrées par le droit de l'Union européenne[39].

Cependant, il est loin d'être certain que les deux cours européennes aient, en l'état actuel de leur jurisprudence, entendu consacrer un tel droit. Le Professeur Bucher admet d'ailleurs qu'une telle construction semble, pour l'heure, « relever de la seule imagination, voire du monde des rêves »[40]. Si cette évolution est certainement souhaitable du point de vue de l'harmonie internationale des solutions pressentie à partir de la position individuelle du sujet du

38 *Ibid.*, n°73.

39 Selon l'auteur, « il ne fait aucun doute que la garantie du principe fondamental de la libre circulation des personnes implique la libre circulation de leur statut familial et, en particulier, des décisions à son sujet » (BUCHER Andreas, « La famille en droit international privé », *op. cit.*, p. 101). Roberto BARATTA propose également de trouver une telle obligation de reconnaissance des statuts personnels dans le droit de l'Union européenne. Ce principe refoulerait l'application des règles nationales de conflit de lois dès lors qu'elle aboutit à la nullité de l'élément de statut personnel (BARATTA Roberto, « Problematic elements of an implicit rule providing for mutual recognition of personal and family status in the EC », *IPrax* 2007, p. 4, spéc. p. 9).

40 Andreas BUCHER admet le caractère fortement aléatoire de la naissance d'un tel droit fondamental : « La portée exacte de ce droit à l'identité est à l'heure actuelle incertaine [...] mais le principe semble s'affirmer clairement. [...] A l'heure actuelle, cela semble relever de la seule imagination, voire du monde des rêves. L'essentiel, c'est de comprendre qu'une telle évolution pourrait se produire, si les esprits et les volontés politiques se dirigent dans cette direction. [...] On doit reconnaître que, sans être un droit, tel est tout au moins un objectif du droit international privé » (BUCHER Andreas, *La dimension sociale du droit international privé*, *op. cit.*, n°69 et s.).

droit, il conviendrait cependant d'en mesurer préalablement toutes les implications, tant sur les règles de conflit de lois que sur les législations et traditions nationales de droit de la famille.

II. Quelle(s) évolution(s) méthodologique(s) pour assurer le respect du droit à la vie privée et familiale ?

Bien qu'elles ne constituent pas une généralité, nous avons pu constater l'existence de situations « boiteuses » lors de la circulation de certains statuts personnels. Cela constitue un facteur d'imprévisibilité et d'insécurité juridique pour les sujets de droit entretenant des liens avec plusieurs ordres juridiques. En doctrine, deux pistes ont été explorées afin de conférer une plus grande stabilité aux statuts personnels des personnes évoluant dans un contexte international : si la solution la plus « radicale » consistant, au stade de l'appréciation de la validité des situations créées à l'étranger, à abandonner la méthode des conflits de lois en faveur de celle dite « de la reconnaissance » semble recueillir l'adhésion d'un important mouvement doctrinal (B.), une modification de la règle de conflit applicable à certains éléments du statut personnel pourrait, selon d'autres auteurs, suffire à satisfaire l'objectif de continuité internationale des statuts personnels et familiaux (A.).

A. La modification de la loi applicable en matière de statut personnel : l'abandon du rattachement à la loi nationale en faveur du celui au domicile ou à la résidence habituelle

Insistons d'emblée sur le mouvement global de recul du rattachement à la nationalité au profit de celui au domicile ou à la résidence habituelle dans la solution des conflits de lois afférents aux éléments de statut personnel. Ce phénomène est particulièrement marqué en droit de l'Union européenne : ainsi, dans son commentaire de l'arrêt *Grunkin-Paul,* rendu par la Cour de Justice des Communautés européennes en 2008 [41], le Professeur d'Avout écrit avoir « le sentiment que la seule souveraineté personnelle juridiquement licite [...] est celle du milieu de vie contemporain de la personne physique ; non pas, comme il est de tradition, celle du pays des origines envers lequel on a gardé l'esprit de retour »[42]. Pour sa part, Fabienne Kauff-Gazin évoque une « citoyenneté européenne de résidence » [43]. En dehors du champ du droit de l'Union européenne, plusieurs éléments confirment ce recul de la loi nationale de l'individu pour régir ses éléments de statut personnel. Ainsi, en matière de partenariat enregistré, la loi nationale des partenaires a, aussi bien au stade de la formation de l'union qu'à celui de ses effets, été évincée des règles de conflits de lois de nombreux Etats[44], alors que l'emprise de la loi nationale lors de la formation du mariage reste, à tout le moins en droit français, prépondérante [45]. Pourtant, la conclusion d'un

41 CJCE, 14 octobre 2008, *Grunkin-Paul*, aff. C-353/06, Rec. 2008, I., p. 7639. Cet arrêt a été rendu en matière de nom patronymique.

42 D'AVOUT Louis, « Commentaire de l'arrêt *Grunkin-Paul* », *JDI* 2009, p. 7, III.

43 KAUFF-GAZIN Fabienne, « Liberté de circulation et nom patronymique », *Europe* 2008, commentaire 397. Le Règlement « Rome III » (Règlement n°1259/2010 du Conseil du 20 décembre 2010 mettant en œuvre une coopération renforcée dans le domaine de la loi applicable au divorce et à la séparation de corps) suit une logique identique : la construction de ses articles 5 et 8 témoigne de la prééminence du rattachement à la résidence habituelle des époux sur celui à leur nationalité commune dans l'esprit du législateur européen.

44 En principe, le partenariat enregistré est intégralement rattaché aux dispositions matérielles de l'Etat de l'autorité qui a procédé à l'enregistrement (en droit français : art. 515-7-1 C. Civ. ; en droit allemand : art. 17b EGBGB ; en droit belge : art. 60 CODIP).

45 Pour un exemple contraire v. le droit suédois, qui prévoit que la *lex fori* suédoise est applicable à tout couple de personnes dont l'une possède la nationalité suédoise ou réside habituellement en Suède. La même règle a été adoptée en Finlande, aux Pays-Bas, au Danemark et en Norvège. Selon un auteur, bien que la règle ne soit pas formulée explicitement, le principe est le même en droits suisse, anglais et espagnol (ROMANO Gian-Paolo, « La bilatéralité éclipsée par

partenariat n'est pas sans entraîner de lourdes conséquences sur le statut personnel des partenaires, tout particulièrement lorsque cette union constitue en réalité un quasi-mariage, comme c'est le cas de la *eingetragene Lebenspartnerschaft* allemande, du *Civil partnership* britannique ou du partenariat enregistré suisse. On constatera cependant que ces éléments s'inscrivent dans un mouvement plus général de fragmentation du statut personnel en DIP[46]. Ainsi, prenant l'exemple d'un couple germano-britannique marié et résidant habituellement en France, Myriam Hunter-Hénin observe que le nombre de questions afférentes au statut personnel des membres du couple qui seront soumises à la loi nationale des intéressés est extrêmement réduit[47] : il s'agira seulement des conditions de fond de la validité de leur mariage[48] et du lien de filiation de leur enfant à leur égard[49]. Par ailleurs, « les droits de l'homme de même que la logique» du droit européen dans son acceptation large feraient, selon l'auteure, « peu de cas de la notion de nationalité », dans la mesure où ils cherchent avant tout à satisfaire des objectifs matériels prédéfinis[50]. Dans le cadre du droit au respect de la vie privée et familiale, l'arrêt *Wagner* constitue une parfaite illustration de ce phénomène, tout comme, en droit de

l'autorité – Développements récents en matière d'état des personnes », *Rev. crit. DIP* 2006, p. 457, n°10).

46 BUREAU Dominique, MUIR WATT Horatia, *Droit international privé,* Paris, L.G.D.J., 2e édition, 2010, t. II, n°640.

47 HUNTER-HENIN Myriam, « Droit des personnes et droits de l'homme : combinaison ou confrontation ? », *Rev. crit. DIP* 2006, p. 743, I, B., 1. En revanche, seraient soumis à d'autres lois que la loi nationale des époux : les effets de leur union (sauf en cas de nationalité commune), les effets du lien de filiation et le divorce (sauf en cas de nationalité commune).

48 Les lois nationales de chacun des époux sont, dans une telle espèce, appliquées tantôt distributivement, tantôt cumulativement. Pour le détail des règles de conflit de lois applicables lors de la formation du mariage, v. MAYER Pierre, HEUZE Vincent, *Droit international privé, op. cit.*, n°548 et s.

49 Par application de la loi nationale de la mère au jour de la naissance de l'enfant, article 311-14 du Code civil.

50 HUNTER-HENIN Myriam, « Droit des personnes et droits de l'homme : combinaison ou confrontation ? », *op. cit.*, I, B., 1.

l'Union européenne, les arrêts *Garcia Avello*[51] et, surtout, *Grunkin-Paul*[52], rendus par la Cour de Justice de l'Union européenne. Enfin, eu égard à la mobilité croissante des personnes, la nationalité ne constituerait plus l'élément le plus approprié pour rendre compte de l'intégration d'un individu au sein d'un milieu social donné[53]. Tirant les conséquences de ces évolutions, des propositions doctrinales tendant à appliquer au statut personnel de l'individu la loi de l'Etat sur lequel est localisé son domicile ou sa résidence habituelle ont été formulées.

Myriam Hunter-Hénin propose de soumettre le statut personnel de l'individu à la loi de sa résidence habituelle, cette dernière étant appréhendée comme le milieu d'intégration pour lequel l'individu entretiendrait un sentiment d'appartenance[54]. La résidence habituelle serait ainsi définie comme le « lieu de convergence des attaches familiales et sociologiques d'un individu avec un pays donné »[55]. Il s'agirait d'une résidence habituelle familiale déterminée en fonction de l'intensité des liens familiaux. Suivant cette proposition, la résidence habituelle d'un futur époux ou partenaire s'apprêtant à rejoindre son futur conjoint ou partenaire sur le territoire d'un autre Etat pour y fixer une résidence habituelle commune serait localisée sur le territoire de l'Etat « d'arrivée »[56], dont le droit régirait dès lors son statut personnel et les conditions de fond de son futur mariage ou partenariat. A cette proposition, Jeremy Heymann préfère celle consistant en un rattachement au domicile de l'individu[57]. D'autres

---

51 CJCE, 2 octobre 2003, *Garcia Avello*, aff. C-148/02, Rec. 2003, I, p. 11613.

52 CJCE, 14 octobre 2008, *Grunkin-Paul*, aff. C-353/06, Rec. 2008, I, p. 7639.

53 HUNTER-HENIN Myriam, « Droit des personnes et droits de l'homme : combinaison ou confrontation ? », *op. cit.*, I, B., 1.

54 HUNTER-HENIN Myriam, *Pour une redéfinition du statut personnel,* Thèse, Presses Universitaires d'Aix-Marseille, 2004, n°413.

55 HUNTER-HENIN Myriam, « Droit des personnes et droits de l'homme : combinaison ou confrontation ? », *op. cit.*, II, A, 1.

56 *Idem.*

57 L'auteur juge en effet que la notion de résidence habituelle est une « notion de fait » fuyante, même si elle a l'avantage de permettre une approche souple, ce qui expliquerait son succès dans le cadre des instruments internationaux et

auteurs proposent d'offrir une option de législation à l'individu, qui serait dès lors libre de choisir entre la loi de sa nationalité et celle de sa résidence habituelle[58].

La soumission du statut personnel à la loi du domicile ou de la résidence habituelle présente certains avantages : l'individu intégré dans un Etat aura, dans la plupart des cas, une meilleure connaissance de la loi de cet Etat, qui constitue son milieu d'intégration, que de celle de l'Etat de sa nationalité, qu'il aura peut-être quitté depuis plusieurs années. De plus, l'Etat de la résidence habituelle n'aura pas à gérer la multiplicité des statuts personnels des personnes résidant durablement sur son territoire. Des impératifs afférents à la protection des tiers et à l'assimilation de l'immigration sont également avancés[59]. Ce critère de la résidence habituelle ou du domicile a été retenu par de nombreux Etats, en particulier anglo-saxons, scandinaves ou encore latino-américains[60], ainsi que par certaines conventions de la Haye[61].

---

européens. Selon l'auteur, des difficultés pourraient être rencontrées dans la détermination de la résidence habituelle d'une personne partageant équitablement sa résidence entre deux ou plusieurs pays. Par conséquent, Jeremy Heymann propose un rattachement du statut personnel au domicile entendu comme « le rattachement d'une personne à un ressort judiciaire, ce qui est pour elle une source de droits et d'obligations », car ce dernier constituerait l'expression d'une « allégeance politique » et de l'« ancrage sur le territoire d'un Etat ». Il devrait être déterminé à l'aune de différents éléments matériels corroborés par un élément psychologique (HEYMANN Jeremy, *Le droit international privé à l'épreuve du fédéralisme européen*, Paris, Economica, 2010, n°441 et s.).

58 CARLIER Jean-Yves, « Autonomie de la volonté et statut personnel », *Cahier des Droits Maghrébins,* vol. 1 (1995), p. 5 ; GANNAGE Pierre, « La pénétration de l'autonomie de la volonté dans le droit international privé de la famille », *Rev. crit. DIP* 1992, p. 425).

59 MAYER Pierre, HEUZE Vincent, *Droit international privé, op. cit.*, n°510.

60 *Ibid.*, n°507.

61 Par exemple, par l'article 4 de la Convention de la Haye du 2 octobre 1973 sur la loi applicable aux obligations alimentaires ; article 13 de Convention de la Haye du 13 janvier 2000 sur la protection internationale des adultes (par le truchement de la compétence) ; article 3 du Protocole de la Haye du 23 novembre 2007 sur la loi applicable aux obligations alimentaires, auquel fait référence le règlement 4/2009 qui traite, entre autres, de cette question.

Si l'on transpose cette proposition aux conditions de validité au fond du mariage ou du partenariat enregistré, celles-ci seraient alors soumises à la loi du domicile ou de la résidence habituelle des intéressés au moment de la célébration ou de l'enregistrement. Il est probable que, dans la plupart des cas, l'Etat de célébration ou d'enregistrement de l'union coïncide avec l'Etat du domicile ou de la résidence habituelle des futurs époux ou partenaires. Un tel mécanisme permettrait donc d'assurer une prévisibilité accrue des solutions ainsi que de prévenir, voire, si un nombre important d'Etats venaient à s'accorder sur ce critère de rattachement, d'éliminer beaucoup de « statuts boiteux ». Appliquée à notre exemple introductif, cette solution reviendrait, pour le DIP français, au stade de l'examen de la validité du mariage célébré en Espagne, à apprécier la validité du mariage d'Alejandro et Giacomo au regard du seul droit espagnol, dans la mesure où les deux époux résidaient en Espagne au moment de la célébration de l'union. De plus, la proposition de Myriam Hunter-Hénin permettrait d'appliquer la loi espagnole à l'époux de nationalité italienne dans l'hypothèse où celui-ci viendrait s'installer en Espagne avec Alejandro peu de temps avant leur mariage, tout en ayant l'intention de s'y établir durablement.

Cependant, cette proposition appelle une réflexion plus générale sur la loi applicable au statut personnel. Bien qu'il ait été évoqué par la Commission européenne dans son Livre vert sur l'état civil[62], ce travail d'ampleur nous paraît peu susceptible d'être amorcé

---

62 Livre vert de la Commission européenne, « Moins de démarches administratives pour les citoyens : promouvoir la libre circulation des documents publics et la reconnaissance des effets des actes d'état civil », 14 décembre 2010, COM(2010) 747 final, p. 14. Le Livre vert évoque, entre autres, la possibilité de faire régir le statut personnel des citoyens européens par la loi de leur Etat de résidence « avec lequel ils ont développé des attaches » plutôt que par leur loi nationale. La Commission européenne aborde également la possibilité de permettre au citoyen « de choisir la loi applicable à un événement lié à l'état civil ». Cette faculté serait cependant encadrée, de telle façon que le choix ne pourrait porter que sur les seules lois avec lesquelles le citoyen entretient des liens suffisamment étroit (loi de la nationalité ou loi du domicile/de la résidence habituelle).

rapidement et de déboucher sur une prise de position des Etats de l'Union européenne à court ou moyen terme. En effet, de nombreux Etats européens sont historiquement attachés au rattachement du statut personnel à la loi nationale[63]. Une seconde voie, qui recueille l'assentiment d'une partie importante de la doctrine, consisterait à étendre la méthode dite « de la reconnaissance » aux situations juridiques familiales créées à l'étranger.

B. L'extension de la méthode de la reconnaissance aux statuts personnels créés à l'étranger

Classiquement, en DIP français, la méthode dite « de la reconnaissance » intervient dans le cadre des questions relatives à la reconnaissance et à l'exécution des décisions judiciaires rendues par les juridictions étrangères[64]. Etendue aux situations familiales, elle consisterait

> à poser comme principe que certaines situations nées à l'étranger en conformité des règles de droit qui y sont applicables doivent être reconnues comme valablement créées dans les autres pays[65].

---

63 A titre d'exemple, en DIP français, cette solution puise ses racines dans l'article 3, alinéa 3 C. civ. selon lequel « les lois concernant l'état et la capacité des personnes régissent les Français, même résidant en pays étrangers », présent dans le Code civil depuis 1804 et bilatéralisé par l'arrêt *Busqueta* rendu le 13 juin 1814 par la Cour de Paris (« Réglée par le statut personnel qui affecte la personne et la suit en quelque lieu qu'elle aille et se trouve, la capacité d'un étranger relève de sa loi nationale », ANCEL Bertrand et LEQUETTE Yves, *Les grands arrêts de la jurisprudence française de droit international privé*, Paris, Dalloz-Sirey, 2008, 5e éd., p. 1).

64 MAYER Pierre, « Les méthodes de la reconnaissance en droit international privé », in *Mélanges en l'honneur de Paul Lagarde*, p. 547, n°5-15.

65 WEISS-GOUT Béatrice, NIBOYET Marie-Laure, « La reconnaissance mutuelle des mariages entre personnes de même sexe et des partenariats entre personnes de même sexe ou de sexe opposé. La situation dans les différents Etats membres. Besoin d'une action de l'UE ? », *PE* 432.731, novembre 2010, p. 10.

Par application de cette méthode au stade de l'éventuelle reconnaissance d'une situation créée à l'étranger et afférente au statut personnel d'un individu, la question du droit applicable à la constitution de la situation, propre au raisonnement reposant sur la méthode des conflits de lois, serait supplantée par celle des conditions de la reconnaissance[66]. Par conséquent, au stade du contrôle de la validité de la situation créée à l'étranger, l'Etat d'accueil devrait rester indifférent à la ou aux loi(s) désignées par ses propres règles de conflit de lois[67]. Son intérêt à l'application de celles-ci céderait le pas devant celui des sujets de droit à la stabilité de leur situation créée à l'étranger[68]. La méthode de la reconnaissance favorise ainsi « l'alignement de la réalité juridique sur le fait »[69], et se fonde sur un objectif de cohérence internationale des rapports juridiques privés[70]. On peut également utiliser le vocable « conflit d'autorités », car cette méthode peut être justifiée par l'intervention d'une autorité de l'Etat membre de constitution. Le Professeur Pataut souligne d'ailleurs que les cas d'intervention d'une autorité administrative constituent

> le champ d'application le plus naturel de cette méthode de reconnaissance des situations parce que précisément l'intervention d'une autorité garantit que la situation considérée a une certaine efficacité dans l'ordre juridique d'origine [...][71].

---

66 NIBOYET Marie-Laure, DE GEOUFFRE DE LA PRADELLE Géraud, *Droit international privé, op. cit.*, n° 227.

67 GOTHOT Pierre, LAGARDE Paul, *Rép. Dalloz Droit international, v° Conflits de lois (principes généraux)*, 2006, n° 47.

68 LAGARDE Paul, « Développements futurs du droit international privé dans une Europe en voie d'unification », *RabelsZ* 2004, p. 225, spéc. p. 232.

69 MAYER Pierre, « Les méthodes de la reconnaissance en droit international privé », *op. cit.*, n°33.

70 PAMBOUKIS Charalambos, « La renaissance-métamorphose de la méthode de la reconnaissance », *Rev. crit. DIP* 2008, p. 513, n°20.

71 Intervention d'Etienne PATAUT dans le cadre du débat faisant suite à sa communication « Le renouveau de la théorie des droits acquis », *Trav. com. fr. DIP* 2006-2008 , p.71, spéc. p. 100.

La méthode de la reconnaissance permet donc de respecter les prévisions légitimes des parties, en particulier lorsque celles-ci ont été confortées par l'intervention d'une autorité étatique lors de la constitution de la situation[72]. De plus, dans ce type de configuration, la *lex auctoris*, loi de l'autorité, qui est aussi la *lex fori*, est le plus souvent appliquée[73]. C'est précisément le cas en matière de partenariat enregistré. Dans le domaine du mariage, cette tendance *lex-foriste* se manifeste de façon plus limitée[74]. Comme nous avons pu l'observer dans le cadre de notre exemple introductif, ou bien encore en matière d'adoption avec l'arrêt *Wagner*, cette solution occasionne une rupture internationale dans le statut familial[75]. Notre faveur va, à l'instar de celle de nombreux auteurs[76], à l'extension de la méthode de la reconnaissance à ce type de situations. En supprimant intégralement les aléas propres au raisonnement conflictuel, elle contribue à garantir la continuité internationale de ces situations, et, partant, l'effectivité des droits fondamentaux tels que le droit au respect de la vie privée et familiale garanti par l'article 8 CESDH[77]. Deux conventions

---

72 NIBOYET Marie-Laure, DE GEOUFFRE DE LA PRADELLE Géraud, *Droit international privé, op. cit.*, n°232.

73 ROMANO Gian-Paolo, « La bilatéralité éclipsée par l'autorité – Développements récents en matière d'état des personnes », *op. cit.*, n°7.

74 V. *supra* note 45.

75 Ce constat peut également être formulé dans d'autres domaines (v. par exemple en matière de nom : CJCE, 14 octobre 2008, *Grunkin-Paul*).

76 En ce sens, entre autres : LAGARDE Paul, « La reconnaissance, mode d'emploi » in *Mélanges en l'honneur d'Hélène Gaudemet-Tallon*, p. 481, n°12 et s. ; « Développements futurs du droit international privé dans une Europe en voie d'unification », *op. cit.* ; MAYER Pierre, « Les méthodes de la reconnaissance en droit international privé », *op. cit.* ; BOLLEE Sylvain, « L'extension du domaine de la méthode de la reconnaissance unilatérale », *Rev. crit. DIP* 2007, p. 307, n°18 ; PAMBOUKIS Charalambos, « La renaissance-métamorphose de la méthode de la reconnaissance », *op. cit.* ; ROMANO Gian-Paolo, « La bilatéralité éclipsée par l'autorité – Développements récents en matière d'état des personnes », *op. cit.*

77 Il faut souligner que, dans le cadre de la reconnaissance en France d'un jugement rendu à l'étranger, la Cour de cassation a choisi de supprimer ce type d'aléa en jugeant que l'identité entre la loi appliquée par le jugement étranger et

internationales font ouvertement usage de cette méthode : la Convention de la Haye du 14 mars 1978 sur la célébration et la reconnaissance de la validité des mariages[78] et la Convention de la Commission Internationale de l'Etat Civil sur la reconnaissance des partenariats enregistrés, ouverte à la signature en septembre 2007[79].

Le recours à la méthode de la reconnaissance dans le cadre de l'appréciation de la validité des situations de statut personnel créées à l'étranger n'est cependant pas synonyme d'abandon de tout contrôle préalable à la reconnaissance : trois conditions sont généralement posées par les conventions précitées, qui permettent de garantir l'équilibre entre les intérêts des sujets de droit et ceux des Etats de reconnaissance. Elles sont peu ou prou identiques à celles prévues dans le cadre de la reconnaissance des jugements étrangers[80]. Tout d'abord, « le respect des prévisions des parties ne s'impos[ant] que si elles sont légitimes »[81], la reconnaissance d'une situation créée par l'autorité d'un Etat avec lequel les intéressés n'entretiennent qu'un

---

celle désignée par la règle de conflit de loi française ne constitue plus une condition de la reconnaissance en France du jugement étranger (v. Civ. 1ère, 20 févr. 2007, *Gaz. Pal.* 2007, p. 1387, commentaire Marie-Laure NIBOYET).

78 L'article 9 de cette Convention formule une règle de reconnaissance des mariages célébrés à l'étranger : « Le mariage qui a été valablement conclu selon le droit de l'Etat de la célébration, ou qui devient ultérieurement valable selon ce droit, est considéré comme tel dans tout Etat contractant sous réserve des dispositions de ce chapitre ». Malheureusement, ce texte n'a été ratifié que par trois Etats : l'Australie, le Luxembourg et les Pays-Bas.

79 En vertu de l'article 2 de cette Convention dite « de Munich sur la reconnaissance des partenariats enregistrés », pour l'heure signée par l'Espagne et le Portugal, « [...] un partenariat enregistré dans un Etat est reconnu comme valide dans les Etats contractants ». Les réserves prévues par l'article 7 sont les suivantes : la polygamie, l'inceste, l'incapacité ou l'absence d'âge légal de l'un des partenaires, la fraude et l'ordre public.

80 Sur les éléments contrôlés en droit international privé français lors de la reconnaissance et de l'exécution des jugements étrangers, v. NIBOYET Marie-Laure, DE GEOUFFRE DE LA PRADELLE Géraud, *Droit international privé, op. cit.*, n°717 et s.

81 GOLDSTEIN Gérald, MUIR WATT Horatia, « La méthode de la reconnaissance à la lueur de la Convention de Munich du 5 septembre 2007 sur la reconnaissance des partenariats enregistrés », *JDI* 2010, p. 1085, n°76.

lien créé artificiellement ne saurait être admise[82]. Dès lors, la validité d'un élément de statut personnel ne pourrait être reconnue que dans la mesure où, du point de vue du DIP de l'Etat de reconnaissance, l'autorité étrangère de création du statut jouissait d'une compétence indirecte fondée sur des liens de rattachement suffisants entre les sujets de droit et cet ordre juridique étranger. Cette condition tend à prévenir les manœuvres frauduleuses des sujets de droit (*marriage shopping*, *registration shopping, adoption shopping*). Une solution pragmatique consisterait à poser une règle uniforme de compétence internationale des autorités de création des éléments de statut personnel[83]. La seconde condition tiendrait à la validité de la situation créée à l'étranger du point de vue des règles tant matérielles que de DIP de l'Etat d'origine. En cas de contestation, il reviendrait à l'Etat de reconnaissance de contrôler la validité du statut au regard du droit de l'Etat de création. Enfin, l'intervention de l'ordre public de l'Etat de reconnaissance ne devrait être permise que de façon très restrictive, par exemple afin de refuser la reconnaissance d'une union incestueuse ou polygamique, ou encore d'un mariage forcé. Chaque Etat resterait cependant libre du contenu de son ordre public, sous le contrôle de la CJUE ou de la CEDH.

Si l'on applique la méthode de la reconnaissance au mariage d'Alejandro et de Giacomo, la France reconnaîtrait la validité de celui-ci, car aucune exception d'ordre public international ne serait prévue pour les mariages entre personnes de même sexe, dans la mesure où le régime du pacte civil de solidarité tend à se rapprocher considérablement de celui du mariage[84]. Par ailleurs, il ne serait pas tenu compte de la loi italienne prohibitive de Giacomo. La seule hypothèse

82 *Ibid.*, n°82.

83 Pour davantage d'éléments, v. notre étude intitulée *Les conflits de qualification en matière de mariage entre personnes de même sexe et de partenariat enregistré dans le cadre européen, Etude de droit international privé de la famille français, allemand, belge et européen*, *op. cit.*, p. 104.

84 CASTAGNE Suzanne, « Mariage, PACS, concubinage – Analyse comparative », *JCP N* 2008, doctr. 1325 ; SIMLER Philippe, HILT Patrice, « Le nouveau visage du Pacs : un quasi-mariage », *JCP N* 2006, n°35, 1266.

de refus de reconnaissance ne pourrait concerner qu'une éventuelle fraude, par exemple dans l'hypothèse où les époux auraient initialement résidé en France, se seraient déplacés en Espagne dans le but exclusif de faire célébrer le mariage, puis seraient revenus s'installer dans l'Hexagone immédiatement après l'acquisition de leur nouveau statut (*marriage shopping*).

Garantissant la cohérence du statut personnel des individus et assurant par là-même le respect de l'article 8 CESDH, un tel assouplissement des conditions d'accueil des institutions créées à l'étranger irait également dans le sens d'une plus grande effectivité de la liberté de circulation des personnes garantie par les traités de l'Union européenne.

Le Pacte Mondial des Nations Unies, un mécanisme efficace de protection et de promotion des droits de l'Homme ?

Jeanne DUPENDANT*

Le Pacte Mondial, plus connu sous son nom anglais « Global Compact », a été initié en janvier 1999 par le secrétaire général des Nations Unies d'alors, Kofi Annan, puis officiellement lancé le 26 juillet 2000. Il a depuis acquis une reconnaissance officielle [1], notamment de l'Assemblée Générale des Nations Unies (AGNU)[2] et du G8[3]. Kofi Annan souhaitait un partenariat fort entre les Nations Unies et la société civile, notamment les entreprises, dont les intérêts n'étaient, selon lui, pas opposés mais pouvaient au contraire

---

* Doctorante à l'Université Paris Ouest Nanterre la Défense, membre du CEDIN.

1 LE FLOCH Guillaume, « Les organisations internationales et le Pacte Mondial », *in* BOISSON DE CHAZOURNES Laurence, MAZUYER Emmanuel (dir.), *Le Pacte Mondial des Nations Unies 10 ans après*, Bruxelles, Bruylant, 2011, p. 33.

2 AGNU, « *Vers des partenariats mondiaux* », 56/76 du 24 janvier 2002, A/RES/56/76 ; 58/129 du 19 février 2004, A/RES/58/129 ; 60/215 du 29 mars 2006, A/RES/60/215 ; 62/211 du 11 mars 2008, A/RES/62/211 ; 64/223 du 25 mars 2010, A/RES/64/223 ; 66/223 du 22 décembre 2011, A/RES/66/223 ; « *Réforme des achats* », Résolution 59/288 du 29 avril 2005, A/RES/59/288 ; « *Document final du Sommet mondial de 2005* », Résolution 60/1 du 24 octobre 2005, A/RES/60/1 ; « *Action préventive et lutte contre la corruption et le transfert d'avoirs d'origine illicite et restitution de ces avoirs, en particulier aux pays d'origine, conformément à la Convention des Nations Unies contre la corruption* », Résolution 60/207 du 16 mars 2006, A/RES/60/207 ; « *Nouveau partenariat pour le développement de l'Afrique : progrès accomplis dans la mise en œuvre et appui international* », Résolution 65/284 du 16 août 2011, A/RES/65/284.

3 <http://unglobalcompact.org/AboutTheGC/Government_Support/recognition_by_the_g8.html> (consulté le 15/05/2012).

mutuellement se soutenir et même se renforcer. Il proposa alors aux dirigeants économiques rassemblés à Davos pour le Forum économique mondial, d'initier *« a global compact of shared values and principles, which will give a human face to the global market »*[4]. Plus concrètement, le Pacte Mondial est un texte énonçant dix principes relatifs aux droits de l'Homme, aux droits au travail, à la protection de l'environnement et à la lutte contre la corruption, que les adhérents sont invités à respecter et promouvoir dans leur sphère d'influence.

Pionnier en la matière, le Pacte Mondial est aujourd'hui, avec plus de 10 300 participants[5], la plus large initiative de responsabilité sociale des entreprises au monde. Bien loin de porter atteinte au mécanisme, la crise économique l'a révélé encore plus pertinent qu'auparavant. Le Pacte Mondial a d'ailleurs enregistré de nombreuses adhésions en 2009[6]. Le Pacte Mondial semble donc « répondre à un réel besoin social, celui de combler une lacune dans la gestion de la mondialisation »[7].

Mais quelle lacune pour quel besoin social ? Un sondage organisé par le Bureau du Pacte Mondial en 2010 révèle que la première motivation d'adhésion au Pacte est d'« *increase trust in company* », alors que

---

4 Discours du Secrétaire Général des Nations Unies, 31 janvier 1999, SG/SM/6881, disponible en ligne : <http://www.un.org/News/Press/docs/1999/19990201.sgsm6881.html> (consulté le 25/06/2012).

5 Le 25/06/2012, il y a 10362 membres du Pacte Mondial. Notons qu'il ne s'agit pas uniquement d'entreprises, qui sont à ce jour majoritaire (6974 entreprises participantes), mais aussi d'agences onusiennes ou étatiques indépendantes, de villes, ou encore d'organisations de la société civile, telles que les Université, les syndicats, les Organisations non gouvernementales, qui sont également autorisées à devenir membres.

6 Bureau du Pacte Mondial, *Annual Review 2009* (Anniversary Edition), pp. 10-12.

7 GHERARI Habib, « Le profil juridique et politique du Pacte Mondial », *in* BOISSON DE CHAZOURNES Laurence, MAZUYER Emmanuel (dir.), *Le Pacte Mondial des Nations Unies 10 ans après*, *op.cit.*, p. 9.

l'« *integration of sustainability issues* » n'arrive qu'en deuxième position et « *address humanitarian concerns* » en cinquième[8]. On comprend alors aisément les inquiétudes et les critiques à l'égard du Pacte. Selon ses détracteurs, il offrirait aux participants un label onusien prestigieux sans grande contrepartie, profitant alors davantage aux entreprises qu'à la société mondiale dans son ensemble[9].

Certes, le Pacte Mondial n'impose aucune obligation de respecter les droits de l'Homme. Reposant sur une approche résolument volontariste – certainement condition de son succès[10] – l'adhésion au Pacte Mondial est facultative et les principes qu'ils comportent ne sont pas contraignants pour les adhérents (I). Ce caractère volontariste permet toutefois la mise en place d'une sanction *via* un mécanisme d'« *accomptabilité* » des participants. Ce mécanisme pourrait effectivement remplir son objectif de promotion des droits de l'Homme, de forum de dialogue et d'identification des bonnes pratiques. Il se révèle toutefois imparfait, notamment en raison de son manque de notoriété (II). Le Pacte pourrait toutefois participer à l'émergence d'obligations, éventuellement internationales, des entreprises en matière de droits de l'Homme (III).

---

8 Bureau du Pacte Mondial, *Annual Review 2009* (Anniversary Edition), p. 13.

9 GHERARI Habib, « Le profil juridique et politique du Pacte Mondial », *op. cit.*, p. 28 ; MAUREL Olivier, *La responsabilité des entreprises en matière de droits de l'homme – II. Etat des lieux et perspectives d'action publique*, études de la Commission nationale consultative des droits de l'homme, 2008, p. 166, disponible en ligne : http://www.cncdh.fr/IMG/pdf/Etude_Responsabilite_des_entreprises.pdf (consulté le 25/06/2012).

10 DEUMIER Pascale, « La question de la sanction dans le Pacte Mondial », *in* BOISSON DE CHAZORNES Laurence, MAZUYER Emmanuel (dir.), *Le Pacte Mondial des Nations Unies 10 ans après*, *op. cit.*, p. 157.

I. Absence d'obligation substantielle en matière de droits de l'Homme pour les participants au Pacte Mondial

L'absence d'obligation résultant du Pacte n'est pas un tabou. En effet, la position du bureau des Nations Unies gérant le mécanisme *via* son site internet est on ne peut plus claire :

> [l]e Pacte Mondial est une initiative à caractère strictement facultatif. Il ne s'agit nullement de contrôler les entreprises ni de leur imposer une conduite ou une activité quelconque.[11]

Il ajoute que :

> [l]e Pacte Mondial n'est pas un instrument de mesure ou d'évaluation. Il ne délivre pas de certificat ni ne juge les mérites des participants.[12]

L'absence d'obligation est également révélée par la formulation incitative des principes :

> [l]e Pacte Mondial *invite* les entreprises à adopter, soutenir et appliquer dans leur sphère d'influence un ensemble de *valeurs fondamentales*, dans les domaines des droits de l'homme, des normes de travail et de l'environnement, et de lutte contre la corruption.[13]

Concernant plus spécifiquement les droits de l'Homme,

> 1. Les entreprises sont *invitées* à promouvoir et à respecter la protection du droit international relatif aux droits de l'Homme dans leur sphère d'influence ; et

---

11 Bureau du Pacte Mondial, « *Foire aux questions* », disponible en ligne : <http://www.unglobalcompact.org/Languages/french/foire_aux_questions.html> (consulté le 25/06/2012).

12 *Idem.*

13 Texte du Pacte Mondial (italiques ajoutées), disponible en ligne : <http://unglobalcompact.org/Languages/french/dix_principes.html> (consulté le 25/06/2012).

> 2. A *veiller* à ce que leurs propres compagnies ne se rendent pas complices de violations des droits de l'Homme.[14]

L'adhésion au Pacte Mondial n'est par ailleurs subordonnée à aucun respect préalable des droits de l'Homme[15].

Dans la mesure où le Pacte Mondial fait explicitement référence aux instruments internationaux dont sont tirés les principes, des obligations pourraient être déduites par renvoi auxdits instruments. En matière de droits de l'Homme, il est toutefois fait référence à la Déclaration universelle des droits de l'Homme, texte lui aussi non contraignant.

Cette approche résolument volontariste du Pacte avait suscité au moment de sa mise en place de vives critiques des Organisations non gouvernementales (ONG) pour qui :

> le global Compact opère un reversement inquiétant : les droits de l'homme sont proposés aux entreprises comme une disposition facultative, alors qu'ils devraient s'imposer à elles, puisqu'ils sont par essence les valeurs communes de l'humanité. Par la proposition du Global Compact, l'ONU accepte, voire encourage l'assujettissement de l'intérêt général à l'intérêt particulier. Elle signe là une grave démission de la communauté internationale[16].

Il semble dès lors important de préciser qu'absence de caractère obligatoire et contraignant du Pacte Mondial ne signifie pas absence d'obligation en matière de droits de l'Homme[17].

D'une part, le Pacte Mondial ne se substitue pas aux mécanismes interétatiques et nationaux de protection des droits de l'Homme et ne

---

14 *Idem.*

15 Seuls les fabricants de bombes à fragmentations ou de mines anti-personnelles, interdites par le droit international, et les entreprises faisant l'objet de sanctions de la part des Nations Unies sont exclues du mécanisme.

16 Propos de la FIDH, cité in GHERARI Habib, « Le profil juridique et politique du Pacte Mondial », *op.cit.*, p. 13.

17 V. notamment la contribution de Caroline BRETON dans ce même ouvrage.

met pas en cause la compétence première des Etats en la matière[18]. Ainsi, le Pacte Mondial n'est qu'un complément à la législation nationale[19]. De plus, les droits de l'Homme déploient aujourd'hui un « effet horizontal » dans les relations interindividuelles et sont devenus « [des] norme[s] de comportement des acteurs privés » par le truchement des obligations positives des Etats[20]. Les Etats ont notamment l'obligation de faire respecter les droits de l'Homme par les entreprises agissant dans le ressort de leurs juridictions[21]. Ainsi, les obligations internationales des Etats en matière de droits de l'Homme

---

18 Le principe est notamment rappelé dans les résolutions de l'AGNU concernant les partenariats privés (A/RES/56/76 ; A/RES/58/129 ; A/RES/60/215 ; A/RES/62/211 ; A/RES/64/223 ; A/RES/66/223 ; A/RES/65/284) et dans les rapports successifs du Représentant spécial du Secrétaire général chargé de la question des droits de l'homme et des sociétés transnationales et autres entreprises, John Ruggie, ainsi que dans les « *Principes directeurs relatifs aux entreprises et aux droits de l'homme : mise en œuvre du cadre de référence 'protéger, respecter et réparer' des Nations Unies* », élaborés par lui puis endossés par le Conseil des droits de l'Homme de l'ONU le 17 juin 2011 (A/HRC/17/L.17/Rev.1).

19 Latham & Watkins LLP, « The Importance of Voluntarism », disponible sur le site officiel du Pacte Mondial : <http://unglobalcompact.org/HowToParticipate/Business_Participation/the_importance_of_voluntarism.html> (consulté le 25/06/2012).

20 V. notamment : CCPR, *Observation générale n°20*, §2 ; *Observation générale n°31*, §6 ; CEDAW, *Recommandation générale n°19*, § 9 ; CEDH, *Ilhan c. Turquie*, arrêt du 27 juin 2000, §76 ; SUDRE Frédéric, *Droit européen et international des droits de l'homme*, Paris, PUF, *2006, 8e édition revue et augmentée*, pp. 237-248 ; VAN DROOGHENBROECK Sébastien, « L'horizontalisation des droits de l'homme », *in* DUMONT Hugues, OST François, VAN DROOGHENBROECK Sébastien (dir.), *La responsabilité, face cachée des droits de l'homme*, Bruxelles, Bruylant, 2005, p. 356.

21 « *Principes directeurs relatifs aux entreprises et aux droits de l'homme mise en œuvre du cadre de référence 'protéger, respecter et réparer' des Nations Unies* », Principes I.A.1., *in* Rapport du Représentant spécial du Secrétaire général chargé de la question des droits de l'homme et des sociétés transnationales et autres entreprises, John Ruggie, 21 mars 2011, A/HRC/17/31, p. 8.

doivent se traduire dans l'ordre juridique interne par des obligations destinées aux personnes privées.

D'autre part, le Pacte Mondial n'empêche nullement l'émergence d'une responsabilité internationale des personnes privées, physiques ou morales, autonome de celle des Etats, et pourrait même y contribuer [22] . Notons que l'existence d'une telle responsabilité internationale des individus est aujourd'hui contestée, tout comme leur qualité de sujet de droit international. Le développement du droit international pénal – qui interdit et punit les violations massives des droits de l'Homme commises par des acteurs non-étatiques – ainsi que le développement du droit international des droits de l'Homme et du droit des investissements, qui confèrent aux individus des droits, nous semblent toutefois confirmer cette qualité de sujet, puisqu'ils ont ainsi la « capacité d'être titulaire de droits et devoirs internationaux et [...] de se prévaloir de [leurs] droits »[23].

Même si une telle responsabilité internationale des entreprises existait, force est de constater l'absence de mécanisme – juridictions pénales mises à part – de mise en œuvre de celle-ci[24]. D'ailleurs, les Principes directeurs relatifs aux entreprises et aux droits de l'homme – qui demeurent frileux sur l'existence de véritables obligations internationales des entreprises en la matière, « responsabilité des

---

22 ASCENSIO Hervé, « L'apparition d'une responsabilité internationale des entreprises », *in* BOISSON DE CHAZOURNES Laurence, MAZUYER Emmanuel (dir.), *Le Pacte Mondial des Nations Unies 10 ans après*, *op. cit.*, pp. 167-184.

23 CIJ, *Réparation des dommages subis au service des Nations Unies*, avis consultatif du 11 avril 1949, CIJ *Rec* 1949, p. 178. V. aussi, DUPUY Pierre-Marie, *L'unité du droit international, cours général de droit international public*, *RCADI*, 2002, t..297, p. 100 ; VAURS-CHAUMETTE Anne-Laure, *Les sujets du droit international pénal : vers une nouvelle définition de la personnalité juridique internationale ?*, Paris, Pedone, 2009, 545 p.

24 Nous ne soulignons pas uniquement ici l'absence de juges compétents pour statuer sur une éventuelle responsabilité internationale mais l'absence même d'engagement de la responsabilité internationale et sa conséquence, la réparation, ne serait-ce que par la satisfaction.

entreprises de respecter les droits de l'homme » y étant synonyme de « faire preuve de diligence raisonnable pour s'assurer de ne pas porter atteinte aux droits d'autrui »[25] – désignent l'Etat comme compétent pour protéger les individus contre les atteintes des entreprises, notamment par la mise en place de voies de recours[26]. Autrement dit, le respect effectif des droits de l'Homme repose essentiellement sur la volonté des Etats de respecter et faire respecter les droits de l'Homme, car l'Etat a en réalité « la compétence du dernier mot et est le 'bras séculier' seul capable de donner vie à la norme internationale»[27].

L'analyse pourrait s'arrêter ici, le Pacte Mondial n'étant ni obligatoire, ni contraignant, il ne peut être efficace. C'est toutefois sous-estimer d'autres éléments qui font l'efficacité de la norme. En effet,

> [l]e souci de notre réputation, c'est-à-dire de nous-mêmes dans le regard et le discours des autres, dirige notre comportement quotidien sans doute plus que les règles du droit ou les maximes objectives de la moralité. L'entreprise n'échappe pas plus que les autres à cette forme de contrôle social. Elle y est même davantage sensible dans la mesure où ses résultats sont largement fonction de son image de marque.[28]

---

25 Rapport du Représentant spécial du Secrétaire général chargé de la question des droits de l'homme et des sociétés transnationales et autres entreprises, John Ruggie, 21 mars 2011, A/HRC/17/31, p. 4.

26 « *Principes directeurs relatifs aux entreprises et aux droits de l'homme mise en œuvre du cadre de référence 'protéger, respecter et réparer' des Nations Unies* », v. notamment Principes I. (Obligation de protéger les droits de l'homme incombant à l'Etat) et III. (Accès à des voies de recours), *in* Rapport du Représentant spécial du Secrétaire général chargé de la question des droits de l'homme et des sociétés transnationales et autres entreprises, John Ruggie, 21 mars 2011, A/HRC/17/31.

27 PELLET Alain, « 'Droits-de-l'hommisme' et droit international », *Droits fondamentaux*, n°1, juillet-décembre 2001, publication en ligne : <http://www.droits-fondamentaux.org/spip.php?article27> (consultée le 25/06/2012).

28 BERNS Thomas, DOCQUIR Pierre-François, FRYDMAN Benoît, HENNEBEL Ludovic, LEWKOWICZ Grégory, *Responsabilités des entreprises et corégulation*, Bruxelles, Bruylant, 2007, p. 22.

Le point de départ du Global Compact est justement l'insuffisance du « *hard law* » et de la contrainte, et tente davantage de séduire les entreprises en leur offrant un partenariat prestigieux. Son objectif est de contourner les Etats et d'encourager les entreprises à devenir des vecteurs de bonnes pratiques, notamment en les incitant à ne plus tirer d'avantages économiques des violations des droits de l'Homme, tolérées dans certains Etats en raison de leur faiblesse ou de leurs failles règlementaires. Outre que la « Soft Law » semble devenir « le mot d'ordre le plus populaire du monde économique globalisé du moment »[29], le caractère facultatif du Pacte nous semble à ce titre une condition *sine qua non* de sa réussite, car il permet d'introduire la sanction par l'exclusion du mécanisme. Le Pacte Mondial serait ainsi « un mécanisme de droit 'doux' (incitatif et sans obligation), sans doute de droit 'flou' (sans précision) mais pas forcément de droit 'mou' (sans sanction). »[30]

II. Le Pacte Mondial, un mécanisme d'*accomptabilité*[31] des entreprises en matière de droits de l'Homme

Comme il vient d'être établi, le Pacte Mondial n'impose aucune obligation substantielle de respecter les droits de l'Homme. Il impose

---

29 THOUVENIN Jean-Marc « Spécificité dans son élaboration : au confluent de la volonté et de la viralité », *in* THOUVENIN Jean-Marc, TREBILCOCK Anne (dir.), *Droit International Social,* à paraître.

30 MAZUYER Emmanuel, « La mise en œuvre du pacte – Quelques leçons d'une étude relative aux principes du travail », *in* BOISSON DE CHAZORNES Laurence, MAZUYER Emmanuel (dir.), *Le Pacte Mondial des Nations Unies 10 ans après*, *op. cit.*, p. 87.

31 Cette expression, proposant une traduction du terme anglais « accountability », est empruntée à Anne Robert, *in* ROBERT Anne, *La responsabilité politique individuelle des membres du gouvernement en France, Allemagne, Grande-Bretagne*, thèse en cotutelle (Universités Paris Ouest Nanterre La Défense et Universität Postdam), en cours.

en revanche une obligation formelle aux adhérents, celle de communiquer.

En effet, depuis 2003, les entreprises adhérentes doivent publier tous les ans une communication sur le Progrès (COP), faisant état de leurs avancées dans l'intégration des dix principes du Pacte[32]. Le degré de communication de l'entreprise détermine son « statut » sur le site Internet du Pacte Mondial. Les entreprises communicant annuellement sont *a minima* « *GC Active* ». Elles peuvent également se déclarer « *GC Advanced* » en décrivant comment elles remplissent ou projettent de remplir les vingt-quatre critères requis pour le niveau[33]. L'avancement substantiel relève donc de l'autoévaluation. Les entreprises ne soumettant pas de COP dans le délai imparti sont désignées « *non-communicating* »[34]. Si après un an, le « *non-communicating* » ne soumet toujours pas de COP, il est radié du Pacte Mondial[35]. Toutes les entreprises expulsées doivent à nouveau postuler pour rejoindre l'initiative.

La sanction, rétrogradation au statut de « *non-communicating* » ou radiation, repose donc exclusivement sur l'exécution d'une obligation formelle de communiquer, mais à aucun moment le contenu des rapports n'est étudié afin de déterminer si l'entreprise intègre effectivement ou non les principes du Pacte Mondial. Certes, communiquer sur le progrès nécessite d'avoir des choses à dire. En ce

32 Les COP doivent comprendre : 1) une déclaration confirmant l'adhésion au Pacte Mondial ; 2) une description des mesures concrètes que l'entreprise a prises depuis son adhésion ou sa dernière communication pour appliquer les principes du Pacte et établir des partenariats qui concourent aux grands objectifs des Nations Unies ; 3) une mesure des résultats obtenus ou attendus. Si une COP n'adresse pas une ou plusieurs des quatre catégories (droits de l'Homme, droit du travail, environnement, lutte contre la corruption), une raison explicative doit figurer dans la COP afin de justifier cette omission (« rapporter ou expliquer »).

33 Pour plus d'informations sur le niveau « GC Advanced » : <http://unglobalcompact.org/COP/differentiation/GCAdvanced_level.html> (consulté le 25/06/2012).

34 Un « délai de grâce » de un an supplémentaire est donné aux entreprises qui viennent d'accéder au Pacte.

35 Procédure introduite en janvier 2011.

sens, le Pacte Mondial pourrait instaurer une obligation de moyen à l'égard des participants[36].

Le système ne tient cependant pas compte des différences fondamentales de structure des différentes entreprises adhérentes. Par exemple, l'élaboration des COP sera plus délicate pour les petites entreprises qui ne sont pas habituées à l'exercice[37], alors qu'une société transnationale élabore généralement déjà un rapport annuel ou un rapport de développement durable, auquel elle pourra intégrer la COP. De même, plus une entreprise est importante, plus sa sphère d'influence, et par là-même ses possibilités de progrès, augmentent. La dimension transnationale de certains adhérents porte toutefois aussi intrinsèquement le risque d'abus du Pacte Mondial. En effet, une société transnationale pourrait soumettre des COP portant sur les améliorations effectuées au siège de l'entreprise, tout en violant les droits fondamentaux de ses employés dans ses usines. Il n'est d'ailleurs pas étonnant que les COP soient généralement rédigées par les services de communication des entreprises.

Afin de lutter contre ce phénomène du « *bluewash* »[38], le mécanisme des COP a été complété par des mesures d'intégrité, dont la mise en

36 ASCENSIO Hervé, « L'apparition d'une responsabilité internationale des entreprises », *in* BOISSON DE CHAZOURNES Laurence, MAZUYER Emmanuel (dir.), *Le Pacte Mondial des Nations Unies 10 ans après*, *op. cit.*, p. 170.

37 La « plateforme d'apprentissage », animée par les réseaux locaux et le bureau du Pacte Mondial, peut en partie pallier à ces écarts en offrant aux entreprises nouvellement adhérentes une assistance pour la soumission des premières COP.

38 Terme utilisé en référence au « *Greenwashing* » (écoblanchiment), pour désigner l'adhésion à des principes sociaux dans le seul but d'améliorer l'image de l'entreprise. V. notamment: BIGGE David M, « Bring on the bluewash: a social constructivist argument against Nike v. Kasky to attack the Un Global Compact », *International Legal Perspective*, 2004, vol. 6, pp. 6-19 ; RASCHE Andreas, « 'A Necessary Supplement': What the United Nations Global Compact Is and Is Not », *Business and Society,* 2009, Vol. 48, No. 4, pp. 511-537.

place alimente malheureusement les soupçons sur le caractère purement marketing de certaines adhésions[39].

Devenir un mécanisme d'évaluation de la performance des entreprises en matière de développement durable ou encore un mécanisme d'engagement de leur responsabilité pour violation des droits de l'Homme n'a certes jamais été une ambition du Pacte Mondial, mais la protection de son intégrité et de sa crédibilité, ainsi que celles de l'ONU, est indispensable. C'est pourquoi toute personne peut contacter par écrit le bureau du Pacte Mondial afin de porter à son attention un comportement manifestement incompatible avec un des dix principes du Pacte. Après un examen de la recevabilité de la plainte, le bureau prend contact avec l'entreprise mise en cause afin qu'elle présente ses observations sur la situation. En l'absence de réponse et aussi longtemps que le silence persiste, l'entreprise sera listée *« non-communicating »*. Le bureau du Pacte Mondial peut également considérer que la participation de l'entreprise au mécanisme porte atteinte à la réputation du Pacte et de l'ONU et, pour cette raison, « expulser » ladite entreprise. Pour être à nouveau « *GC active* », l'entreprise devra démontrer que son comportement est à présent en adéquation avec les valeurs du Pacte. Cette procédure manque toutefois de transparence puisqu'elle est totalement confidentielle.

Ce « dispositif juridique minimaliste »[40] est-il efficace ? Il pourrait l'être car il joue sur l'effet « *shaming* », or « en droit des affaires, il est souvent soutenu que l'atteinte à la réputation est une sanction bien plus redoutable que la sanction pécuniaire »[41]. Encore faut-il que le dispositif jouisse d'une notoriété suffisante pour que la perte du statut « *GC active* » et l'exclusion portent effectivement atteinte à la

---

39 DEUMIER Pascale, « La question de la sanction dans le Pacte Mondial », *op. cit.*, p. 163.

40 GHERARI Habib, « Le profil juridique et politique du Pacte Mondial », *op. cit.*, p. 10.

41 DEUMIER Pascale, « La question de la sanction dans le Pacte Mondial », *op. cit.*, p. 164.

réputation. Or, c'est là la principale faiblesse du Pacte Mondial : il est trop peu connu, y compris dans le milieu académique[42].

Quant aux autres sanctions associées à la perte du statut « *GC active* », elles n'apparaissent pas plus dissuasives. Les membres « *non-communicating* » et, *a fortiori*, les entreprises radiées, ne sont pas autorisés à participer aux activités du Pacte Mondial ou à utiliser son logo. Or les évènements sont peu nombreux[43] et le logo est d'ores et déjà très peu utilisé par les participants. Ceci est peut-être du aux conditions, extrêmement restrictives, d'utilisation de ce logo[44]. Les participants doivent notamment demander l'autorisation du bureau du Pacte Mondial pour chaque utilisation qu'ils souhaitent en faire. Cette politique évite certainement que les Nations Unies soient associées à des événements qu'elles ne cautionnent pas. Elle réduit cependant d'autant les occasions de faire connaitre le Pacte Mondial, via les sites Internet des entreprises ou encore des évènements médiatisés. Le logo, à l'instar du Pacte Mondial, est d'ailleurs totalement inconnu du grand public.

Renforcer la notoriété du Pacte Mondial apparait nécessaire pour lui offrir les outils juridiques à la hauteur de son ambition politique. Car un mécanisme inconnu finit par perdre de son importance, même marketing, et le Pacte Mondial risque tout simplement de tomber dans l'oubli. Les chiffres révèlent du reste peut-être d'ores et déjà un désintérêt des participants pour l'initiative. En juin 2012, il y avait 6974 entreprises participantes. Parmi elles, 1410, soit près d'un quart des participants, étaient « *non-communicating* »[45]. Depuis la mise en

42 DAUDET Yves, « Perspectives », *in* BOISSON DE CHAZOURNES Laurence, MAZUYER Emmanuel (dir.), *Le Pacte Mondial des Nations Unies 10 ans après*, *op. cit.*, p. 185.

43 Pour une liste des événements de l'année 2010 : Bureau du Pacte Mondial, *Annual Review 2010*, p. 56.

44 Pour en savoir davantage sur l'utilisation du logo, v. : <http://www.unglobalcompact.org/AboutTheGC/Global_Compact_Logo/index.html> (consulté le 25/06/2012).

45 La liste des participants est consultable en ligne : http://unglobalcompact.org/participants/search (consulté le 25/06/2012).

place du Pacte, 2048 entreprises, soit un quart des participants, ont été expulsées[46].

Comme indiqué sur son site internet :

> [l]e Pacte Mondial n'évalue pas lui-même les performances des entreprises. L'objectif est de mettre au point une plateforme publique permettant aux parties prenantes (par exemple, les investisseurs, les employés et/ou les consommateurs) de faire des choix plus éclairés, afin que les entreprises soient à la hauteur de leur engagement envers le Pacte Mondial.[47]

Les COP sont d'ailleurs envisagés comme des communications avec les parties prenantes des participants. C'est pourquoi elles doivent être intégrées à un rapport public (rapport annuel, rapport de développement durable) et à défaut être publiées sur le site Internet de l'entreprise, en plus de leur publication sur celui du Pacte Mondial.

Or, dans les conditions actuelles, la relation redditionnelle ne joue pas pleinement son rôle. En effet, « [l]'élément essentiel dans une relation redditionnelle n'est pas l'obligation de rendre des comptes, c'est l'existence d'une autorité qui peut les exiger »[48]. Il s'agit donc d'impliquer davantage les ONG afin qu'elles jouent pleinement leur rôle en évaluant les rapports et en soulevant d'éventuels abus. Une telle action des ONG permettrait également d'identifier les bonnes pratiques, afin d'identifier un cadre transparent et stable à la responsabilité sociale des entreprises.

---

46 Bureau du Pacte Mondial, *Annual Review 2010*, p. 19.

47 Bureau du Pacte Mondial , rubrique « *Communications sur le progrès* », disponible en ligne : <http://unglobalcompact.org/Languages/french/communication_progres.html> (consulté le 25/06/2012).

48 Stan CORBETT, « La responsabilité ministérielle et la loi sur la gestion des finances publiques : l'obligation constitutionnelle de rendre compte des dépenses gouvernementales », CISPAA, vol. 3 (Liens : responsabilité et reddition de comptes), p. 271, disponible en ligne : <http://publications.gc.ca/collections/Collection/GomeryII/Etudes3/fr_CISPAA_Vol3_5.pdf> (consulté le 25/06/2012).

L'implication du grand public nous semble en revanche illusoire, en l'absence d'évaluation et d'un véritable label en résultant[49]. Il ne faut bien sûr pas minimiser le rôle des « consommateurs politiques »,

> qui ne déterminent plus leur choix en fonction du prix et de la qualité intrinsèque des produits, mais également en tenant compte des conditions dans lesquelles l'entreprise réalise ses activités[50].

Le succès des labels « BIO » ou « commerce équitable » en témoigne. Mais pour que cette nouvelle « main invisible » fasse son œuvre, l'information est indispensable pour que le choix soit éclairé. On imagine toutefois mal un consommateur consulter les COP des entreprises avant de faire ses courses. Dès lors, le développement d'indicateurs fiables permettant de mesurer le degré d'engagement des participants du Pacte Mondial et, idéalement, d'un label y associé permettrait une véritable implication du consommateur dans le mécanisme et renforcerait certainement l'efficacité du Pacte.

III. Vers des obligations internationales des entreprises en matière de droits de l'Homme ?

La mondialisation a indéniablement conduit à l'émancipation des entreprises et au recul de l'Etat providence. La règlementation mondiale n'a cependant pas suivi. Dans ce contexte, il était clair pour Kofi Annan que :

---

49 Notons qu'il existe d'ores et déjà des labels sociaux, en Belgique notamment. Il est donc possible d'évaluer la durabilité et la citoyenneté d'un produit ou d'une entreprise.

50 BERNS Thomas, DOCQUIR Pierre-François, FRYDMAN Benoît, HENNEBEL Ludovic, LEWKOWICZ Grégory, *Responsabilités des entreprises et corégulation*, *op. cit.*, p. 20.

> sans l'engagement et le soutien actif des entreprises, les valeurs universelles [...] risquaient de demeurer lettres mortes, régulièrement célébrées mais tout aussi régulièrement bafouées ou ignorées.[51]

Or, sans les Etats, il serait impossible pour l'ONU d'imposer des obligations internationales aux entreprises en la matière, et encore moins de sanctionner leurs violations.

> Dans ce contexte peu satisfaisant et peu contraignant, le mouvement de la responsabilité sociale des entreprises encourage les entreprises à affirmer et à assumer volontairement, indépendamment de toute obligation juridique, une responsabilité au moins morale en matière sociale, de protection de l'environnement ou de respect et de promotion des droits de l'Homme.[52]

Ces engagements sociaux ou moraux pourront-ils un jour se muer en obligations juridiques ? Plusieurs éléments vont dans le sens d'obligations futures, voire d'obligations d'ores et déjà en gestation[53].

En premier lieu, l'Etat peut toujours intervenir dans sa fonction régulatrice pour imposer ou favoriser un comportement respectueux des droits de l'Homme. La commission européenne travaille notamment actuellement sur un futur texte européen imposant aux

---

51 GHERARI Habib, « Le profil juridique et politique du Pacte Mondial », *op. cit.*, p. 21.

52 BERNS Thomas, DOCQUIR Pierre-François, FRYDMAN Benoît, HENNEBEL Ludovic, LEWKOWICZ Grégory, *Responsabilités des entreprises et corégulation*, Bruxelles, Bruylant, 2007, p. 11.

53 Pour une présentation détaillée des possibles réceptions des codes de conduite par les sources « classiques », v. : FRYDMAN Benoît, LEWKOWICZ Grégory, « Les codes de conduite : source du Droit global ? », *in* CARTUYVELS Yves et al., (ed.), *Les sources du droit revisitées*, Bruxelles, Presses des facultés Universitaires de Saint Louis, à paraître en 2013 ; MAZUYER Emmanuelle, « La force normative des instruments adoptés dans le cadre de la responsabilité sociale de l'entreprise », *in* THIBIERGE Catherine et alii, *La force normative – Naissance d'un concept*, Paris, LGDJ / Bruxelles, Bruylant, 2009, pp. 580-584.

entreprises cotées la publication de rapports non financiers[54]. La directive 2003/51/CE incite d'ores et déjà les entreprises à présenter des informations non-financières dans leur rapport annuel [55]. L'existence d'une contrainte règlementaire de présenter des informations concernant la politique sociale de l'entreprise pourrait emporter

> des conséquences juridiques non négligeables, dans la mesure où l'entreprise qui néglige de fournir les informations requises ou qui fournit des informations inexactes, peut s'exposer à des sanctions, notamment pénales, prévues de longues dates par les lois sur la publication des comptes des entreprises[56].

De même, une entreprise qui ferait de la publicité sur sa participation au Pacte sans en être signataire ou en ayant un comportement manifestement incompatible[57] avec les principes qu'il édicte, pourrait être sanctionnée pour publicité ou pratique commerciale trompeuse[58].

---

54 V. la page Internet relative à la Responsabilité sociale des entreprises : <http://ec.europa.eu/enterprise/policies/sustainable-business/corporate-social-responsibility/index_fr.htm> (consulté le 25/06/2012).

55 Directive 2003/51/CE du Parlement européen et du Conseil du 18 juin 2003 modifiant les directives 78/660/CEE, 83/349/CEE, 86/635/CEE et 91/674/CEE du Conseil sur les comptes annuels et les comptes consolidés de certaines catégories de sociétés, des banques et autres établissements financiers et des entreprises d'assurance (Texte présentant de l'intérêt pour l'EEE).

56 BERNS Thomas, DOCQUIR Pierre-François, FRYDMAN Benoît, HENNEBEL Ludovic, LEWKOWICZ Grégory, *Responsabilités des entreprises et corégulation*, *op. cit.*, 2007, p. 34.

57 C'était notamment le cas dans la célèbre affaire *Kashy v. Nike* devant les juridictions américaines.

58 V. également la Directive 2005/29/CE du Parlement européen et du Conseil du 11 mai 2005 relative aux pratiques commerciales déloyales des entreprises vis-à-vis des consommateurs dans le marché intérieur et modifiant la directive 84/450/CEE du Conseil et les directives 97/7/CE, 98/27/CE et 2002/65/CE du Parlement européen et du Conseil et le règlement (CE) n°2006/2004 du Parlement européen et du Conseil («directive sur les pratiques commerciales déloyales») (Texte présentant de l'intérêt pour l'EEE).

En second lieu, le Pacte Mondial pourrait être un catalyseur de processus coutumier. En effet, le mécanisme favorise

> les comportements mimétiques pour dupliquer ce que fait la concurrence, surtout si l'on croit que l'action en cause est porteuse commercialement parlant[59].

A ce titre, il semble bien institutionnaliser les deux éléments du processus coutumier[60] : la pratique, en ce qu'il incite les entreprises à avoir un comportement respectueux des droits de l'Homme, et l'observation, en ce qu'il les incite à observer la pratique des autres par l'organisation de réseau et la publication des COP. Si le mécanisme était accompagné d'un mécanisme d'identification des bonnes pratiques, il inciterait encore davantage à l'uniformisation autour de l'observation d'une pratique de référence. Cette observation provoquera, potentiellement, la conviction en l'existence d'une obligation justifiant ladite pratique, conviction du droit constitutive de la norme coutumière. A l'issu de cette opération coutumière, les personnes privées morales seraient destinataires d'obligations internationales en matière de droits de l'Homme. Il s'agira ensuite de déterminer quel forum international ou global pourrait être compétent pour institutionnaliser la norme coutumière ainsi formée et en contrôler le respect.

Ainsi, le Pacte Mondial, à l'instar de tout mécanisme de responsabilité sociale des entreprises, incite ces dernières à concilier, à leur rythme, rendement économique et civisme. Il joue ainsi pleinement son rôle de gestion des risques et d'anticipation des éventuelles réformes – qu'elles soient nationales, internationales ou globales – qui leur imposeraient des obligations qu'elles ne seraient pas encore en mesure

---

59 GHERARI Habib, « Le profil juridique et politique du Pacte Mondial », *in* BOISSON DE CHAZORNES Laurence, MAZUYER Emmanuel (dir.), *Le Pacte Mondial des Nations Unies 10 ans après*, *op. cit.*, p. 28.

60 SOUSSAN Audrey, *L'identification de la coutume de droit international pénal*, thèse (Université Paris Ouest Nanterre la Défense), en cours (soutenance prévue en décembre 2012).

de remplir. Cela peut paraître décevant et il est légitime d'attendre du mécanisme une avancée substantielle pour la société mondiale dans son ensemble. Davantage d'engagement politique de la part des entreprises et des Etats, qui se montrent sans doute trop conciliants avec leurs entreprises, notamment lorsqu'elles agissent en territoire étranger[61], serait sans doute bienvenu. Toutefois, le Pacte Mondial a le mérite de les inciter à faire un pas en direction des droits de l'Homme. Le mécanisme serait ainsi, à l'instar de l'Organisation des Nations Unies, à laquelle il appartient, « *not created to take mankind to heaven, but to save humanity from hell*»[62].

61 V. la contribution de Caroline BRETON dans ce même ouvrage.

62 Propos de Dag Hammarskjöld au sujet de l'Organisation des Nations Unies dont il était alors le Secrétaire Général.

La responsabilité civile extraterritoriale des entreprises multinationales au regard des droits de l'homme

Caroline BRETON *

Depuis les revendications pour un « Nouvel ordre économique mondial » dans les années 1970, la question du contrôle des activités des sociétés transnationales eu égard aux droits de l'homme est devenue récurrente. En effet, différents instruments de *soft law*, adoptés par la suite[1], les ont fortement encouragées à s'y conformer. Le débat s'est de nouveau intensifié dans les années 1990 grâce aux initiatives lancées par les Nations Unies dans le cadre du Pacte mondial (*Global Compact*)[2] ou adoptées par la Sous-commission pour la promotion et la protection des droits de l'homme des Nations Unies[3]. Ces initiatives, entièrement volontaires, ont certes eu le mérite

* Doctorante à l'Université Paris Ouest Nanterre la Défense, membre du CEDIN.

1 Tels que les Principes directeurs de l'Organisation de coopération et de développement économiques (OCDE) à l'intention des entreprises multinationales, ou encore la Déclaration de Principes tripartite sur les entreprises multinationales et la politique sociale préparée par l'Organisation internationale du travail (OIT).

2 V. la contribution de Jeanne DUPENDANT dans le présent ouvrage.

3 Notamment la résolution définissant les « Normes sur la responsabilité en matière de droits de l'homme des sociétés transnationales et autre entreprise », v. Organisation des Nations Unies, Commission des droits de l'homme, Sous-commission de la promotion et de la protection des droits de l'homme, *Normes sur la responsabilité en matière de droits de l'homme des sociétés transnationales et autres entreprises*, E/CN.4/Sub.2/2003/12/Rev.2, adoptées à la 22e séance, le 13 août 2003 ; v. également : HARRISON James, « Human Rights and Transnational Corporations: Can More Meaningful International Obligations be Established? », *in* FAUNDEZ Julio & TAN Celine (dir.), *International Law, Economic Globalisation and Developing Countries*, Cheltenham/Northampton, Edward Elgar Publishing Ltd, 2010, p. 205-233.

d'attirer l'attention des Etats, des entreprises, et de la société civile en générale, sur cette problématique et de contribuer à la reconnaissance et à la diffusion d'une certaine éthique dans le monde des affaires. Elles ont cependant été vivement critiquées précisément parce qu'elles n'étaient pas contraignantes et donc peu susceptibles de modifier le comportement des entreprises les moins vertueuses.

Il aurait été alors envisageable que des obligations puissent naître dans le chef des Etats d'origine de ces sociétés (qui leur accordent leur nationalité) ou des Etats d'accueil de leurs activités (qui se déroulent sur leur territoire). Effectivement, des plaintes pour violations des droits de l'homme peuvent être déposées à l'encontre de cette seconde catégorie d'Etats devant le Comité des droits de l'homme des Nations Unies ou grâce aux mécanismes mis en place par l'OIT[4]. Néanmoins, il faut encore noter que ces instruments internationaux, qui ne sont obligatoires que pour les Etats Parties, voient les procédures qu'ils instituent dépourvues de l'efficacité dont elles auraient pourtant dû faire preuve, minées par le manque de moyens financiers de ces organisations, leur mauvaise accessibilité aux particuliers, ou encore par l'absence de tout suivi efficace. Ce sont les principales raisons pour lesquelles ils ont été jusqu'à présent si peu utilisés afin d'engager la responsabilité des Etats lorsque des entités opérant sur leur territoire commettent des violations en matière de droits de l'homme. Dans ce contexte, imposer directement des obligations aux sociétés transnationales est devenu un enjeu crucial.

Or, dans l'ordre juridique international, les entreprises transnationales ne disposent pas, en vertu du droit international, de la personnalité juridique, de sorte qu'elles semblent bénéficier d'une certaine immunité[5], bien sûr vivement critiquée[6]. Il n'en demeure pas

4 V. FIDH, « Section I Les mécanismes intergouvernementaux », *Entreprises et violations des droits de l'homme. Un guide pratique sur les recours existants à l'intention des victimes et des ONG*, mars 2012, p. 183, disponible en ligne : <www.fidh.org> (consulté le 06/06/2012).

5 Certains considèrent même qu'elles n'auraient que des obligations morales. v. VAN GENUGTEN Willem J.M., « The Status of Transnational Corporations in International Public Law. With Special Reference to the Case of Shell », *in*

moins que leur responsabilité peut être engagée au niveau interne dans l'Etat d'origine de la société mère ou dans l'Etat d'accueil de leurs activités. Toutefois, comme il l'a été relevé :

> les personnes affectées par les activités de l'entreprise ont une probabilité souvent faible d'obtenir réparation dans leur propre Etat, pays hôte de l'investissement. L'absence de volonté politique ou de moyens juridiques suffisants des autorités locales (absence de législation adéquate, manque d'infrastructures, politisation ou corruption du système judiciaire, inexistence de l'assistance judiciaire, etc.) – due en partie à la pression exercée par l'attrait des investissements étrangers – sont en effet courants en ce domaine. En outre, il n'est pas rare que l'intermédiaire local de l'entreprise (filiale, sous-traitant ou partenaire commercial), auteur des faits, soit insolvable ou ne soit pas assuré, ou encore que les preuves soient localisées dans le pays d'origine de la multinationale, lorsqu'elle est elle-même l'auteur des faits incriminés ou, à tout le moins, à l'origine des décisions qui ont conduit à la violation[7].

Force est alors de constater que la responsabilité civile extraterritoriale des sociétés multinationales est difficile à mettre en œuvre devant les tribunaux internes qui, d'une part, ne se déclarent encore que trop rarement compétents (I.), et qui, d'autre part, éprouvent des difficultés à retenir la responsabilité des entreprises eu égard à la structure de ces dernières (II.).

EIDE Asbjorn, BERGESEN Ole, GOYER Pia Rudolfson (Ed.), *Human Rights and the Oil Industry*, Antwerpen/Groningen/Oxford, Intersentia, 2000, pp. 71-89.

6 V. notamment : BRABANDERE Eric de, « Human Rights Obligations and Transnational Corporations: The Limits of Direct Corporate Responsibility », *Human Rights and International Legal Discourse,* vol. 4, No. 1, 2010, pp. 66-88 ; PENTIKÄINEN Merja, « Changing International 'Subjectivity' and Rights and Obligations under International Law – Status of Corporations », *Utrecht Law Review*, vol. 8, No. 1, janvier 2012, pp. 145-154.

7 FIDH, « Section II Mécanismes judiciaires », *Entreprises et violations des droits de l'homme. Un guide pratique sur les recours existants à l'intention des victimes et des ONG*, mars 2012, p. 183, disponible en ligne : <www.fidh.org> (consulté le 06/06/2012).

I. Une responsabilité civile extraterritoriale hors du champ de compétence des tribunaux

Des actions en responsabilité civile sont régulièrement dirigées à l'encontre d'entreprises multinationales au sein des deux systèmes juridiques les plus représentatifs : celui des Etats-Unis et celui des Etats membres de l'Union européenne, qui sont à la fois les deux entités qui disposent de la législation la plus développée en la matière et celles qui accueillent généralement sur leur territoire les sociétés mères des multinationales dont les activités de leurs filiales locales sont en cause[8]. Pourtant, il apparaît que le système américain (A.), comme le système européen (B.) sont encore largement insuffisants pour traiter correctement de cette question.

A. Un système américain adapté mais restrictif

Aux Etats-Unis, le principal instrument utilisé afin d'engager la responsabilité de sociétés transnationales pour les violations des droits de l'homme qu'elles auraient commises à l'étranger est l'*Alien Tort Claims Act* (*ATCA*) de 1789. Pourtant, cet instrument n'était à l'origine absolument pas destiné à fonder de telles actions[9]. Ce dernier

---

8 Pour une comparaison entre les systèmes américain, canadien, australien et anglais, v. CHOUDHURY Barnali, « Beyond the Alien Tort Claims Act : Alternative Approaches to Attributing Liability to Corporations for Extraterritorial Abuses », *Northwestern Journal of International Law & Business*, vol. 26, No. 43, 2005.

9 V. REGAN Paul, « Human Rights Compliance and Accountability for U.S. Multinational Enterprises: A Principled Step Forward after Sosa and Kiobel », *Widener Law School Legal Studies Research Paper*, No. 12-11, disponible en ligne : <http://papers.ssrn.com/sol3/papers.cfm?abstract_id=2017997> (consulté le 06/06/2012) ; TRIPONEL Anna, « Comparative Corporate Responsibility in the United States and France for Human Rights Violations Abroad », in MORRIS Andrew P. & ESTREICHER Samuel (dir.), *Global Labor and*

dispose en effet simplement que « the district courts shall have original jurisdiction of any civil action by an alien for a tort only, committed in violation of the law of nations or a treaty of the United States »[10]. Ainsi, les tribunaux américains sont compétents pour connaître de toute action civile intentée par un étranger (c'est-à-dire un individu ne disposant pas de la nationalité américaine) pour un délit civil commis en violation du droit international conventionnel, comme coutumier[11].

La jurisprudence est cependant venue imposer des conditions supplémentaires pour qu'une telle action soit recevable. Ainsi, outre la nécessité de respecter un délai de prescription qui court généralement à partir de la commission de l'acte préjudiciable ou de la découverte du dommage, le requérant doit encore établir la compétence personnelle du tribunal à l'égard de la société défenderesse. Cette condition est satisfaite à partir du moment où il existe une « sufficient connection »[12] entre le tribunal et la société, c'est-à-dire qu'il est prouvé que la société entretient des liens de rattachement suffisants avec l'Etat du for, soit que son siège social est situé dans l'Etat du tribunal compétent, soit, s'il est situé sur le territoire d'un autre Etat, qu'elle conduit ses affaires de manière continue et systématique dans l'Etat du for. Par ailleurs, il est également exigé, dans certains cas, que la société en cause ait agi de concert avec un acteur étatique, ou avec

---

Employment Law for the Practicing Lawyer, Alphen aan den Rijn, Kluwer Law International, 2010, pp. 59-158.

10 First Judiciary Act, 1789 (ch. 20, §9(b)), codifié dans 28 U.S.C. §1350.

11 Les tribunaux américains avaient toutefois rencontré quelques difficultés pour définir les termes « law of the nations », v. notamment : United States Court of Appeals, Second Circuit, June 30, 1980, *Filartiga v. Peña-Irala*, (630 F.2d 876); United States Court of Appeals, Second Circuit, October 13, 1995, *Kadic v. Karadzic*, (70 F.3d 232, 64 USLW 2231) ; United States Court of Appeals, Ninth Circuit, September 18, 2002, *John Doe v. Unocal*, (395 F.3d 932); Supreme Court of United States, June 29, 2004, *Sosa v. Alvarez-Machain*, (542 U.S. 692).

12 United States Court of Appeals for the Second Circuit, September 17, 2010, *Kiobel v. Royal Dutch Petroleum*. (621 F.3d 111).

son aide, pour les commettre[13]. Enfin, une dernière difficulté doit être surmontée : celle du *forum non conveniens*[14]. Les tribunaux doivent alors déterminer si un forum alternatif adéquat existe pour régler efficacement le différend (et notamment si celui du lieu de survenance du dommage ne constituerait pas un forum plus naturel en raison de sa proximité avec les preuves ou les témoins par exemple)[15]. Cependant, la Second Circuit Court a fait remarquer, à juste titre, qu'une fin de non-recevoir opposée à une action fondée sur l'*ATCA* par application de l'exception de *forum non conveniens* reviendrait à contrarier l'intention du Congrès qui avait précisément voté cette loi pour qu'un tribunal américain puisse connaître de faits qui se sont déroulés à l'étranger et qui ont porté préjudice à des étrangers[16]. Malgré ce tempérament, il est évident que ces conditions restrictives et fluctuantes posées par les tribunaux sont pour le moins difficiles à satisfaire par le requérant. D'autant qu'il faudrait encore que les tribunaux s'accordent sur le champ d'application de l'*ATCA*.

En effet, dans l'affaire *Sosa v. Alvarez-Machain*[17], première décision prise par la Cour suprême américaine sur le fondement de l'*ATCA*, cette dernière a adopté une approche restrictive pour interpréter et définir le champ d'application de celui-ci. Elle remarque notamment qu'il doit être utilisé normalement pour « [a] relatively modest set of actions alleging violations of the law of the nations » et

---

13 V. notamment l'affaire *Kadic v. Karadzic* (1995), *op. cit.*, qui vient expliciter les cas dans lesquels l'*ATCA* peut s'appliquer à des personnes privées.

14 V. par exemple : United States Court of Appeals, Second Circuit, October 5, 1998, *Jota v.Texaco*, (157 F.3d 153, 41 Fed.R.Serv.3d 1282, 29 Envtl. L. Rep. 20,181).

15 V. par exemple : Supreme Court of United States, December 8, 1981, *Piper Aircraft Company v. Reyno*, (454 U.S. 235, 102 S.Ct. 252, 70 L.Ed.2d 419).

16 United States Court of Appeals for the Second Circuit, September 14, 2000, *Wiwa v. Royal Dutch Petroleum Co. and Shell Transport and Trading Co.*, (226 F.3d 88), at 105 ; United States Court of Appeals, Second Circuit, October 5, 1998, *Jota v.Texaco*, (157 F.3d 153, 41 Fed.R.Serv.3d 1282, 29 Envtl. L. Rep. 20,181), at 159.

17 Supreme Court of United States, June 29, 2004, *Sosa v. Alvarez-Machain*, (542 U.S. 692).

préconise de restreindre la création de nouvelles causes d'action sur son fondement, ce qui signifie que l'*ATCA* ne donne pas nécessairement aux tribunaux compétence pour connaître d'affaires impliquant des multinationales. Ainsi, encore récemment, dans l'affaire *Kiobel v. Royal Dutch Petroleum*, le tribunal concluait :

> that imposing liability on corporations for violations of customary international law has not attained a discernible, much less universal, acceptance among nations of the world in their relations *inter se*. Because corporate liability is not recognized as a « specific, universal, and obligatory » norm [...], it is not a rule of customary international law that we may apply under the ATS[18].

L'ATCA ne pouvait dès lors permettre d'engager la responsabilité de sociétés transnationales pour violation des droits de l'homme. Au contraire, dans l'affaire *Doe v. Exxon Mobil*, la D.C. Circuit Court of Appeals fait valoir que

> it would create a bizarre anomaly to immunize corporations from liability for the conduct of their agents in lawsuits brought for shockingly egregious violations of universally recognized principles of international law[19]

et accepte que l'*ATCA* s'applique. Il en résulte donc une jurisprudence aléatoire qui ne fonde la compétence des tribunaux américains que dans des cas très restreints et prive les requérants de toute sécurité juridique.

B. *Un système européen plus ouvert mais inopérant*

La responsabilité civile des sociétés multinationales pour violations des droits de l'homme commises en dehors du territoire de l'Union

---

18 United States Court of Appeals for the Second Circuit, September 17, 2010, *Kiobel v. Royal Dutch Petroleum*, (621 F.3d 111).

19 United States Court of Appeals for the District of Columbia Circuit, July 08, 2011, *Doe v. Exxon Mobil* ; confirmé par United States Court of Appeals, Seventh Circuit, July 11, 2011, *Flomo v. Firestone*, (643 F.3d 1013).

européenne ne peut, quant à elle, être engagée, devant les tribunaux de ses Etats membres, sur le fondement d'une législation spécifique, mais principalement sur celui du Règlement n° 44/2001 concernant la compétence judiciaire, la reconnaissance et l'exécution des décisions en matière civile et commerciale (autrement dénommé Bruxelles I)[20].

Conformément aux articles 2, 3 et 4 du règlement, la juridiction en principe compétente est celle de l'Etat membre sur le territoire duquel le défendeur, quelle que soit sa nationalité, possède son domicile (c'est-à-dire, pour les personnes morales, le lieu de leur siège statuaire, de leur administration centrale ou de leur principal établissement, selon l'article 60). Néanmoins, si le défendeur n'y est pas domicilié, sont prévues des compétences spéciales, définies à l'article 5, qui dispose notamment qu'

> une personne domiciliée sur le territoire d'un Etat membre peut être attraite, dans un autre Etat membre : […] 3) en matière délictuelle ou quasi délictuelle, devant le tribunal du lieu où le fait dommageable s'est produit ou risque de se produire ; 4) s'il s'agit d'une action en réparation de dommage ou d'une action en restitution fondées sur une infraction, devant le tribunal saisi de l'action publique, dans la mesure où, selon sa loi, ce tribunal peut connaître de l'action civile ; [et] 5) s'il s'agit d'une contestation relative à l'exploitation d'une succursale, d'une agence ou de tout autre établissement, devant le tribunal du lieu de leur situation.

Ce dernier cas implique, de surcroît, une dépendance de l'entité secondaire par rapport à la société mère qui est, elle, domiciliée sur le territoire européen, et son implication effective dans la conclusion des affaires réalisées [21]. L'exception de *forum non conveniens* peut

---

20 Règlement (CE) n°44/2001 du Conseil du 22 décembre 2000 concernant la compétence judiciaire, la reconnaissance et l'exécution des décisions en matière civile et commerciale.

21 Sauf en matière délictuelle où le tribunal du lieu où le fait dommageable s'est produit ou risque de se produire peut être compétent, mais dans les cas de violation des droits de l'homme par des entreprises multinationales, le dommage se déroule le plus souvent hors du territoire européen, ce qui rend cette disposition inopérante.

également être soulevée dans ce cadre si elle est prévue dans le droit interne de l'Etat du for.

Il semble donc que le Règlement élargisse la compétence des tribunaux européens qui auraient à connaître d'actions intentées par un étranger à l'encontre d'une société transnationale, mais cet instrument n'est en réalité que peu adapté. En premier lieu, il n'envisage au principal que le cas d'une responsabilité directe de la société mère tout en exigeant qu'elle soit domiciliée sur le territoire d'un Etat membre. Or, les entreprises domiciliées en dehors de l'UE ne peuvent voir leur responsabilité engagée devant un tribunal européen[22]. En second lieu, il ne tient pas compte de l'hypothèse la plus répandue qui est celle d'un recours intenté à l'encontre d'une entité locale qui aurait, à l'étranger, un comportement contraire aux droits de l'homme. En effet, le Règlement ne prévoit la compétence des tribunaux européens que si ces entités sont situées sur le territoire européen, mais ces dernières sont le plus souvent implantées dans des pays en développement bien éloignés de l'Union européenne.

Le Règlement se trouvant écarté, il faudra alors, pour déterminer la compétence du tribunal, appliquer le droit interne qui ne la prévoit pas nécessairement. Il a donc été proposé une refonte de Bruxelles I[23] afin d'étendre son champ d'application aux défendeurs non européens et notamment « to include a forum necessitatis in the Brussels I Regulation in an attempt to prevent déni de justice and ensure access to justice »[24], et de restreindre les cas de *forum non conveniens* ou de

---

22 V. CJCE, arrêt du 6 octobre 1976, *A. De Bloos, SPRL c. Société en commandite par actions Bouyer*, aff. 14-76, *Rec.*, p. 1497 ; CJCE, arrêt du 22 novembre 1978, *Somafer SA c. Saar-Ferngas AG*, aff. 33/78, *Rec.*, p. 2183 ; CJCE, arrêt du 18 mars 1981, *Blanckaert & Willems PVBA c. Luise Trost*, aff. 139/80, *Rec.*, p. 819.

23 Commission européenne, *Proposition de règlement du Parlement et du Conseil concernant la compétence judiciaire, la reconnaissance et l'exécution des décisions en matière civile et commerciale (Refonte)*, COM(2010) 748 final, 14 décembre 2010.

24 EECKHOUT Veerle Van Den, « Corporate Human Rights Violations and Private International Law. The Hinge Function and Conductivity of PIL in Implementing Human Rights in Civil Proceedings in Europe: a Facilitating Role

litispendance. Mais cette réforme apparaît encore insuffisante pour faire rentrer dans la compétence des tribunaux des Etats membres de l'Union européenne des violations commises hors du territoire européen, en matière de droits de l'homme, par des sociétés multinationales.

II. Une responsabilité civile extraterritoriale exclue en raison de la structure des sociétés multinationales

Etablir la responsabilité directe des sociétés multinationales, dans un pays autre que celui dans lequel elle opère, semble déjà pour le moins compliqué dans la mesure où, sur le plan juridique, les tribunaux ne disposent pas des instruments suffisants pour fonder leur compétence, et où, sur le plan factuel, il est difficile de prouver que la société mère a causé le dommage ou a directement participé aux faits qui les ont causés. Mais, tenir la société mère responsable des agissements de ses filiales, ou autres entités qui en dépendent, relève, puisqu'elles sont autonomes (A.) quasiment de l'impossible, et ce, malgré le développement de la théorie du voile corporatif (B.), alors même que cela constituerait un moyen efficace de lutter contre l'impunité de ces entreprises et d'indemniser les victimes.

---

for PIL or PIL as a Complicating Factor? », 26 juin 2011, disponible en ligne : <http://papers.ssrn.com/sol3/papers.cfm?abstract_id=189569> (consulté le 06/06/2012) ; v. également KESSEDJIAN Catherine, « Commentaire de la refonte du règlement n°44/2001 », *Revue trimestrielle de droit européen*, No. 1, janvier-mars 2011, pp. 117-129.

A. Une absence de responsabilité de principe de la société mère pour les violations des droits de l'homme commises par ses filiales

En pratique, il est rare que ce soit la société mère qui effectue directement ses opérations à l'étranger. En règle générale, elle opère grâce à la constitution d'un établissement stable, c'est-à-dire, « une installation fixe d'affaires par l'intermédiaire de laquelle une entreprise exerce tout ou partie de son activité »[25] (un bureau, une agence ou une succursale). Or, ces entités ne sont pas autonomes et ne disposent pas d'une personnalité juridique distincte de celle de la société mère[26]. Cependant, si l'on applique le règlement Bruxelles I, on s'aperçoit que la seule possibilité offerte aux demandeurs, dans le cadre d'un litige concernant l'exploitation de cette entité, est celle d'attraire la société, domiciliée dans un autre Etat membre, devant le tribunal du lieu de situation de la succursale, de l'agence ou de l'établissement (article 5.5). Le règlement s'avère donc inutile car, comme il l'a été déjà été développé précédemment, ces entités locales sont situées en dehors du territoire européen et aucun recours ne peut donc être intenté devant les juridictions des Etats membres parce qu'elles ne sont pas compétentes.

Une société mère peut également opérer à l'étranger grâce à la création d'une filiale (soit par la constitution d'une nouvelle société, soit par la participation à une société existante – par sa prise de contrôle par exemple) qui, « de nationalité locale, […] agit sur son marché d'implantation en son nom propre et à ses risques et périls »[27].

---

25 OCDE, *Modèle de convention fiscale concernant le revenu et la fortune : Version abrégée*, OECD Publishing, 22 juillet 2010, disponible en ligne : <www.oecd.org> (consulté le 06/06/2012).

26 MOUSSERON Jean-Marc, RAYNARD Jacques, FABRE Régis, PIERRE Jean-Luc, *Droit du commerce international. Droit international de l'entreprise*, Paris, Litec - Editions du juris-classeur, 2003, 3e éd., p. 388 et s.

27 BARELIER André (dir.), *Exporter : pratique du commerce international*, Paris, Foucher, 2000, 16e éd., p. 160.

La société mère ne conserve qu'un lien financier avec sa filiale en participant à son capital, tandis que cette dernière dispose notamment d'une autonomie structurelle et décisionnelle. Cela signifie donc, qu'en raison de sa personnalité juridique distincte, seule la filiale pourra en principe répondre des actes qu'elle commet, même si la société mère est impliquée.

Or, dans la mesure où il est complexe d'engager la responsabilité d'une filiale devant les tribunaux de l'Etat d'accueil de ses activités tant pour des raisons juridiques que politiques (le droit interne doit prévoir la possibilité d'un recours pour des victimes qui peinent généralement à accéder à la justice), et où, lorsque cette responsabilité peut être engagée, il est parfois difficile d'octroyer aux requérants une réparation satisfaisante pour les dommages qu'ils ont subis (notamment quand les actifs de la filiale qui a été reconnue responsable sont insuffisants), ces requérants ont plus souvent cherché à engager la responsabilité de la société mère. Toutefois, si le lien entre cette société mère et l'évènement ayant causé les dommages n'est pas direct, le principe de l'autonomie de la personnalité juridique de la filiale s'oppose à ce que les actes de cette dernière puissent être imputables à la société mère qui ne peut dès lors pas en être tenue responsable. Une exception cependant a permis de renverser le principe : la levée du voile corporatif.

B. *Une exception notable mais très limitée : la levée du voile corporatif*

Si l'on écarte la responsabilité directe de la société mère pour manquement à son devoir de *due diligence* à l'égard de sa filiale[28], sa

28 Eu égard à son devoir de *due diligence*, concept juridique anglo-saxon qui impose de « prendre toutes les précautions nécessaires et raisonnables pour éviter la survenance d'un dommage », l'entreprise « doit évaluer les risques d'atteintes aux droits de l'homme, s'informer sur ses partenaires commerciaux et sur le contexte dans lequel elle exerce ses activités à l'étranger », v. FIDH, « Section II Mécanismes judiciaires », *Entreprises et violations des droits de*

responsabilité ne pourra être engagée pour les violations commises par cette même filiale que par la levée du voile corporatif. En effet, comme il l'a déjà été relevé : « [p]iercing the corporate veil essentially means disregarding the separation between entities organized in corporate form with limited liability of shareholders »[29], ce qui signifie que ce procédé permet une rare exception au principe de l'autonomie de la personnalité morale de la filiale vis-à-vis de celle de la société mère.

Les tribunaux américains, pour retenir la responsabilité de cette dernière (notamment dans le cadre de l'*ATCA*), vont pouvoir recourir soit à l'*instrumentality doctrine* (en cas de domination totale de la société mère sur sa filiale), soit à l'*alter-ego doctrine* (s'il y a une unité d'actionnariat et d'intérêt entre celles-ci). Certaines conditions doivent alors être satisfaites pour que « le voile soit levé ». Le requérant doit, tout d'abord, établir que la filiale ne dispose pas d'une personnalité morale indépendante (c'est-à-dire qu'elle ne jouit pas d'une autonomie financière, décisionnelle ou structurelle, ce qui est le cas si elle n'a pas d'avoirs ou de locaux qui lui sont propres par exemple). Il doit démontrer, ensuite, qu'elle est utilisée afin d'accomplir des actes frauduleux, injustes ou inéquitables au bénéfice de la société mère et, prouver, enfin, qu'un lien de causalité existe entre le comportement reproché et le dommage allégué. Ainsi, dans l'affaire *Doe v. Unocal*[30], la théorie de la levée du voile social invoquée par le demandeur a pu être retenue par la Cour. Cependant, les conditions posées, qui s'apprécient *in concreto*, sont difficiles à remplir et il apparaît que « [s]eul le contrôle par la maison mère des

---

l'homme. Un guide pratique sur les recours existants à l'intention des victimes et des ONG, mars 2012, p. 259, disponible en ligne : <www.fidh.org> (consulté le 06/06/2012).

29 KRYVOI Yaraslau, « Piercing the Corporate In International Arbitration », *Global Business Law Review*, vol. 1, 2011, p. 5.

30 United States Court of Appeals for the Ninth Circuit, April 27, 2001, *John Doe v. Unocal Corporation & Total S.A.*, (248 F.3d 915), p. 926.

opérations quotidiennes de sa filiale autorisera, certainement, une levée du voile social »[31].

En droit de l'Union européenne, il n'existe aucune disposition spécifique réellement adaptée au sujet traité, mais l'on peut se fonder sur le droit européen de la concurrence pour ce qui concerne la levée du voile corporatif. La responsabilité de la société mère peut être retenue pour les actes commis par sa filiale sur le territoire européen quand cette dernière « ne détermine pas de façon autonome son comportement sur le marché, mais applique pour l'essentiel les instructions qui lui sont imparties par la société mère »[32]. Une fois encore c'est l'intensité du contrôle qui va déterminer la mesure dans laquelle le voile va pouvoir être levé.

Néanmoins, les obstacles demeurent encore nombreux, tels que par exemple :

> la difficulté de prédire si ces différents enseignements [...], pourront être facilement exportés à la question de la violation extraterritoriale des droits de l'Homme ; [le fait que la preuve de] la levée du voile social [soit] à charge des demandeurs, ce qui est particulièrement lourd à rapporter et, [que] la possibilité de lever le voile social [soit] une question factuelle, et pourrait inciter les sociétés-mères à ne plus exercer de contrôle sur leurs filiales afin d'échapper à la levée du voile social[33].

---

31 FIDH, « Section II Mécanismes judiciaires », *Entreprises et violations des droits de l'homme. Un guide pratique sur les recours existants à l'intention des victimes et des ONG*, mars 2012, p. 249, disponible en ligne : <www.fidh.org> (consulté le 06/06/2012).

32 CJCE, arrêt du 21 février 1973, *Europemballage Corporation et Continental Can Company Inc. c. Commission des Communautés européennes*, aff. 6-72, *Rec.*, p. 215, §15.

33 FIDH, « Section II Mécanismes judiciaires », *Entreprises et violations des droits de l'homme. Un guide pratique sur les recours existants à l'intention des victimes et des ONG*, mars 2012, p. 259, disponible en ligne : <www.fidh.org> (consulté le 06/06/2012).

III. Conclusion

Aucun des mécanismes existants ne permet de respecter le droit à un recours effectif des victimes des violations des droits de l'homme commises par des entreprises multinationales. Certes, des législations telles que l'*ATCA* ou le règlement Bruxelles I offrent la possibilité d'engager leur responsabilité afin d'obtenir réparation pour les dommages qu'elles ont causés. Cependant, obtenir du tribunal qu'il accepte simplement de connaître de l'affaire s'avère on ne peut plus complexe, et qu'il accède à la requête bien plus encore. Il faut également noter que les parties ne sont pas placées sur un pied d'égalité et que les sociétés n'hésitent pas à investir des sommes conséquentes pour assurer leur défense face à des requérants vulnérables. C'est d'ailleurs un règlement amiable qui vient très souvent solder le litige, ce qui n'incite guère les entreprises à respecter les droits de l'homme.

Parallèlement à cette responsabilité civile extraterritoriale, il existe une responsabilité pénale extraterritoriale qui n'est guère plus satisfaisante. De nombreux instruments internationaux et régionaux ont invité les Etats à légiférer en la matière, mais le droit pénal interne demeure là encore insuffisant. Les tribunaux américains[34] retiennent ainsi la responsabilité de l'entreprise pour les violations commises par ses employés agissant dans le cadre de ses fonctions et au bénéfice de celle-ci (*theory of agency*) ; par ses dirigeants ou ses cadres (*theory of identification*) ; ou par des individus extérieures à celle-ci mais avec sa complicité (*theory of accomplice liability*). Or, aucun critère clair et

34 Leur compétence peut être aussi bien territoriale si le comportement reproché s'est déroulé sur le territoire américain, ou à l'étranger s'il a un effet direct, substantiel et prévisible sur ce dernier ; personnelle active ou passive ; ou universelle en la fondant sur des conventions internationales visant à protéger les droits de l'homme, comme la Convention contre la torture et autres peines ou traitements cruels, inhumains ou dégradants par exemple, ou en la fondant sur des lois spéciales nationales telles que le *Foreign Corrupt Practices Act – FCPA*, et le *Racketeering Influenced and Corrupt Organizations Act – RICO*.

précis n'a été défini pour leur application à un cadre de responsabilité pénale extraterritoriale. En droit de l'Union européenne, il n'existe pas d'équivalent en matière pénale au règlement 44/2001 régissant les affaires civiles. Chaque Etat membre organise donc son propre droit interne comme il l'entend, ce qui entraîne que les résultats ne sont pas ceux escomptés. L'exemple le plus significatif est celui de l'affaire *Total*, dans laquelle les demandeurs, des réfugiés birmans, avaient été obligés de soutenir devant un tribunal français, que le travail forcé dont ils avaient souffert pour le bénéfice de Total (dans le cadre de la construction d'un pipeline en Birmanie) avait été constitutif de l'infraction d'enlèvement, en l'absence d'une infraction spécifique définie dans le Code pénal français. Ainsi, une ordonnance de non-lieu a été rendue le 22 juin 2006[35] aux motifs que les éléments constitutifs du crime d'enlèvement n'étaient pas réunis en l'espèce et qu'en droit français, le travail forcé ne pouvait être, même s'il était prouvé, qu'un élément factuel destiné à corroborer le crime et non constituer le crime lui-même. Par suite, dans le cadre d'un accord amiable, Total, ainsi que son partenaire Unocal, avaient décidé de créer un fonds de solidarité d'un montant de 5,2 millions d'euros destiné à soutenir les efforts humanitaires locaux en Birmanie et à octroyer une indemnisation à toutes autres personnes pouvant apporter la preuve d'avoir été dans une situation similaire à celle des demandeurs. Cela paraît totalement inacceptable compte-tenu du fait que les droits dont il est question ici sont des droits humains fondamentaux qu'il conviendrait de protéger et sur lesquels on ne devrait pas pouvoir transiger. Diverses propositions ont été faites pour remédier aux carences des droits internes (créer une cour internationale dédiée aux violations commises par les sociétés transnationales[36] ou impliquer davantage

35 Cette ordonnance n'a pas été publiée.

36 V. CHOUDHURY Barnali, « Beyond the Alien Tort Claims Act : Alternative Approaches to Attributing Liability to Corporations for Extraterritorial Abuses », *Northwestern Journal of International Law & Business*, vol. 26, No. 43, 2005.

l'Organisation mondiale du commerce[37] par exemple), mais aucune n'a été retenue pour le moment.

Si la voie judiciaire ne fonctionne pas de la manière la plus efficace, il ne reste plus qu'à se tourner vers l'éthique des entreprises[38]. Les mécanismes volontairement mis en place par les Etats et les entreprises présentent, en effet, un potentiel prometteur pour contribuer à la prévention des violations des droits humains. Mais, là encore, ils restent limités dans leur portée[39] et, s'ils ne sont pas conjugués avec des réformes du régime juridique dont bénéficient ces sociétés, ils ne peuvent conduire qu'à des résultats dérisoires.

---

37 V. DEVA Surya, « Human Rights Violations By Multinational Corporations and International Law: Where from Here?, Connecticut Journal of International Law », vol. 19, 2003, pp. 1-57.

38 V. MCBARNET Doreen, « Corporate Social Responsibility beyond Law, through Law, for Law », *University of Edinburgh School of Law – Working Paper Series*, 2009/3.

39 V. MCINERNEY Thomas, « Putting Regulation Before Responsibility: Towards Bindings Normes of Corporate Social Responsibility », *Cornell International Law Journal*, vol. 40, 2007, p. 171.

Table of Contents

HUMAN RIGHTS AND CRIMINAL LAW AND ENFORCEMENT

HUMAN RIGHTS AND PRIVATE ACTORS

ATTEINTES AUX DROITS DE L'HOMME DANS LE MONDE CONTEMPORAIN

Atelier trinational, Tbilissi, septembre 2011

A l'occasion du 60e anniversaire de la Déclaration universelle des droits de l'homme, l'Assemblée générale des Nations Unies a déploré qu'« aucun pays ni territoire ne peut prétendre que tous les droits de l'homme y sont pleinement réalisés, en permanence et par tous. Des êtres humains souffrent, aujourd'hui encore, du fait du non-respect et de la violation de leurs libertés et droits fondamentaux. » En Géorgie notamment, les violations des droits de l'Homme font partie de l'Histoire récente. L'atelier trinational organisé par l'Université du Caucase (Géorgie) et les Universités de Paris Ouest Nanterre La Défense (France) et de Potsdam (Allemagne) a ouvert de nouvelles perspectives sur la façon de prévenir efficacement de telles violations.

Des mécanismes de prévention sont-ils nécessaires ? La soft law est-elle plus efficace que la hard law ? Existe-il une contradiction entre le droit des peuples à l'autodétermination et l'intégrité territoriale ? Qui est lié par des droits de l'Homme dans les conflits armés ? Les droits de l'Homme jouent-ils un rôle en droit pénal ? Quel mécanisme permet la prise en compte des droits de l'Homme en droit international privé ? La responsabilité des sociétés transnationales peut-elle être engagée pour violations des droits de l'Homme ? Ces problématiques et d'autres sont analysées dans douze articles en anglais, français et allemand.

VERLETZUNG VON MENSCHENRECHTEN IN DER HEUTIGEN WELT

Trinationaler Workshop, Tiflis, September 2011

Anlässlich des 60. Jahrestags der Allgemeinen Erklärung der Menschenrechte beklagte die Generalversammlung der Vereinten Nationen, dass „kein Land oder Hoheitsgebiet behaupten [kann], dass dort alle Menschenrechte uneingeschränkt zu allen Zeiten und für alle verwirklicht worden sind. Nach wie vor leiden Menschen unter der Vernachlässigung und Verletzung ihrer Menschenrechte und Grundfreiheiten." Insbesondere in Georgien sind Menschenrechtsverletzungen ein schmerzhafter Teil der jüngeren Geschichte. Der trinationale Workshop, der von der Caucasus School of Law (Georgien) gemeinsam mit den Universitäten Paris Ouest Nanterre La Défense (Frankreich) and Potsdam (Deutschland) organisiert wurde, hat neue Perspektiven auf den effektiven Schutz von Menschenrechten eröffnet.

Sind präventive Mechanismen notwendig? Ist „soft law" effizienter als „hard law"? Steht das Selbstbestimmungsrecht der Völker im Widerspruch zur territorialen Integrität der Staaten? Wen binden Menschenrechte in bewaffneten Konflikten? Wie beeinflussen Menschenrechte das Strafrecht? Welche Mechanismen erlauben die Anwendung von Menschenrechten im Internationalen Privatrecht? Können transnationale Unternehmen für Menschenrechtsverletzungen haftbar gemacht werden? Diesen und anderen Aspekten wird in zwölf ausgewählten Beiträgen auf Englisch, Französisch und Deutsch nachgegangen.

Cultures juridiques et politiques

Vol. 1 Stephanie Rohlfing-Dijoux (éd)
La Transmission de Terminologie et de Concepts Juridiques dans l'espace Européen. *Allemagne / France / Russie*
2012, ISBN 978-3-0343-1094-9

Vol. 2 Otmar Seul & Tomas Davulis (éds./Hrsg.)
La Solidarité dans l'union Européenne / Solidarität in der Europäischen Union. *Actes de la 5ème Université d'été franco-germano-lituanienne et européenne en sciences juridiques Vilnius, 3-10 juillet 2008 / Tagungsband der 5. Deutsch-Französisch-Litauischen und Europäischen Sommeruniversität in den Rechtswissenschaften, Vilnius 3.-10. Juli 2008*
2012, ISBN 978-3-0343-1122-9

Vol. 3 Ralf Alleweldt, Raphaël Callsen, Jeanne Dupendant (eds.)
Human rights abuses in the contemporary world.
Tri-National Workshop, Tbilisi, September 2011
2012, ISBN 978-3-0343-1147-2